I Shudder

Also by Paul Rudnick

NOVELS

Social Disease
I'll Take It

PLAYS

I Hate Hamlet
The New Century
Valhalla
The Most Fabulous Story Ever Told
Jeffrey

ESSAYS

If You Ask Me (as Libby Gelman-Waxner)

PAUL
RUDNICK

I Shudder

And Other Reactions
to Life, Death,
and
New Jersey

HARPER
An Imprint of HarperCollins*Publishers*

The essay "I Hit Hamlet" is reproduced
with permission of *The New Yorker*

Designed by Eric Butler

Library of Congress Cataloging-in-Publication Data
is available upon request.

ISBN-13: 978-1-61523-502-5

For John Raftis

Contents

CONTENTS

x

Author's Note

I have changed a few names in the nonfiction pieces,
to allow private citizens to remain private.
All of the fictional pieces are true.

I Shudder

The Sisters

1.

My first apartment in New York was a fifth-floor walk-up on Charles Street in the West Village. On the first Saturday after I'd moved in, I got a visit from my mother and her sisters, my Aunt Hilda and my Aunt Lil. All of these women were stylishly dressed, including leather handbags and silk scarves, and they all wore those oversized eyeglass frames which are known as "Tootsie" glasses, because Dustin Hoffman wore them when he was in drag. Actually, Dustin Hoffman in *Tootsie* could have been a fourth sister, because he wore such nice wool challis skirts and exhibited a proud, feminist outlook.

The Klahr sisters—their maiden name—always wore their hair slicked back in matching buns, like their mother, and their many steel hairpins sometimes set off the metal detectors at airports. They were all brunettes; blondes, along with anyone who spent too much time on their hair, were considered suspect, trivial, and, inescapably, Gentile. The sisters aimed for a certain dignity and finesse; they resisted the trophy minks of their outlying cousins and preferred heavier ethnic jewelry over anything gold and garish.

My mother, Selma, is the baby, and she was considered rebellious and even bohemian. This was because she read poetry and had moved, with her family, to the New Jersey suburbs; Jersey was considered exotic when compared to Long Island. Hilda was the elegant middle sister who tended to be the peacemaker, despite her dry and often subversive sense of humor. Hilda was the person to sit next to at a Passover seder, because she'd murmur, "Oh, come on already, get those Jews out of Egypt. Let's eat!"

Lil was the all-powerful eldest sister, a compact, solidly built dynamo with the staunch, gimlet-eyed mien of a Navajo priestess. Lil was an accomplished person. During the Depression, with no money, she'd founded a nursery school, aided by my Uncle Rudy, a peppy gym teacher, and she'd continued to rise, ultimately becoming a Superintendent of Schools. Lil had also recently departed from the sisters' code of subdued good taste. She'd started having a local dressmaker whip up a closetful of polyester tube dresses in bold, almost tropical prints, sometimes with bobbing ball fringe at the hemlines. These dresses had high necklines and short sleeves, and they resembled colorful, off-season covers for patio furniture. "These dresses are so practical," she'd tell her siblings, "you should get some." Lil's greatest gift was her magnetic, raw confidence. She had strong opinions, and she knew exactly what you should be doing with your life, and she had no problem with letting you know.

I could hear the sisters climbing the many flights up to my apartment, with expressive groans and remarks like, "How much further?" "Why does he live here?" and "I think I'm having a stroke."

"Look who's here!" my mother called out, entering the apartment and kissing me.

"Look who's here!" said Hilda, hugging me.

"Look who's here!" said Lil, adding, "So there's no elevator?"

"Of course not," explained my mother. "That's why he lives up here—so we won't come and visit him."

"Well, I guess we showed him," Hilda chortled.

"I'm not kidding, there's no elevator?" asked Lil.

"There is," I replied, "but it's restricted. This is a nice building."

"Oh, very funny," said my mother.

"Mr. Ha-Ha," said Hilda, grinning.

"So this is your apartment?" said Lil, looking around. With the addition of a bed, myself and my relatives, the ten-by-fifteen-foot studio was packed.

"Of course this is his apartment," said my mother.

"What else?" said Hilda.

"Is this the whole thing?" asked Lil. "Or is this the foyer?"

"Actually, there are five more bedrooms," I explained, "but they're being painted."

"There are not," said my mother, "he just graduated. This is perfectly fine; it's a studio."

"It's lovely," said Lil. "See, I'm being nice."

"She's being nice." said Hilda, "Write that down."

"Hil?" said Lil, wary of insubordination.

"I didn't say anything!" Hilda insisted.

"So it's a studio?" asked Lil. "Why do they call it that? So it'll sound fancy? Why don't they just say, it's a broom closet up a lot of stairs with a bed and, I hope to God, a bathroom. Is there a john?"

"I just go out in the hall," I said. "There's a bucket."

Hilda laughed, but after Lil glanced at her she stopped, claiming, "I'm not laughing, it's not funny. I'm sure there's a john."

"It's right in here," said my mother, supportively opening the bathroom door. "Come on in, we'll take the grand tour."

The three women peered inside a bathroom the size of half a phone booth.

"Look, he has a toilet," said Hilda, approvingly. "Very nice."

"And a sink," added my mother.

"It's like the Waldorf," Lil concluded. "Are there bugs?"

"Of course not!" my mother protested, and then, to me, "You don't have bugs, do you?"

"I can't afford them," I said. "It's sad."

"You know," said Lil, "when Mama and Papa first came to this country, they lived on the Lower East Side, in a tenement, just like this. And now here you are."

I'd never really known my grandparents, who'd died when I was little. My grandfather had been a tireless garment factory worker, a cutter who skillfully sliced through many layers of tweed and gabardine; he was also known for such remarks as, "Like the monkey said when he peed into the cash register,

'This is running into money.'" My grandmother, who made Lil look like a trembling ingenue, had been especially concerned with her family's internal cleanliness. For Hilda's eighth birthday, without telling Hilda or her guests, she'd frosted a batch of cupcakes with melted Ex-Lax, so that the kids would all stay regular.

"Look what we brought you!" said Hilda, handing me a shopping bag. Gifts are like passports in my family, since no one is allowed to travel without carrying many wrapped packages. My aunts always bring something, even if the gift makes no sense. "It's the gesture," Lil would say, "it marks the occasion." Over the years I've received, among other things, Mexican papier-mâché marionettes, a tennis sweater, a notepad with an appliquéd felt cover depicting a man in a vest playing a banjo, and a bamboo back scratcher. Hilda would find many of these treasures at an outlet store on Long Island called Girl Meets Buy.

At my apartment, I opened Hilda's shopping bag to find washcloths, a wicker cover for a box of Kleenex, and a plastic toilet brush. While these were actually thoughtful purchases, the women began handling the various housewares as if they were uncut rubies, or newborn infants, to be adored and inspected for flaws.

"This is a very nice toilet brush," Lil told Hilda. "Where did you get this?"

"At the store near me," said Hilda. "It also comes in taupe."

"I love these washcloths," said my mother, nuzzling one first to her own cheek, and then to mine. "Feel how soft."

"And look, wicker," said Lil, holding the Kleenex caddy up to the light. "I could use this."

"Give me that," I said, snatching it away.

"So you're going to climb all those stairs," said Lil, "and then you're going to sit here, probably on that bed, since I'm not noticing a chair, and you're going to write something. So what are you going to write?"

"Leave him alone," said Hilda, "he just got here."

"He has to make a living," said Lil, who had a point.

"He's going to write whatever he wants to write," said my mother, "and it's going to be wonderful and we're all going to love it, as long as it's not disgusting."

While my mother was concerned about, in ascending order of importance, how I was going to support myself, what I was eating, and bugs, I think she was thrilled that I'd moved to New York. She'd been raised in a home where, while culture had been revered, it wasn't practiced. Money was scarce, so schooling, and finding both a husband and a Job With A Future had been paramount. Throughout her life, to the distrust of her sisters, my mother had worked at places like a literary magazine, an organization that booked orchestra tours, and a ballet company. As her sisters would delicately inquire, "And they'll pay you for that?"

"You know what you should write?" Lil advised me. "Those thrillers, like you can buy at the airport. The people who write those books, they do very well. I love those books."

"Or you could write children's books," suggested Hilda, who was an ardent grade school librarian, "like Dr. Seuss."

"Or you could write a diet book," said Lil. "Those books make a fortune. Although, personally, I always want to tell people, here's a diet tip: stop eating."

Happily, my father, who'd been parking the car, arrived to interrupt this discussion. My dad was a very supportive, good-natured man who'd been attracted to my mother's vitality, although he was somewhat overwhelmed, not to mention outnumbered, by the full sisterly onslaught. All of the men the sisters had married shared this quality, of having to brace themselves for holidays, or any occasion, when the women reunited. Lil was a particular challenge. Once, my parents were in the front seat of our car as my dad was looking for a parking space in midtown. I was in the backseat with Lil, who was championing her greatest cause, Israel. "When there's a cure for cancer," she told me, "it's going to come from Israel." Then she leaned over the front seat, informing my father, "If we were in Israel right now, there'd be parking."

"I love this apartment," my father told me, back on Charles Street, "but who are all of these strange women? Are they staying?"

"Norman," Lil asked my father, "be honest. Do you think that a person can actually live in this apartment?"

"Yes," my father decided, "I think it's just fine. And look at all of those nice, big, healthy bugs."

"Where?" Hilda asked, panicking.

"I told you!" said Lil, triumphantly.

"NORMAN, THAT'S NOT FUNNY!" said my mother, as my father and I laughed. "See," she continued, disgusted with both of us, "they think that bugs are funny."

"Maybe late at night, while I'm asleep," I proposed, "maybe the bugs will write something for me, like Rumpelstiltskin."

"We're going," my mother announced. "Hil, Lil, let's go."

7

After more debate about whether I should buy a chair, where I should buy a chair, whether I owned a bedspread, whether my bedspread had any matching accessories, whether my relatives would be able to make it back down all those stairs without having heart attacks, whether there were any good restaurants in the area, without bugs, and whether I needed more toilet paper, a subject which the ladies discussed as if toilet paper might not be readily available in Greenwich Village, Lil and Hilda departed, while my parents held back.

"Call me up when we get back to New Jersey," said my mother, kissing me, "and don't talk to strangers or stay out all night or do anything I wouldn't do."

"And have fun," said my father, hugging me.

"How?" I asked.

Once everyone was gone, I sat on my bed in a room which somehow felt palatial, because the apartment was mine, because I was brandishing a sparkling new toilet brush as if it were a royal scepter, and because I was finally alone. I heard a noise, and I looked out my tiny window. Across the courtyard, on a lower floor, I saw two men having very verbal sex, atop a butcher-block kitchen table.

"Fuck me, you bastard!" one of the men demanded.

I was home.

About eight months later, in January, I had to move because so much snow and ice had accumulated on the roof of my building that my ceiling caved in, dumping large chunks of filthy, sopping wet plaster right onto my bed, which I luckily wasn't in at the time.

"It was a sign from God," Lil told me the next time I saw her, "and do you know what God was telling you?"

"What?"

"Never live on the top floor."

2.

I moved to an even smaller apartment a few blocks away, on the ground floor of a deeply ugly building on Perry Street, next to a parking garage. This apartment was basically a short hallway with a slight bulge at the end, for a bed, and it was so depressing that the sisters were not allowed to visit, for fear it would upset them too much.

"Is it that bad? Worse than the other one?" Lil asked me, at a family get-together back in New Jersey.

"It's like living in a drawer," I told her.

"I don't even want to think about it," said my mother.

"I'm sure it's not that bad," said Hilda. "How could it be that bad?"

"It's so bad," I told the group, as if I were sitting atop a bunk bed and delivering the capper to a summer camp ghost story, "that even the bugs spend the weekend somewhere else."

There was a silence.

"Now all I'm going to think about are the bugs," said my mother.

"So where do they go on the weekends?" asked Lil, weirdly interested.

And then a few weeks later I was robbed. I wasn't home when

a junkie broke into my apartment. A helpful neighbor, hearing some commotion, called the police, who came right over and arrested the burglar while he was still on the premises. As they were putting him in handcuffs, the phone rang, and one of the officers picked it up. It was my mother.

The officer explained the circumstances to my mom, who had only one question: "Oh my God," she said, "this guy, the burglar, what did he do to the apartment? Did he destroy things, did he turn everything upside down?"

"Well, ma'am," said the officer, glancing around, "the place looks pretty terrible. There's clothes and boxes everywhere. It kinda looks like a tornado hit it."

"Oh my God," said my mother.

When I finally got home, the apartment was of course exactly how I'd left it. Which I never told my mother.

A police detective arrived the next day to take my deposition. He was unbearably handsome, with a mustache; to this day, I'm convinced that the police and fire departments deliberately staff gay neighborhoods with especially hunky men, as a vicious tease.

The detective couldn't have been nicer or more professional, and I couldn't have been more swoony and hideously embarrassing. I fell all over myself thanking him, and I offered him free tickets to an Off-Broadway play I was working on. He thanked me but said that he wasn't allowed to accept gifts in the line of duty, though he added that if I wanted to, I could write a letter of commendation for his departmental file.

After he left, I composed at least fifteen drafts of this letter, each of which would've gotten the detective fired. "Dear New York Police Department," one draft began. "Let me tell you, from the first time I laid eyes on Lieutenant Ramirez, I understood what they mean by 'New York's finest.'"

I eventually came up with a version that didn't sound as if it were being written in hot pink Magic Marker, on lined and scented notebook paper, to a member of a boy band, and I sent it off. A week later I got a phone call from a woman who identified herself as the girlfriend of my burglar/junkie. "You know, Jimmy was already breaking his parole, so he's gonna go back to jail anyways," she said, in an impatient whine, "so do you really wanna press charges?" She thought that Jimmy's already being a convicted felon somehow made him more sympathetic. I didn't want her to rush right over and kill me with a rusty razor blade, so I told her that I'd think about her request, and I hung up. Here's the saddest part: Jimmy wasn't a very bright junkie, because I didn't own anything worth stealing. He'd tried to heist, among other items, a ceramic mixing bowl half-filled with pennies, and a huge rhinestone which a friend had sent me as a gag birthday gift.

I did still wonder what I would do if I became the target of Jimmy and his girlfriend and their inept but possibly bloodthirsty drug ring. I decided that maybe I'd call up Lieutenant Ramirez and beg him to come over right away, claiming that I was too scared to spend the night in my apartment alone. But then I concluded that if I ever really needed serious protection from armed criminals, the person I should call was my Aunt Lil.

3.

My next apartment, a few years later, was an improvement—it was a one-bedroom on Christopher Street. It was only on the second floor, so the sisters had no trouble climbing their way up.

"This is so much nicer," said Lil, inspecting my living room; she was absolutely right, since this was the first time I'd ever had a separate living room.

"I love this!" said Hilda. "And there's a kitchenette!"

"Are we allowed to look in the bedroom," asked my mother, "or did you clean up for us by taking everything and throwing it in there?"

"Excuse me," I said, deeply offended, opening the door to my sliver of a bedroom. "See? It's a showplace." Then I quickly shut the door, before my mother or my aunts could actually take too close a look and find either my porn or the moldy laundry which was in fact lumped under both the bed and the bedspread.

"So what's that place next door?" asked Lil. "Is it a bar?"

"It's a leather bar," I said; it was called Ty's, and it was one of the oldest, and busiest, such places in the city.

"A leather bar?" asked Hilda.

"He means it's an S and M bar," said my mother, trying to sound both sophisticated and nonchalant.

"S and M," said Lil, nodding her head. "That's when people like to have other people beat them up, right? Like on a date?"

They were all looking at me, as if I were suddenly a bondage authority, and I'd never even been in the bar. Like any decent citizen, I'd only watched S&M porn, with titles like *Dungeon Daddy* and *Stableboy II: The Revenge*.

"I don't think that they necessarily beat each other up," I replied, haltingly. "I think that they do all sorts of things, like . . . I don't know, bondage and discipline."

"You know," said Hilda, "when some of those rowdy kids come into my library and they're yelling and they won't sit still or choose a book, I could use a little S and M."

"S and M," Lil repeated. "Does that stand for, what— sadomasochism?"

"Or slave and master," I said.

"How do you know so much?" my mother asked me, warily.

"They're my neighbors," I said, as if that explained everything.

"So who decides who's the slave and who's the master?" Lil wondered. My mother, Hilda, and I exchanged a glance, and I'm pretty sure that we were all thinking the same thing: Lil was definitely a top.

"I think people just naturally pick," I told Lil.

"That makes sense," said Hilda.

"And look at all of your nice things," said Lil, now zeroing in on the main function of the visit. For the sisters, any fresh location could become a gallery or, even better, a store.

"You've been buying things," my mother said, approvingly, "where do you find all of this stuff?"

The sisters were, it must be said, world-class shoppers. They weren't spendthrifts, they didn't shop recklessly, and they didn't hoard; they weren't like those women who can be found sobbing on daytime talk shows as they watch videotape of their crammed closets, bloated with twenty-eight unworn ponchos and fifty-three sets of baby clothes for their childless homes.

The sisters shopped with a scientific delight. Every item held the potential to surprise and amaze, from a chipped yard-sale saucer to an enameled pillbox in a Parisian department store. They rarely spent large amounts of money, because they'd feel too guilty, and unable to shop again later that afternoon. They especially loved shopping for others; that way they got the high without the crash. They were retail Mother Teresas.

Lil was the Ali, the Michael Jordan, the legendary presence. Lil could leave Bloomingdale's with an armload of possible outfits for her grandchildren, all unpaid for; the salespeople knew her and trusted her to pay for what she kept and return the rest. Lil knew that at a discount store, if a dress had a missing button or belt, she could point out the defect to a clerk and receive additional money off. I don't believe for a second that she ever surreptitiously removed a button and slipped it into her purse, but there were rumors.

I considered myself to be merely the sisters' humble trainee, their bungling intern. But I do have the gift. By the time I'd moved to Christopher Street, I was making just enough money for some oddball purchases, and plenty of foraging. I'd haunt the city's junk shops, weekend flea markets, and lowest-end antiques stores, unearthing stuff like plaster forearms, circular oil paintings of Roman ruins, and abandoned souvenirs, like a tiny alabaster model of the Leaning Tower of Pisa. My apartment was half dull-gray industrial shelving bought used at a restaurant supply store on the Bowery, and half what can only be called tchotchkes. "Tchotchke" is a Yiddish word meaning "something peculiar which you don't need, and which has no discernible purpose or value, but which you can't live without."

Lil eyed my tchotchkes with a hungry, practiced eye, as if beneath a velvet throw pillow or a carved wooden deer head she'd find a gold doubloon, or the secret of perpetual motion. She moved from one object to the next, sometimes letting her hand linger flirtatiously, as if she was murmuring, "Do I love you? Or you? My, aren't you pretty." Finally, she picked up a heavy brass paperweight, in the shape of a prominent Roman nose. She examined it, as if through some invisible jeweler's loupe, and then turned it over, assuming there'd be a price tag underneath. There wasn't. Lil wasn't cheap, or obsessed with money, but still, she liked to know what things went for. It told her where she stood.

"This is very nice," she commented, holding the paperweight, as if we were in some Cairo bazaar and I was crouched nearby, wearing a fez. Then, with an even more surpassingly bogus not-that-I-care attitude, she asked, "So, what did you pay for this?"

"That's none of your business," I said, raising the ante.

"No, come on, seriously. I'm just curious—what did you pay for this?"

"I'm not going to tell you."

My mother and Hilda were getting nervous; they loved Lil but almost never stood up to her. It was too risky.

"Why aren't you going to tell me?" Lil asked.

"Because it's private, and you don't need to know."

The atmosphere became dangerously electric.

"You should tell her," Hilda advised me. "Just tell her."

"You don't have to tell her," my mother said, her voice quavering. "But you could."

"No, no," said Lil, putting the paperweight back down onto my desk. "He's absolutely right, it's his personal business, and I don't need to know."

My mother and Hilda looked at each other, staggered. Had we entered some parallel universe? Had the earth just spun off its axis? Had Lil surrendered?

"Thank you," I said, with just a little too much premature smugness.

"But tell me," said Lil, picking the paperweight back up, "just out of curiosity, you know, what would you pay for something . . . *like* this?"

Sometimes you just want to applaud.

4.

Some years later Lil's husband, my Uncle Rudy, who was in his seventies, died what I can only call the Platonic ideal of a Jewish death: he had a fatal heart attack on the ninth hole of a golf course in Miami Beach. Rudy and Lil had both been very athletic, so his death was unexpected: like his wife, Rudy had seemed unstoppably vigorous and up for any tennis match or Vermont bicycle ride or hike through a kibbutz.

At Rudy's funeral, Lil stood with one hand on her husband's coffin and the other around my shoulders. "Your Uncle Rudy always loved you, you know that, don't you?" she said. "He never understood why, in your writing, you had to use that kind of language, but he loved you."

Less than two years later, Lil shocked her sisters by remar-rying. She had been living in Florida, where she'd met Bernie, a widower who'd been married for many years to an extremely gutsy, opinionated woman, not unlike Lil. Bernie's late wife had also enjoyed crafts, and had left behind many unfinished projects, all of which Lil thoughtfully wrapped up and mailed off as gifts, so various friends and relatives soon received a dead woman's half-completed tissue-paper-and-glue collages, and translucent, oversized, plastic-resin daisies.

Lil surprised the family in other ways as well: she broke the sisterly edict against wearing fur by buying a large white mink stole. Lil wasn't a tall woman, and she refused to drape the stole across her back and bunch it in the crook of her arms, as many women do, with a slouchy, champagne-at-the-country-club élan. Lil preferred to wear the mink slung around her neck, with the two square-cut ends hanging straight down, almost to the floor, like a white mink prayer shawl, or a polar bear carcass.

I, meanwhile, had been pursuing marriage material of my own. I was on the dance floor of a downtown club when I was introduced to John, and I had the most romantic response pos-sible: I knew instantly that he was far too self-possessed and good-looking for me, and that I'd be completely ignored. When we danced and talked and then actually began to go out, the scenario felt like a rip in the time-space continuum. But here's why it all began to make sense: John was a doctor, with a spe-cialty in rehabilitative medicine and head injuries. I was obvi-ously a test case.

When I told my mother that I was dating a doctor, her ancient tribal DNA kicked in, and she almost imploded with happiness. "He sounds wonderful," she said, and then, inevitably, she asked, "Is he Jewish?" I said no, and there was a distinct pause. Finally she asked, "Is he smart?"

I think my mother was just getting back at me because, a few years earlier, she'd called me with the welcome news that Hilda had hit the true Jewish-American jackpot: her son Carl, who was a doctor, had become engaged to another doctor, a terrific woman named Marcie Levine. That's when I'd taken a distinct pause and then asked, "Jewish?" And that was when my mother hung up on me.

Soon John invited me to visit him at his rehab center, out in New Jersey. I was nervous about going because, while I found head injuries fascinating, I was squeamish about almost all medical procedures. John, however, being a professional, was thoroughly at home with even the most graphic physical symptoms, and he loved watching cable shows like *The Man with the 25-Pound Face-Eating Tumor* and a drastic weight-loss documentary called *A Trash Can Full of Skin*. This latter program was the genuinely moving story of an Englishwoman who, after losing hundreds of pounds, traveled to America for radical surgery to remove her many yards of hanging flesh, and she'd titled the show herself. I had trouble watching the scalpel slice into her abdomen and thighs, but John was riveted.

"But what do they do with the excess skin once they cut it off?" I asked, while watching the show with my hands covering my eyes. "Is it like fabric or more like fruit roll-up? Could they fold it up and store it in a freezer for skin grafts? Is there enough to make a really unusual carry-on bag?"

John looked at me. "I won't answer you," he decided, "unless you take your hands away and watch the surgery." My Aunt Lil was right: as she'd once told me, the goyim are crafty.

John's rehab center was a pleasant, campus-like brick complex, and as he walked me through the halls, all of his patients approached him adoringly.

"Well, hello, Doctor," said one middle-aged woman, with a meaningful wink. John had told me that after this patient had been in a car wreck, she'd recovered physically but had become sexually insatiable. This sounded like an urban legend, concocted online, but there she was. "Last week," John said, "the nurses found her in one of the other patients' rooms, with this man who, because he was having severe balance problems, needed to be tied to his bed. She was all over him, and we had to call the orderly to drag her out."

"Lookin' good, baby," the woman told John, wriggling her shoulders appreciatively, "Mm, mm, mmmm . . ."

"Vicky," said John, "do you remember what we said? About boundaries and inappropriate behavior?"

"Oh, come on, Doc," the woman scoffed. "All I need is a man and a beer."

We moved on, and John spoke with another patient, a man who, following a motorcycle mishap, looked fine but could no longer determine what was food and what wasn't. His family had caught him nibbling golf balls.

"Is this food?" the man asked, cradling a small brushed-steel lamp.

"Not food, Frank," John replied, and the man gratefully put the lamp back on an end table.

"You see," John told me, "Frank is fine, because he's learned that he just has to ask."

"But that lamp might be food if you were really, really hungry," I pointed out.

John stared at me. "Did you even finish high school?" he asked. Then he was called away, because a new patient, an extremely dazed, near-comatose eighteen-year-old, was being admitted. This boy was from rural Pennsylvania, where he'd locked himself in his bedroom for the better part of a week, chugging a homemade brew incorporating grain alcohol. His family, which had somehow permitted this spree, had brought him in and reported that he was "foamulating" at the mouth. John had also told me about another family he'd met while he was in medical school, who had referred to the fibroid tumors in the mother's uterus as "fireballs of the Eucharist."

John left me alone in his office, where I instantly tried on one of his extra white jackets and pretended to write prescriptions on one of his pads. "Here you go," I told an imaginary sufferer, "just take this entire bottle of pills all at once." Then I made a major strategic error, when I left the office to get a sip of water from a nearby fountain, not realizing the office door would lock automatically behind me. As I stood outside the door to John's office, a cluster of his patients began to circle me, with grave and increasingly belligerent suspicions. I remembered a scene from the fifties B-movie *Shock Corridor*, in which a reporter infiltrates a mental hospital, only to find himself trapped in a ward filled with sexually predatory women. "Nymphos!" he mutters.

"What were you doing in the doctor's office?" asked one man, who had a noticeable dent in his forehead.

"I'm . . . visiting," I replied.

"Does the doctor know you were in there?" asked a sturdy-looking woman, rubbing her knuckles.

"Oh yes," I said, "he left me in there."

"Then why did you come out here?" asked the man with the food-recognition issues; it occurred to me that, from his point of view, I might be a tasty ham sandwich or a plate of his mom's ziti.

"I came out here to get a drink," I said, knowing I sounded defensive.

"I don't think you're supposed to be here," said the guy with the dent.

"I'm going to call the orderly," said the foodie, and I wondered if he was going to ask the orderly to bring condiments and sharp utensils.

"Ain't you somethin'," said the woman with the boundary problems, eyeballing me, with her hands on her hips. "Me likee."

"*He's not supposed to be here,*" growled a newcomer, a hulking college athlete with a bandaged head and a menacing cast on his arm.

"It's fine, guys," John told the mob, as he came to my rescue. "This is Paul, and we're still not sure what's wrong with him."

John proved himself again, because when I went with him to a medical conference in Florida a few months later, he insisted that we stop in West Palm on our way back, so that he could meet Aunt Lil and my new Uncle Bernie.

John drove our rental car out to Heritage Acres, the retirement community where the couple was living. My mother and

Hilda had been down for a few visits, and while Hilda had been polite, the place was my mother's worst nightmare. "It's like a warehouse for old people," she'd told me, "where all they do, all day long, is play golf and compare their diseases. I love my sister, but if I had to live there, I'd cut my throat."

John and I drove through the gates, and we saw hundreds of identical, single-story bungalows, lined up in neat rows beside narrow canals. The sun was merciless, and there weren't many trees. Everything seemed to be covered with stucco and painted the color of a faded Band-Aid. Heritage Acres was like a well-tended terrorist training camp, filled with eighty-five-year-old women in roomy, quilted floral housecoats, and pot-bellied, cigar-smoking men in Sansabelt slacks. We pulled up to Lil's bungalow, and she greeted us at the front door. Lil was now in a wheelchair, which was being pushed by the astound-ingly compliant Bernie.

"Look who's here!" cried Lil, and, as we entered the smallish front hallway, she managed to back her wheelchair directly over Bernie's toes. He didn't wince or complain in the slightest, and she continued to crush his toes throughout our visit. His refusal to gripe, or even mention the torment, pretty much defined their relationship—Bernie was a total sweetheart, and utterly devoted to Lil. "So this must be the doctor," she said, motioning John into the living room, where she could take a better look.

The house was small, but sunny and cheerful. Lil had filled the pastel walls and wicker shelving with a mix of framed family photos, ornamental, hammered-brass Passover plates, and pot-tery and wall hangings collected on her travels; there was also a lumpy but impressive, almost life-sized, brown ceramic bust of Golda Meir. A shaded rear sun porch overlooked a canal. While I understood my mother's fears, for a couple like Lil and Bernie, Heritage Acres was warm, wheelchair-accessible, and even lively; it was the modern shtetl, with cable, medical facilities, and a nearby airport.

"And you must be Lil," said John, "I've heard so much about you."

"Don't listen to him," said Lil, gesturing to me. "So tell me, Doctor, what's wrong with me?"

John took a deep breath and entered the arena by offering both his credentials and free medical advice. About a year earlier, Lil, who was now in her eighties, had been driving and her legs had gone numb. John quizzed her on her symptoms, which involved spinal problems and difficulties in adjusting her many medications. John agreed with her current doctor's diagnosis, and he mentioned all of the most recent research on Lil's condition. I stood by, proudly and nervously, like the spouse of a hopeful immigrant during his citizenship exam.

Lil listened attentively and then, after a dramatic pause, she told John, "You're a very good doctor. Have some candy. Bernie, get him some candy."

This offer meant that John had performed exceptionally well, and Bernie fetched and opened a large, flat box of fussy candies with elaborate icing and questionable centers. I was horrified when John actually ate one of these treats, because, as I told him later, once we were alone, "Those were *ornamental* candies. Lil's had that same box for over fifty years, because everyone knows that they're just for show, to prove she's a good hostess. What did it taste like?"

"Like a very old eraser."

"Look, he's having a candy," Lil said, as John manfully swallowed the prehistoric goodie. "But you're a doctor, isn't candy bad for you?"

"Everything's bad for you," John replied, jovially. "Breathing is bad for you. But we all need some candy."

"He's very smart," Lil informed me, as if John had left the room. "Why is he so smart?"

"You mean for a Gentile?" I asked. "I don't even know why they bother letting them go to school. They can't learn, and all they do is drink."

"That's a terrible thing to say," Lil scolded, "even if it's true. So your specialty is head injuries. What is that, like if I hit someone in the head with a hammer?"

"Arlene, next door, she had a head injury," said Bernie.

"Arlene has two fake hips, a neck brace, and she needs a kidney," said Lil, "but I don't think she has a head injury. She's just not very bright."

"No," said Bernie, "before she got her new hips, she fell in the tub and hit her head on the sink. That's how she got that terrible scar."

"That's not a scar," said Lil. "She just wears too much lipstick. I told her, I said, 'Arlene, you look like a streetwalker, except you're riding around on that little scooter.'"

Lil's Jamaican housekeeper provided a lunch of cold cuts and fruit, while Lil spoke about her new marriage: "It's important to have a relationship. It keeps us both young, and there's always someone there to call 911. Bernie and I, we have fun, you should stay for a few days and come with us. We get up at six a.m. and Bernie drives us to the mall for the Early Bird Special on breakfast, and then we hit the Stop and Shop—you can find incredible deals, last week we got fifty cans of tuna, ten for a buck fifty."

"So maybe some of the cans were a little dented," Bernie added. "Who cares?"

Every beat of this narrative terrified me, but I was especially alarmed at the thought of Bernie, who was nearing ninety, behind the wheel of a car.

"So show me," Lil asked John, as we got ready to leave. I knew just what she was talking about, because my mother had told her about the tattoo John had gotten a few weeks earlier. On his right shoulder there was now a heart, with a dagger through it, dripping blood, and there was a banner stretched across the heart with my first name on it.

The tattoo had been entirely John's idea, and I'd been stunned. We'd gone to the tattoo parlor together, and I had checked out the many tattoo options that were pictured in the sketches lining the walls. My favorites were the Chinese characters for "to vomit," and a large-scale body mural, suitable only for someone's entire chest or back, of a bare-breasted native Alaskan hottie, shrugging off her fur-trimmed parka as she rode a cresting ocean wave, balanced on twin dolphins; I tried to imagine the guy who'd say, "Oh, yeah, man, that's what I want—the Alaska chick with the dolphins! Forever!"

As we waited, I could hear a twenty-something girl in the back, wailing pitiably as she was marked with only the tiniest navy blue heart on her ankle. I then watched in agony as the tattoo artist began to dig his many needles, each filled with a different color, into John's flesh, as John sat calmly, without even the mildest groan or wince. "But doesn't that hurt?" I asked, through clenched teeth.

"Of course it hurts," John scoffed. "It's a needle. Aren't you going to get one? Maybe a skull, or maybe that topless butterfly woman who looks like she's having sex with a saber-toothed tiger."

"I tell you what," the tattoo artist told John, as he meticulously outlined the heart on John's shoulder. "If you want, I'll throw in some purple on this for free."

"Sure," said John, "why not?"

"AHHHH!!!" I moaned, as if the needle were piercing my eyeball. I have trouble getting a flu shot, so I wasn't about to opt for something more sustained and elaborate. "But am I a coward, and a terrible person," I asked John, "because I'm not getting your name tattooed on my shoulder?"

"Yes," said John, and then he faked torture by chanting, "Ow ow ow ow!"

I was, of course, thrilled beyond belief by John's tattoo, because I somehow imagined that it made *me* tougher, as if I were now a Hells Angel or an especially unrepentant serial killer on death row. I loved John even more because he never expected me to return the favor; he was being permanently inked with the name of a real wuss. There was only one problem: at the beach, people tended to look at John's tattoo, ask, "Is that real?" and then they'd spit on their fingers and rub the tattoo, to check whether it was temporary.

"Yes, it's real," John would tell these people, "and why are you spitting on me?"

"Look at that," said Bernie, in West Palm, as John rolled up the sleeve of his T-shirt, "a doctor with a tattoo."

"So, Aunt Lil," I asked, "what do you think?"

Lil considered the situation. "I like it," she decided. "And do you know why? Because it's a gesture. And so it means something. And, most of all, it's permanent. Which is important," she concluded, right to me, "because you can take a ring off."

5.

A year later, Lil died. John and I went to her funeral, and the service was held at a white marble temple in Queens. My mother, Hilda, other relatives, and Lil's many friends had gathered; but because Lil had been living in Florida for so long, the rabbi hadn't known her. He spoke in generalities, which was a shame, because Lil was such an impressive and full-voltage woman. "Life is like a sandwich," the rabbi intoned, in his plummy, pleased-with-himself rabbi voice, "the two slices of bread don't matter, it's what's in the middle that counts."

The mourners were puzzled by this, because none of us could follow the metaphor—if you don't have the two pieces of bread, then it's not a sandwich, it's just loose meat. And if the rabbi was referring to birth and death, well, those do seem rather necessary events, even in the life of a BLT.

After the service, everyone piled into their cars and drove out to one of those vast roadside cemeteries on Long Island. I always find these places incredibly depressing, not because they're filled with dead people, but because the stone markers and careful landscaping have so little to do with those dead people's lives or personalities. These cemeteries seem like filing systems, like some bland, hellish vision of a peculiarly American eternity, a Levittown for the deceased.

Lil's coffin was lowered into the ground, and her sisters and her daughter each tossed a shovelful of dirt into the grave. Usually, the mourners leave after this, and the cemetery staff fills in the rest of the grave, but Lil had left very specific, alternative instructions. Lil had felt that, under the usual procedure, after the mourners depart, the grounds crew gets sloppy, and often toss empty soda cans and cigarette butts into the graves along with the soil. Lil stipulated that at her funeral, her friends and relatives should wait until the grave was completely filled in, just to keep the gravediggers honest.

This took a while. It was even a little annoying, but it was very Aunt Lil, and it certainly gave her the last word. I looked at my mother and Hilda, who were dissolved in tears. Lil had sometimes terrorized them, but the three sisters had always been a team. Now there was no one to advise them or bully them or praise them for bringing back such thoughtful gifts from London or Montreal or Albuquerque.

Bernie looked lost; he knew that he'd been very lucky to have found two such appealingly forceful wives. Lil's daughter, Martha, a vital woman, with a loving, what-the-hell attitude—she's Lil without the Uzi—was surrounded by her four kids, Lil's adored grandchildren. I sometimes wondered if Martha had been sure to have lots of children, to give Lil the maximum number to shop for.

John hadn't known Lil for long, but he seemed very moved. I saw how much John had respected Lil, as a kindred spirit.

They were both exceedingly tough cookies. John, as I was discovering, was a very no-bullshit guy, who, when asked, would offer very specific, stop-whining advice. He was a fallen Catholic from Spokane, Washington, and Lil was a Depression baby from Queens, but they had more than understood each other. They were both passionate travelers who didn't need particularly luxurious accommodations. Lil had once taken a package tour of Israel which had promised that the participants would get to serve in the Israeli army. She had been bitterly disappointed, because, "They didn't really let us do anything. We just dusted off little bits of pottery at an archaeological dig." I could tell that she'd wanted at least a skirmish.

During the years following Lil's death, I've noticed that when my mom and Hilda get together, or talk on the phone, they take turns becoming Lil. They tell each other what to do, in no uncertain terms, and they both get irate when the other one won't listen; this heartfelt battling keeps Lil alive. I don't particularly believe in heaven, but I like the concept; I especially like the picture of Lil chatting with God, because she has some ideas.

Lordy

1.

Just about all writers share one titanic, all-consuming, and eternal source of inspiration: the rent. Enter Hollywood, which is UNICEF for playwrights.

I was lying on my couch, trying to come up with an idea for a screenplay, and I began thinking about drag, and wondering why a guy in a gown is so often funnier than a woman in, say, a dapper three-piece suit. I tried to imagine a disguise or transformation that might be more fun, for a female star. And so I started thinking about nuns. Nuns can seem dictatorial, sexually repressed, and scary, and therefore entertaining. I pictured a lower-rung showgirl who witnesses a gangland hit. To protect her, the feds stash our doll in a convent, and, because it's a comedy, she's forced to wear a habit. I was obviously sparked by such gender-swaps as *Some Like It Hot*, and by Barbara Stanwyck as a burlesque queen invading a college campus in *Ball Of Fire*. But I wanted nuns, so I called my notion *Sister Act*.

I brought *Sister Act* to the producer Scott Rudin, and we agreed that the leading role was a natural fit for Bette Midler, then, in the late 1980s, the delicious, dependably rowdy star of such hits as *Ruthless People* and *Outrageous Fortune*. Bette's production company was based at Disney, so Scott set up a meeting in New York with a studio chieftain. I pitched *Sister Act* and a deal was struck. I was stunned at how rapidly the project came together, but then, the Lord works in mysterious ways. He may even work for Disney.

I wrote a treatment, which is a studio term for "summarize the story in under two pages, so that an executive's assistant can boil it down to one paragraph on a Post-it, and please refer to all characters by the names of the stars who should play them but never will." The treatment, like any activity in the studio sector, is designed to make the project appear not merely attractive, but surefire. It's an ironclad guarantee, assuring every staff member that his or her job, home, second home, spouse and vehicle upgrades are in the bag.

I was still new to this process, so my treatment was probably worrisome. I wanted *Sister Act* to be a satire of sugary family perennials like *The Sound of Music*, *The Singing Nun*, *The Flying Nun*, and such parochial school romps as *The Trouble with Angels* and its sequel, *Where Angels Go, Trouble Follows*. These mainstream nun flicks were filled with sage, older nuns who, after offering their wisdom, would die serenely off-screen; with younger, guitar-strumming "rebel" nuns, sometimes riding Vespas; and with feisty novices, who either had to be broken, via missionary work, or farmed out to the Von Trapp compound.

My favorite nun saga is *The Song of Bernadette*, a biopic that follows a humble French peasant girl who experiences a vision of the Virgin, as portrayed by an immaculately brunette Linda Darnell. A bubbling, healing spring bursts forth at the site of Bernadette's epiphany, and ultimately becomes the millions-served holy shrine of Lourdes.

I planned for *Sister Act* to subvert all of this prissy uplift. I wanted our heroine, Terri Van Cartier, to embody raunch, sex, and the unstoppable gospel of cheap showbiz. It would be pop versus pope, and pop, in a barrage of sequins, wisecracks, and Marlboro Lights, would win. That's how addled or innocent or crazy I was, because I actually believed that Disney would make a movie that tried to defeat the Catholic Church.

Treatment in hand, I was flown to Los Angeles for an early meeting blitz. Such meetings are what most people would consider gossip with a buffet interrupted by phone calls, but what Hollywood calls work. Since I couldn't drive, I arranged for a cab to the Disney lot in Burbank. I love taking cabs in L.A., because it's like heading out on an extended cross-country family vacation. In New York, a cab passes buildings, buses, and other cabs, but in L.A. you can see used car lots, redrock canyons, and mesquite. From a Beverly Hills mansion, I once saw a seven-year-old girl emerge, dressed in the short black satin skirt, fishnet stockings, and frilly starched apron of a naughty French maid, and I was outraged: Where were the child labor laws? Then I remembered that it was Halloween.

The Disney headquarters, like everything else Disney, was

enchanted and disturbing. Everything was themed. There were topiaries clipped into eerily threatening boxwood Mickeys and Minnies, and street signs pointed bicycle messengers along Goofy Avenue and Dopey Drive. Some of the buildings were modestly scaled and retro, but carved above the entrance to a more recent office tower was a monumental, ten-foot-high, limestone grouping of the Seven Dwarves, with their arms raised, as if they were holding up the many upper floors. This effect was adorable and grotesque, because if the figures are that tall then they're not dwarves anymore, plus they were enslaved and suffering, as if after they'd built the pyramids Doc and Grumpy had been shipped to L.A. in chains. I should mention that during this period, Disney's obsessively hands-on micromanagement style had justified the nickname Mousechwitz.

I entered the sleek, impersonal office of an ebullient vice-president. All of the Disney execs at this time wore exclusively black or navy blue, costly but unconstructed Armani or Comme des Garçons suits, for a Rodeo Drive ninja feeling. The studio was about to release what would become its blockbuster animated musical *The Little Mermaid*, and the VP was holding what looked like a brightly colored cardboard purse. "Paul, look!" he exclaimed, tilting his purse this way and that, "it's the Little Mermaid Happy Meal!" He was friendly and welcoming, and I noticed a framed photo of a softball team on the ledge behind him. "That's from our company picnic," he explained. "It was so much fun!" I asked about the other grinning, sunburned people in the picture, all wearing Team Disney sweatshirts and Mouseketeer ears, and the VP, thinking about it, realized that they'd all since been fired.

Another, equally gung-ho, executive appeared, carrying, in his palm, a four-inch-high collectible plastic figurine of the Little Mermaid herself, with her chunky cascade of red hair and her skimpy seashell bra. "Look at her!" this exec crowed. "Isn't she hot? I'd do her!" Other staffers approached, all agreeing that the figurine was indeed hot and doable, and I tried not to ask, "Do you want to do the action figure, the cartoon, or the mermaid herself? How exactly do you do a mermaid, anyway? Wouldn't you drown?"

As in all decent studio meetings, everyone was "totally stoked" about *Sister Act* and eager to "fast-track" the property. The execs tended to sound like skateboarders, and their primary notes were about shaping the material for Bette and about how much we all loved nuns. "Nuns!" I declared, "I'd do 'em!" and everyone cheered.

I returned to New York and completed a first draft. I handed it in, and there were questions. With Bette considering the role, the movie could now become an all-out musical, so what should she sing? Original material or Motown standards? As Terri chafes at convent life, could she smuggle some of the other nuns, with a few stashed in the trunk, into a drive-in? A whorehouse? A McDonald's, for product placement? Could the nuns get high? What about sex? I felt that enforced chastity should be a logical source of comedy—wouldn't Terri get itchy? What if there was a guy who felt turned on, and terrified, by his yen for a nun? And where should the convent be located—on an isolated prairie, or somewhere more urban?

I flew out for more meetings. Bette and her staff were now present, and Bette was indecisive. She was, and is, a fabled

35

performer, having kicked off her career before gay audiences at a bathhouse in New York. She was also extremely well-read, and was conflicted about her image. Did she dare play a nun? Everyone, for many months to come, continually explained to Bette that she wasn't risking blasphemy by portraying an actual nun, yet she remained uneasy.

A word about stars. Many are appealing, but the greatest exhibit a transformative gift. In a meeting, Bette, with a cold, could seem bedraggled or distracted, and thoroughly human. But she could also, as a sheer act of talent and will, become something more, and something that doesn't necessarily require a squadron of tireless hair and makeup people. Bette could suddenly, and to startling and enthralling effect, become the real deal, the most interesting person in the room—or the galaxy. I'd watch and realize, Oh, of course, that's what stardom is. That's how she earns her salary and the fascination, and patience, of the world.

I've learned to be shy about meeting actors, or writers, or just about anyone I admire. Sometimes a star is subdued or not particularly verbal, or as dumb as a post. I once asked Scott Rudin, who's worked with everyone from Tom Cruise to Meryl Streep, which stars, in his experience, delivered off-camera, which personalities continued to impress. One of the first names he offered was Bette.

Months passed, and I produced draft upon draft. One morning I found myself seated before a borrowed typewriter, in a tower suite at the Chateau Marmont in Los Angeles. The hotel room had open windows on four sides, looking out to the valley, the hills, and a Diet Coke billboard. As I worked, a monsoon breeze came up and the stacks of pages flew around my head. I felt like either the beleaguered, soon-to-be-hard-drinking, downtrodden screenwriter of any number of black-and-white movies, or a sparkling Disney heroine, a Cinderella or a Snow White, as she's visited by twittering, animated blue jays and robins.

About a year in, Team Disney, Team Bette, Scott and I sat in a meeting, discussing Catholic teaching regarding vows of silence, poverty, and chastity, and the specifics of a Franciscan versus a Benedictine order. Glancing around, I saw that I was analyzing papal dogma with a room almost exclusively filled with Jews. At a loss, someone suggested that I should be sent for some hands-on research to a convent. "Yes!" cried Bette, a firm believer in continuing education. "Paul, you really need to go to a convent!"

So I was shipped, by bus, to the rural Regina Laudis convent on the outskirts of Bethlehem, Connecticut. I'd read that this convent had been the home, for decades, of the actress Dolores Hart, who, as an ingenue, had appeared as a spring-break coed in *Where the Boys Are* and opposite Elvis Presley in *King Creole*. Ms. Hart had left Hollywood to become a nun, taking her final vows in 1970, when she told an interviewer, "There is a promise given in a vocation that is beyond anything in your wildest dreams. There's a gift the Lord offers and He is a gentleman." Ms. Hart insisted that she'd thoroughly enjoyed her sojourn in California, although in 1959 she'd said, "Elvis is a young man with an enormous capacity of love . . . but I don't think he has found his happiness. I think he is terribly lonely."

I couldn't wait to meet such a prescient, ponytailed starlet-turned-sister. The convent was a series of rambling, mostly clapboard buildings set amid trees and pastures, and I was assigned a bed in a gender-appropriate bunkhouse. This was a somewhat cloistered order, meaning it wasn't an ecclesiastical petting zoo. The nuns weren't readily available for conversation, as they received no funding from the Vatican and supported themselves by running a farm, a dairy, and a ceramics workshop; they were far too busy to talk to anyone except their husband, Jesus. As a heretic, it occurred to me that a convent could be seen as an extremely sacred, industrious harem.

Wandering into the surrounding woods, I came upon a shed that showcased an elaborate nativity scene composed of over a hundred hand-carved, nineteenth-century Neapolitan dolls. It was holy yet garish, like the set for a PBS children's show using puppets for the baby Jesus and his buddies. Back in my dorm, I went through my research. Convents in America, I found, were like charm schools, because enrollment was way down. In prefeminist years, a young woman was expected to get married, and her employment options were limited, so back then becoming a nun could actually be a route to independence. But lately, if you asked your average teenager to abandon boys, fluffy duvets, and downloads of all her favorite bands, she'd rather not.

Convents and monasteries were closing everywhere, and their land and buildings were being sold and bulldozed. The few remaining abbeys often echoed with teetering seventy-year-old nuns tending to ailing ninety-eight-year-old nuns. Vatican II had caused additional attrition. Once nuns were encouraged to wear more conventional outfits and to work in the community, many decided: Why not just become a teacher or a social worker with a livelier Saturday night? I worried that *Sister Act* might be the final crude iron nail in the Sisterhood's simple pine coffin.

I decided to stalk Dolores Hart. I hoped that there'd been a papal dispensation, allowing her to pray in a sleeveless shell top and a pert, highlighted flip. I skulked around, and eventually found a cottage that turned out to be the convent's gift shop—so as a gay Jew, I finally felt embraced. The stock was skimpy, mostly pottery, organic skin creams, greeting cards, and several "Women in Chant" CDs, one seductively titled *Virgin Martyrs.* At first I almost overlooked a tiny, gnarled creature, perched on a stool behind the cash register, like a bat or a long-fossilized chimp.

"I hate this!" the chimp yipped, and I saw that she was trying to watch a soap opera on a black-and-white portable mini-TV, the perfect accessory for a nun. "The G.D. reception keeps going out!" she cawed. "I can't see my show!"

I hoped that this wasn't what remained of Dolores Hart, so I instantly turned myself into an accomplished investigative journalist. "Good afternoon, Sister," I began, as if I were suddenly wearing a blue oxford-cloth button-down and a safari jacket.

"What?" she croaked.

"I said, good afternoon. I'm visiting. So, is this the gift shop?"

"What does it look like?"

I detected an unspoken "asshole" in her remark, and I was taken aback. Weren't nuns supposed to be wholesome, accepting, and chipper, all the livelong day? "It's so lovely out here," I ventured.

"We're not 'out here.' We're inside. And it's cold. What's wrong with this thing?" She pounded the set with her arthritic knuckles, as if she were boxing its ears.

"So, how long have you been a nun?" As I asked this, I felt like I was hitting on her, and that we both needed to be holding long-necked beer bottles and scanning the room for someone hotter.

"Since before you were born, boy. What would you know about it?"

Maybe this was a wicked nun, exiled for her harsh personality to the gift shop, to heal herself through selling keychains and calendars. I would reach out. "Is it a hard life?" I asked.

"Yeah, it's a hard life. I'm a nun. It's supposed to be a hard life. What are you?"

"I'm a writer."

"What?"

"I'm a WRITER."

She laughed because, of course, every nun's a critic. "That's good," she said, still chortling. "A writer! I like that."

"So why did you become a nun?"

"Why? Why? I was sixteen. I had eight brothers and sisters. I liked to pray, I believed in God, I had a calling. End of story."

I was running out of probing topics, and I didn't think she wanted to dish about where to meet monks. "So, do you ever wish you weren't a nun? That you'd chosen a different life?"

She stared at me, in wonder and disgust. "Only when my G.D. TV doesn't work!" A final swat caused a grainy image to reappear, and she turned away from me, instantly far more absorbed in a studly young doctor's flirtation with a heavily mascaraed nurse.

At five a.m. the next morning, I attended the second-earliest Mass, in a rough wooden chapel, which reminded me of a finished basement or a cedar-lined humidor. As everyone bowed their heads, I did just what I do at any religious service: I sort of respectfully but noncommittally bowed my head and mumbled gibberish, except for the word "amen." I'm a garden-variety lapsed suburban New Jersey Jew; for my bar mitzvah, I'd learned the Hebrew for my Torah portion phonetically, from a record. After my bar mitzvah, I never went back. Catholicism always seemed more exotic, the way your friends' parents can seem more interesting than your own; your friends' parents also have no power over you.

The Mass was heartfelt, unadorned, and a little boring. The nuns prayed constantly when alone, and at up to eight services throughout the day. The room was icy and dim, lacking any vivid stained glass or theatrical velvet. This is why I'm not a nun, I decided. If you felt truly summoned, this extremely spare and focused existence would be all you hungered for, a personal completion. Becoming a nun reminded me of having a sex change. If you wanted something that extreme, if you felt certain about that degree of transformation, you really had to want it.

That afternoon, I was permitted a brief audience with, if not the Mother Superior, then someone highly placed in the nun command. She spoke to me through some shadowy grillwork in a central office. She was kind and helpful, although she didn't waste time. "Welcome to Regina Laudis," she said. "What are you doing here?"

I paused, and then I told the nun that I was researching a novel about a woman seeking a more pure, prayerful life, within convent walls. I suspected that replying "Oh, I'm writing a Disney farce about a tramp in a habit" wasn't quite the ticket. I asked the Sister about the convent's history, and she supplied basic, informative answers. She was accustomed to ignorant outsiders, and she let me down easy.

At first I decided that deliberately lying to a nun had finally guaranteed my passage to Hell. I thought again, and knew that, as always, I was being entirely self-absorbed, and that the nun most likely couldn't care less. She wasn't a cartoon nun, a harridan with a ruler, but someone who'd consciously devoted herself to a difficult life, of sacrifice, contemplation, and service. She didn't want any of the things I wanted. She wouldn't pray for an unlimited supply of chocolate-covered pretzels or brawnier shoulders or the ability to fly. We worshiped entirely different Madonnas. I wanted to tempt her, with a Snickers bar or a copy of *Us Weekly*, just to see if she'd crack. Years later, I did hear about a nun who'd somehow managed to acquire and hide a closetful of designer evening gowns in her otherwise nondescript apartment—she was like a very private, devout Cinderella.

As I was leaving the convent, on my way out to the bus, I caught sight of an older woman carrying a tin pail of milk from the convent barn. She was wearing high, mud-spattered rubber boots and a down vest over her habit. She was smiling and working hard, and she just might have been Dolores Hart. I decided not to approach her, since she was busy and probably didn't need to be asked any more questions about Elvis. She'd done something unheard of for an American: she'd been offered the life of a celebrity and, quietly and politely, she'd said no.

On my ride back to New York, I read a book called *Lesbian Nuns: Breaking the Silence* and learned that for gay women, especially of earlier generations, religious life had often been a true sanctuary, although the higher-ups would push to separate lesbian couples, citing a ban on "particular friendships," which struck me as just plain mean.

I shared all of my discoveries at my next Los Angeles meeting with the Disney people, and the information about the lesbian nuns was deemed especially not useful. My contract expired and wasn't renewed. Bette had finally abandoned the role and *Sister Act* was dead in the water, but then, just like with Bernadette on that bleak French crag—a miracle!

2.

Whoopi Goldberg accepted the part of Terri, although she asked to have the character's name switched to Deloris because, I was told, she'd always wanted to play someone called Deloris. I was asked to return, and despite the prospect of more meetings and more notes and, most likely, a discussion of whether to include a sparkly, Day-Glo, strawberry-scented Communion wafer in the *Sister Act* Happy Meal, I said yes.

I flew out and was introduced to the movie's just-hired director, Emile Ardolino, a sweet-tempered, silver-haired man who'd devised a superb camera technique for capturing ballet on many episodes of the PBS series *Dance in America*, and who'd worked with Scott Rudin on their Oscar-winning documentary about Jacques D'Amboise, *He Makes Me Feel Like Dancing*. Hollywood had found all of this suspiciously high-brow, so Emile had fought his way to directing the chick-friendly Catskills romance *Dirty Dancing*. Further casting for the supporting nuns in *Sister Act* began, and I was included in the process.

The script called for actresses of all shapes and ages, although the Disney execs still squabbled over which nuns should be "fuckable." Under Deloris's supervision, a core group of nuns would form a choir, so the women auditioning were asked to prepare a song. The film's musical director was Marc Shaiman, who'd worked with Bette for years, and who was much admired for his many film scores; a few years later he'd write the score for *Hairspray*. For the wannabe nuns, Marc brought in dozens of the most amazing Broadway, cabaret, and recording artists from the past fifty years. Marc, Scott, Emile, and I were all intravenous users of original cast CDs, so let's not mince words: in that room, Angela Lansbury was Spiderman.

The auditions became a blissful, one-time-only Gay Jeopardy Tournament of Champions. Susan Johnson would enter, and we'd all rush to compliment her on her work in *The Most Happy Fella*, a show which had first been produced before most of our panelists were born. We didn't need a vision of the Virgin, because we saw Mary Wickes, who'd sung opposite Bing Crosby onscreen in *White Christmas*. A Jedi Master was declared when an actress appeared and Emile, his eyes shining, gushed, "I loved you in *Donnybrook*!" I bowed to Emile, because I'd never even heard of *Donnybrook*.

My rewrites were less rewarding. The studio notes poured down: "Deloris needs to be more sympathetic." "Deloris needs to teach the nuns, but she needs to learn something, too." "The movie isn't about nuns, it's about friends." "Could Deloris help a needy child?" "Does Deloris need a dog?" "Can we have a montage where Deloris and the nuns bond while painting a colorful anti-drug mural?" "Can two of the nuns coax Deloris into a threeway behind the altar?" Okay, I made that last suggestion up, but only to avoid diabetes. The Disney notes were always phrased in the most positive, supportive, gee-wouldn't-it-be-great-if tone, and that was the problem. It was like being trampled to death by cheerleaders.

The studio deadlocked over casting Whoopi's love interest. Any sexual content had become all but nonexistent, but there was still a by-the-book police officer who supervised Deloris's transfer to the convent, while developing the most tame, Disneyfied crush. The question became, should the officer be caucasian or African-American? The studio was in a dither of political correctness, mixed with business concerns. Was interracial love a brave step forward, or would the black audience object? What about the white, southern demographic? How could the studio keep every possible moviegoer happy? Finally a honcho burst into a meeting, burbling, "I've got it! I've got the guy! I know exactly who Whoopi's boyfriend should be— Edward James Olmos!"

I stared at him and asked, "Excuse me. Do you think that if a black person and a white person have a baby, it's a Hispanic?"

"*Yes!*" he shouted triumphantly, and, to this day, I'm not sure if he was kidding. Either way, I couldn't take the process, or the notes, or the prospect of all those nuns hugging, so I quit.

After I left, *Sister Act* was rewritten by half of Southern California. Even as shooting began, writers came and went, and working on the film became a form of jury duty. I'd get occasional updates, from friends and gossip columns, as the star, the studio, and the script erupted. Whoopi, it was rumored, had eventually shipped one of the execs a boxed set of heavy brass balls.

I was still a beginner, and I wanted desperately to avoid Whining Screenwriter Syndrome. I'd signed a contract and cashed the checks, which were underwriting my work on a new play. No one has ever jammed a gun to a screenwriter's head, demanding another extended car chase. I was in such Manhattan denial that it hadn't occurred to me that, at some point, *Sister Act* would be released.

I was FedExed a final draft of the script, which was now the product of many hands. Good or bad, it was no longer my work, so I asked to have my name removed from the credits. The studio was concerned, and I got a series of urgent calls, offering me a videocassette of the final cut, asking me to watch it and reconsider. I kept refusing, because even if the movie was terrific, it wasn't my script. I was extremely uncomfortable about accepting the praise or blame for something I hadn't written. An exec finally proposed, "Paul, don't watch the movie alone.

Get a bunch of your friends and have them all come over and make popcorn and watch it together. You'll have a blast!"

I answered, "You know, I could invite my friends over and bring out a dead puppy. And we could toss it around, but we really couldn't say it was flying."

After that, Disney agreed that I could use a pseudonym, pending their approval. I first went for "R. Chasuble," explaining to an executive that Reverend Chasuble was a priest in another farce, Oscar Wilde's *The Importance Of Being Earnest*. He was skeptical. I came up with "Screenplay by Goofy." He wasn't amused. Thinking aloud, I joined the first name of a character from a story I'd written to my brother's middle name, and arrived at the blandly inoffensive "Joseph Howard," which was rubber-stamped by the studio and which still sounds like someone who helped found the Mormon Church.

Sister Act opened and was, improbably, a great success. It hadn't been an expensive production and so everyone made money, including me. I had nothing to do with the sequel, *Sister Act II: Back in the Habit*, but there's a credit line reading "Based On Characters Created By Joseph Howard." A stage version is in the works. In interviews, Bette has expressed regret about not appearing in the film. A year after it opened, I ran into one of the original executives assigned to the project, and he said, "Paul, you know, you should really write something for Bette."

"I did," I told him.

"What?"

"*Sister Act.*"

"Oh, that's right!" he replied, giggling.

I can't vouch for the quality of the original film, for one reason. *Sister Act* may very well be just fine, but I've never been able to watch it.

As for Dolores Hart, I've read that she's now the Prioress of Regina Laudis, and that she has also, over all her years in the convent, kept up her membership in the Academy of Motion Picture Arts and Sciences. She loves being sent DVDs of all the latest movies, because she's the only nun who's allowed to vote for the Oscars.

I Shudder:

An Excerpt from the Most Deeply Intimate and Personal Diary of One Elyot Vionnet

Hallie Tesler

As this is my most deeply intimate and personal diary, I am assuming that it will one day be introduced into evidence at my trial.

I am Elyot Vionnet. I am sixty-three years old, and for all of my adult life I have lived in my perfect studio apartment on a high floor of a building which almost overlooks Gramercy Park. My home is furnished with a polished cherrywood antique Venetian chair in the shape of a human skeleton, a small French writing desk and a brass campaign bed which can be completely disassembled for travel, and which once belonged to Napoleon Bonaparte. I am semiretired from my career as a substitute teacher in the Manhattan school system, I sleep in crisply starched one-hundred-percent cotton pajamas with the thinnest, palest blue stripe, and I have had just about enough.

You see, there are people in this world without manners, kindness, or common decency, and sometimes I want to kill these people, but I don't. Not always.

Because, you see, I'm here to help.

For example:

There's a twenty-eight-year-old woman in my neighborhood whom I have never seen without a phone welded to her ear. I have glimpsed her on the street, at the supermarket, picking up her dry cleaning and ordering coffee, all without ever interrupting her wireless conversations to pay the slightest attention to the actual human beings behind the various counters and cash registers involved. A week ago I watched as this woman crossed a busy intersection, against the light, without glancing up from her call. I was of course hoping that a drunk driver or a speeding getaway van would send her flying, just so that I might find her phone in the gutter and tell the caller, "I'm sorry, but your call has been interrupted—by divine justice." But, sadly, traffic swerved, and the woman looked up with a brief, annoyed grimace, as if she was blaming the universe for threatening to interrupt her social life. I had to do something.

The woman's doorman told me her name: Hallie Tesler. And a quick Google gave me her cell-phone number. Sitting in my apartment, I decided to start easy. I dialed, and when Hallie answered, I said, "You don't know me, but please don't hang up, just keep your friend, or whoever it is, on hold. Here's my guess:

right now you're sitting in the backseat of a cab, where your incessant, mindless chatter has made you ignore not merely the glorious city right outside your window, but also the fact that you're just about to arrive at your destination. And because you've been so relentlessly attached to your phone, only once the cab has stopped will it suddenly occur to you that it might be time to start rummaging through your immense designer shoulder bag, in order to dig out your wallet and begin calculating the lowest possible tip, all while you continue to take calls, thus wasting so many other people's time, especially that of the elderly woman on the corner, who's been waiting for a cab in the rain for forty-five minutes. So I want you to think about your behavior, and I also want you to study your shoulder bag and wonder why anyone in their right mind would ever buy, even at sixty percent off, an item with quite that many useless grommets, straps, and buckles, in grimy beige cowhide, an item which resembles nothing so much as a low-level Long Island mafioso's finished basement convertible sofa." As Hallie began to sputter, I quietly hung up.

Two days later, I sat on my campaign bed, munching from a paper bag filled with unsalted, jumbo cashews, each as sweetly curved as a fetus, and another bag of chocolate-covered raisins. I believe in a benevolent God not because He created the Grand Canyon or Michelangelo, but because He gave us snacks.

I called Hallie. "It's me," I began, "and I know that right now you're at work, in your cubicle, chatting on the phone to various friends about what you thought about doing last night but didn't do because you were so tired, what you watched on television instead, what the people you watched on television were wearing, and why it made them look dumpy, what you dreamed about, what you were wearing in your dream, what you're planning on wearing tonight, and many similar topics, each so equally and exquisitely tedious that even you must assume that whoever you're talking to is just grunting in robotic agreement while they check their e-mails."

"Who is this?"

"Mr. Vionnet."

"Who?"

"Here's what I want you to do. First, use your computer to find your Facebook page, the one with those photos of you and your posse in Cancún from last spring, where you're all wearing those tragically undersized bikinis and those grotesquely oversized sunglasses, and hoisting Big Gulp plastic cups filled with lite beer, the pictures where everyone looks so identical that it takes five of you to equal one still-trying-desperately-to-party-while-veering-dangerously-close-to-thirty-single-gal. And I want you to scroll down to the section titled 'My Interests,' where you've listed 'friends, family, hanging out,' and I want you to add, 'lying to myself about everything.'"

"Shut up! I'm calling the police!"

"And you'll report me for doing what? For knowing everything about you, from just one look at your bulging, painfully side-zippered purple suede boots with the stacked heel and the stains from the drips of lo-cal ranch dressing?"

"I love my boots! Everyone loves my boots!"

"Everyone? Do you know *that* many seventies hookers? Let's face it, you've bought your boots, and all of your ideas about life, at the wrong strip mall. So here's how we'll start to fix all that.

After I hang up, you won't make any more calls, and you will in fact actually get some work done, with a surprising sense of satisfaction. Then, on your way home, you won't instantly suck on your cell and begin trading overnight agendas. You won't inhale your iPod either, as you will actually walk home without an artificial soundtrack. You will look at other people, at buildings, at shop windows, at animals, and at New York City. You will actually experience the dusk, rather than narrating it to your friends."

"I don't do that!"

"Not anymore," I said, as I clicked off, and pictured Hallie as she moved through fury, frustration, and finally her first moments of acceptance, as she unwrapped a mini Tootsie Roll and, for the first time in years, actually savored its delicious chemical bouquet.

The next evening, which was Saturday night, I was wearing my pajamas and lying beneath my chaste white cotton sheets, with my head supported by four nondecorative pillows. I imagined that I was an impossibly wealthy patient suffering nobly from some fatal yet appealingly nonsymptomatic illness in an elite Swiss clinic high in the Alps. I lay absolutely still, as if I was being painted for posterity by a gifted surrealist. As I looked at my ceiling, appreciating my chandelier, I felt so blissfully clean and weightless that, once more, I decided to share my good fortune. I phoned Hallie, and the background hubbub gave me all the clues I needed. "It's Elyot," I said, "and I realize that you're slouched on a banquette at a club which has lost just enough of its exclusive, first-three-months trendiness so that it now has to begin admitting yearning acolytes like you and your friends, who are all wearing desperately short, spangled black dresses, which are all cut low enough to reveal that each of you has a matching, tiny navy blue star tattoo, a spray-on tan, and a light dusting of body glitter."

"Shut up! Shut up!"

"And of course, because you've spent your entire evening on the phone, receiving updates from other nearby clubs and hangouts, no man has dared approach you, especially not that deeply cute, just-tousled-enough, possible-art-director, possible-bass-player across the room, who really does have a great crooked smile and whose jeans fit him with such sexual-yet-baggy nonchalance that they might be either plain ol' Levis or $1,200 Japanese custom-fit. But that man will never give you a second glance, and here's why: because while a man might pursue a woman with a few extra pounds or a few missing fingers, and while he might even lust after a woman who looks completely out of place in a nightspot filled with so much painfully processed hair swinging in front of so many Lasik-surgeried eyes, that man will never, and you know I'm right, he will never speak to a woman with even the tiniest, shiniest, most current phone permanently slapped to her ear, like a growth that could only be successfully removed along with a sizable chunk of skull. That omnipresent phone tells him that this woman is eternally hedging her bets, forever seeking some mythical better offer, that this woman does not exist in the moment, which is the essence of flirtation, that this woman has the world on permanent hold."

There was a pause, and then a small voice wondered, "Is that really true?"

"Here's how you'll find out. In thirty seconds, you will place your phone inside your teeny metallic leather clutch bag, beside the lip gloss, the condom, the ATM card, and your doubts. Then, rather than immediately turning to your friends to initiate a point-less, shouted-over-the-DJ conversation, you will sit quietly, but with interest. You will lean forward, watching the room, not with judgment but curiosity. You won't panic, or affect some hideously false come-hither allure. You will not play with, chew on, or flip your hair, or your hair extensions. You will not sip provocatively from your $8 bottled water. You will simply appear engaged in the night. Then I guarantee that within ten seconds that man will smile at you, and instead of immediately beginning to select pri-vate schools for your future children, you will smile back."

I hung up and settled against my pillows, with my arms atop the sheets in perfect, unbent symmetry. I was now the sculpted marble figure of a saint atop my bier in St. Peter's in Rome; I was the saint everyone touched for good luck, and I tried not to be repulsed by all of those sticky, crippled fingers, and all of those gelato-scented, moistly murmured prayers.

Hallie called me the next day, on Sunday afternoon, to thank me, I assumed, for being both so rude and so mind-bendingly accurate. "I need to meet you in person," she said, and I took this as an excellent portent of the new Hallie, choosing human con-tact over technology. We arranged to meet at 4 p.m. in a small park near both our homes. I love city parks, because they're the most artificial version of nature possible. Parks are nature with a falafel cart and a view of the boutique across the street which offers sunglasses for the price of a condominium.

I perched on a bench and watched as Hallie approached. She was not using her phone, and I detected a fresh rigor to her step, a clearness in her eyes, and she was even dressed simply; she looked ten years younger, just out of high school. She easily located me, maybe because I was the only person holding a hand-lettered cardboard sign reading, "You're Welcome."

"Mr. Vionnet?"

"Yes?"

"I did everything you told me. Over the past week, whenever I've taken a cab, I've looked out the window, and I've always had my wallet out and ready at least a block before I got to wherever I was going."

"Hallie," I said, deeply touched, because I find anything involving proper cab etiquette ineffably moving.

"When I was at work, I stayed off the phone and I got way more done, and my boss even noticed and now she's going to recommend me for a raise and a promotion. And on my lunch break, I took my apple and cheese to Washington Square Park and I watched people. I listened to street musicians, I gave helpful directions to out-of-towners, and I even eavesdropped on a tour group, and I learned all of this amazing stuff about the history of the Square, like about which corner was a Potter's Field, and which tree was used to hang Civil War deserters. And I watched three incredible kids on their skateboards, while another bunch of guys did a poetry slam, topping each other with their descriptions of the fountain and the dogs and the sky."

"I love New York," I said with complete sincerity, because Manhattan has never lied to me.

"And last night, at the club, I put my phone away, just like you said I should, and I leaned forward and I smiled. And I thought about how lucky I was, to be young and healthy and to be living in the greatest city on earth. And I started laughing, I was just sort of elated, and that cute guy did come over. He's a novelist who also teaches at NYU and today we had brunch at this place overlooking the river."

"Bravo!" I cried, humbled by her imminent gratitude, and by the gift which she'd most likely brought along—perhaps a small, blank diary bound in alligator, or a candleholder of colorful Mexican tin.

"Fuck you," Hallie continued, her eyes suddenly the steely gray of a Home Depot poured-resin, look-of-granite countertop. "When I wasn't on my phone, I noticed how disgusting the backseat of a cab really is. There's almost always somebody's half-empty plastic thing of take-out salad, and somebody else's used tissues and one grimy pink mitten. And a driver started hitting on me because he thought I didn't have any friends so I'd be an easy mark, and he was sixty-two years old and he smelled like air freshener and corned beef!"

"Excuse me?"

"And because I wasn't making personal calls all the time at work, my boss saw how much free time I had and gave me three times more shit to do, and she kept hanging around my desk and telling me about her divorce and showing me creepy Polaroids of her fucking parrot! Dressed in different outfits for different holidays! And when I took my lunch to the park, because I wasn't on my phone, this one guy kept trying to sell me a phone card and this other guy kept trying to tell me about the

Jehovah's Witnesses and another guy kept telling me about how he only needed five more dollars so he could get his babies out of Darfur! And because I wasn't on my phone I couldn't just politely ignore everyone and I had to talk to them!"

"Perhaps a different park . . ."

"Then, last night at the club, that guy who came over to me? Sure he was cute, but he's a fucking *aspiring* novelist! He has two chapters done, after ten years! He's a teaching assistant who makes ten grand a year and he wants to move to Alaska and live off the grid! And if I'd been using my phone I would've heard about another party just a block away, where all of these lawyers were celebrating their quarterly six-figure bonuses and were buying cars for strangers! And now all of my friends have dumped me because for the past week I haven't been taking their calls so they think that I feel superior to them and that I'm a bad friend and a fucking loser, and now they've changed all of their numbers and they won't give them to me, although I heard that someone used their phone to take a picture of me sitting by myself and laughing at the club, and now it's been posted all over the Web with the caption 'Got Meth?' And it's all your fault! Just because I talk on my phone, it doesn't mean that I'm shallow or useless or stupid! It means I have friends! It means I'm alive! I love my phone, and I think that you're just some nasty, bitter, backwards old fart who's jealous of anyone who knows how to speed-dial! So if you ever call me again, I will use my phone to call the police and have you arrested for trying to ruin my life! You fucking fuckwad fuckhead!"

With that she reached into her purse and grabbed her phone, which flew to her ear like a hummingbird to a gardenia. Hallie spun away from me, chattering ferociously as she marched across the street, sadly unaware of the oncoming double-decker hop-on/hop-off sightseeing bus, which mowed her down, killing her instantly, as the tourists on the upper level captured the tragedy with their picture phones, to the instant delight of their grandchildren back in Oslo.

Hallie was buried later that week in her Long Island hometown, where all of her friends gathered, discreetly text-messaging each other at the graveside to indicate sightings of any totally cute mourners at nearby interments.

Hallie was buried with her phone, and sometimes I still like to call her, first to hear the ringtone echoing off the metallic walls of her casket, and then to hear her last, strangely prophetic recorded greeting: "Hi, this is Hallie, and I'm either screening or on the other line, but please leave a message because I'm dying to talk to you! Luvya lots!" Although I'm sure that by now the microchip is full, I always leave a message, saying, "Darling, this is Mr. Vionnet. Call me."

Hewen and Schifty

1.

New York may be the city of ambition, but it's also a safe harbor for many full-tilt eccentrics. Small towns sometimes embrace their acceptably unhinged cat ladies or irascible gun collectors, especially if they're members of solid local families, but New York all but recruits the most defiantly bizarre personalities, the people who couldn't possibly live anywhere else, at least not without police protection.

As a child, I'd always imagined that simply living in New York, and getting to meet such people, would be my career. As a recent college graduate, I was broke, so I begged my way into a meeting with Helen Merrill, who was known as not just a radically independent-minded literary agent, but as a force of mystery and terror. She lived and worked in an apartment on the second floor of a brownstone in Chelsea, and as I entered, a heavily accented German voice barked, "Vait!"

The apartment was arranged with a cozy but deliberate mix of family antiques, Danish modern sofas, and offbeat touches: all of the curtains were made from hanging ropes of linked soda-can pop tops. After waiting for twenty minutes, I stood and peered into the tiny galley kitchen. Helen was standing over a large, steaming, battered metal stewpot on the stove. She was small and slender, with a silver pageboy haircut, a stained *Ms.* magazine T-shirt, white canvas pants, and faded blue Keds. She was using a metal ladle to stir what I assumed was enough soup to feed a regiment; taking a closer look, I saw that the pot was filled with boiling water, and floating with envelopes. "I am steaming off the stamps and the postage-meter labels," Helen informed me, "so I can use zem again. It saffs money, and I am just a poor German lady." This was how I discovered that Helen was notoriously cheap; I found out later that, after gluing the secondhand postage onto new packages and letters, she'd send an assistant out for hours to deposit the goods, only a few items at a time, in different mailboxes many blocks apart. Helen believed that this canny technique would help her to elude the attention of the FBI.

"Go! Sit!" she commanded, wiping her hands on a dishtowel. Then she lit the first of many, many unfiltered Camels, and unwrapped a Reese's Peanut Butter Cup; over time I learned that cigarettes and Reese's were Helen's entire diet. She was then in her early sixties, but she looked both ancient and age-less, like a particularly hard-living sphinx. Her face was lined with spidery wrinkles and there were serious rumors that she was, in fact, Greta Garbo. Several friends insisted that Garbo, having abandoned her film career, had changed her life and her name, and moved downtown. Helen would sometimes repeat this rumor, laugh, and do nothing to discourage it.

"So," she said, after lighting a fire in her fireplace, taking a few calls, and finally sitting in an armchair opposite me, "why on earth would you want to be a playwright? It is a tewwible life!" At this point Helen had lived in New York for over forty years, and her accent had only deepened; it was particularly effective and intimidating over the phone. When the accent grew especially regal, she'd say, "Oh, I was just being the Countess," and she'd usually add, "You know, I actually am a countess, but I would never use my title, it would be so pwetentious." She'd arrived in America just before World War II, and I later asked her what life had been like back then, for a girl who spoke no English during wartime, and she'd replied, all aglow, "Oh, it was marvelous!"

"I . . . I want to be a playwright because I love the theater," I told Helen, "and because it's all I've ever wanted to do, and because—I don't know how to do anything else."

"Aha!" Helen cried. "So you want to be a playwright because you are totally useless!"

"Yes."

"Well, we shall see."

I felt like, by admitting both my affection for the theater and my complete ineptitude, I had passed a test. Helen liked honesty, although rarely in herself. Like all good New Yorkers, Helen believed in complete and constant self-creation. Helen had come to New York in search of options, of infinite possibilities.

She had wanted to see who she might become, through a combination of hard work, communion with other, equally driven people, and extravagant lying. It sounded good to me.

I began writing plays, which weren't very good and which no one, wisely, was willing to produce, so I supported myself with many odd jobs. These included:

1. In coveralls, I'd lie on my back on a dolly and be shoved underneath the stage at the Juilliard School of Music to paint the underside with thick, black, fire-retardant goo. I'd become coated with this foul-smelling sludge, and people would move away from me on the subway. I felt strangely powerful.

2. A Broadway production of *The Importance of Being Earnest* decided to use real plants for a massive greenhouse scene. I was hired to water the foliage every day, and then lower a bank of ultraviolet lights to keep everything alive indoors. Despite my best efforts, the plants kept dying, and I began using my meager salary to replace the corpses with plastic plants. Finally the grow-lights jammed and I accidentally flooded the dressing rooms and I ran away and I never went back and that's why no one should ever use live plants onstage.

3. When a publisher hired me to write dust-jacket copy, I'd diligently read the manuscripts of all the books I was assigned, so that I could summarize their contents in a paragraph or two. I soon learned that this was an unnecessary step. On the

inside flap of their dust jackets, all first novelists were to be declared "the voice of a new generation," all second or third novelists were to be called "a national treasure," and every nonfiction author was "a champion of truth whom we ignore at our peril." Each work from a genre writer—mysteries, thrillers, romance novels, etc.—was boosted as "an un-put-downable, page-turning, spine-tingling, edge-of-your-seat roller-coaster ride."

4. A soon-to-be-extinct magazine hired me to cover the auction of the Joan Crawford Estate. Among the available items was a pair of the star's legendary fuck-me pumps, which went to an eleven-year-old child actress, who was using the event to attract personal publicity, and who distributed photos of herself as a supporting orphan in *Annie*, and who told reporters that Joan was her role model, "as an actress and a star." The auction peaked when a security guard couldn't stop laughing as he dangled a dusty plastic bag filled with dozens of pairs of Ms. Crawford's pitchfork-caliber false eyelashes. The bidding was fierce, but the lashes eventually went to a guy who ran a housecleaning service and who swore that he only wanted to admire the lashes, as holy relics, and not wear them. I wondered if, in the future, Joan's lashes might heal those born without lashes, or with pale, puny, unbattable lashes.

Since I wasn't making Helen any money as a playwright, she put me to work as a sort of indentured servant. I'd deliver packages for her, and then she began calling me at random times to escort her on mystery trips. She'd never tell me where we were going, but, for example, one afternoon she brought me to the apartment of an eager young composer/lyricist. Without any warning, Helen pointed to me and told the guy, "This is my nephew, Hanschen."

The composer/lyricist wanted Helen to represent both him and his latest project, a rock-opera adaptation of James Joyce's *Ulysses*. He sat down at his piano and played and sang the entire score himself, pummeling the keys and singing his guts out, while Helen chain-smoked and I sat, as I'd been instructed to, cross-legged at her feet.

After howling his rock opera's thunderous climax, the exhausted but hopeful composer/lyricist turned to Helen and asked, "So what do you think?" Helen took a long, slow drag on her cigarette, exhaled deeply, and finally replied, nodding toward me, "He will tell you. Hanschen will tell you what I tink."

I was dumbfounded, but I knew that somehow, through mental telepathy, I was supposed to become Helen's mouth-piece. That's why she'd brought me along; it turned out that the composer/lyricist was a friend of a friend, and Helen had agreed to hear his work as a favor. Therefore, she didn't feel obliged to come up with a coherent opinion. That was my job.

"Well," I began, at a total loss, "Helen thinks that your work is extremely promising…" As I went on, in terms of vague encouragement, Helen would nod sagely, and occasionally smack me on the back of my head to indicate agreement. After we left, I asked Helen why I'd been renamed Hanschen. "Today you are Hanschen." she replied loftily, "Next time you will be Otto."

We repeated this ventriloquist routine at a number of auditions.

One woman proclaimed that her new musical would be a sure-fire blockbuster because "it combines *A Chorus Line* with *Star Wars*." The weird thing was, she was right: the piece was never produced, but it was in fact the story of starving, unemployed actors on other planets.

As my relationship with Helen developed, I learned never to ask her any personal questions, as she maintained her Teutonic allure by remaining militantly private. Once in a very rare while, she'd drop some tidbit regarding her past, so I gradually found out that she'd had many passionate attachments in her life, and that they'd almost all ended badly. I began to understand why it was painful for her to talk about these attachments, but here's what I began to unearth:

Back in Germany, Helen had adored her architect father and battled constantly with her mother, "who wanted me to be a good girl." Helen had a sister who was also now living in New York, on the Upper East Side, and another sister who she said was "cwazy." "How is she crazy?" I asked, assuming that Helen meant she was stubborn or flighty. "Oh no, she is actually cwazy," Helen said. "She's in a mental hospital in Austwia, because she thinks she's a Mother Superior."

Helen had been married to a handsome pianist, and she claimed that they had sometimes met in a confessional at St. Patrick's Cathedral for clandestine lunchtime sex. The pianist had cheated on her, and when she'd tried to leave him, he'd locked her in a closet for three days. There was a stepdaughter, the marriage had ended, and Helen wouldn't permit any more questions. I'm not sure what really went on, but with Helen, sometimes the most unlikely details turned out to be true.

Before becoming an agent, Helen had been a successful photographer, and she'd been friends with people like Diane Arbus. There was a long-boarded-up theatrical hangout on Eighth Avenue, a restaurant called Downey's. It briefly reopened in the nineties, and the walls were still lined with large, moodily lustrous black-and-white portraits of such stage stars as Richard Burton and Jessica Tandy, and it turned out that many of these pictures were Helen's work. Helen only spoke to me once about this career. She said, "One night, I decided, no, I knew, I chust knew, that I wasn't good enough, that I'd never be a gweat photographer. So I said, fine, alwight, then I will never take another picture. So that same night, I took all of my pwints, hundweds of them, and my negatives, and all of my contact sheets, and I took them out into the stweet, and I shoved them into the public garbage cans. Done! But that night it wained, and the next morning I found all of my pictures, glued to the sidewalk, up and down Fifty-seventh Street. Can you imagine?"

After abandoning photography, Helen spent some time in Connecticut, studying printmaking with the artist Josef Albers; Helen had a signed Albers print on her wall. But soon she became an agent, first with a partner and then on her own. I never felt that Helen still wanted to be an artist. She didn't seem regretful, because reinvention and a rigorous lack of nostalgia were always her route to a happier future.

While she was still taking celebrity portraits, Helen had met the very young, rising movie and theater star Tony Perkins. Perkins, whom Helen always referred to as "Toh-neee," had been a teen heartthrob who was eager to pursue more serious work, and he was sexually conflicted. He had long-term affairs with men, including another screen idol, Tab Hunter, but he eventually married and had kids. During his early years, he and Helen had been extremely close, and had shared an apartment. Helen had helped manage his career, and Tony had managed Helen's nose.

Her nose, at the time, had been much longer and curved downwards. "Oh," she told me, "it was a big one." While Perkins was filming *Psycho*, he and the movie's director, Alfred Hitchcock, both kept pressing Helen to have a nose job. She ultimately told them, "Fine, if you will pay for it." They did, and Helen, her face heavily bandaged, had recuperated in one of her favorite vacation spots, the seaside Massachusetts town of Truro. Because of her trouble pronouncing the letter "r", I absolutely loved to hear Helen's interpretation of "Twuwo."

Helen's friendship with Perkins dissolved; she once claimed that a psychic had told Perkins to distance himself from Helen. Whatever the cause, they became estranged, even though Perkins still lived only a few blocks away, with his new family. This was the pattern for many of Helen's bonds, both personal and professional: she'd become tumultuously devoted to someone, and chaos would follow.

Becoming an agent, as a woman in her fifties, must have been a struggle, but Helen was more than up for it. She especially relished being a one-man band; she represented mostly writers and theater designers, and there were no contracts. Helen had her own quirky business practices, based on trust and insanity. She would work tirelessly on a client's behalf, but sometimes she'd drop clients without telling them. She hated confrontation, so if she decided to stop handling someone, she'd just stop taking their calls. Sometimes clients weren't sure if they were still in fact clients; I completely understood when one crazed playwright appeared at Helen's door waving a meat cleaver.

Helen liked to think of herself as both impeccably well-mannered and devilishly raw. The high-toned Helen, when discussing someone's new girlfriend, would say, "Oh, I am sorry, but I simply do not care for her. She is what I would call the 'c' word." Then, after a beat, "You know, a cunt." Helen would also augment her budget-wise wardrobe of rumpled T-shirts and threadbare pants with, say, an Art Deco brooch, set with diamonds. "All you weally need," she'd comment, "is one piece of weally good jewelwy."

As a proud bohemian, Helen was disdainful of her profession. One night, during our early years, she had me accompany her to a fancy dinner party at a producer's apartment. The guest list was high-powered, and I didn't know a soul. Helen was seated beside another agent, a trendily shaggy-haired young hotshot from one of the mammoth uptown agencies, and he kept going on about all of his blue-chip clients and his eight-figure deals. Helen finally turned to him and asked, as loudly as possible, "My darling, tell me, how does it feel to be a pawasite on the awtist?"

"Oh, schnookie," Helen said to me, as I walked her home afterwards. When Helen was slightly drunk, I became "schnookie"; when we were talking business, I was "Wudnick." "Oh, schnookie, all of those tewwible people, at that tewwible party—what did you tink of it?"

"I thought it was wonderful," I said, just to provoke her.

"You did not!" she all but spat. "But why do those people

70

even exist? Oh, I suppose they are making a lot of money. But let us stop for a moment."

Helen then sat on the front steps of her building, and looked up at the sky. I wondered if she was plotting her next career, and her next personality, and her next life.

"I am so old," she said, "but I never complain. Not once. Tell me, haf you ever heard me complain?"

"No," I lied.

"Gudt, that was the correct answer. But if I was to complain, do you know what I would say? I would say, here is the pwoblem, with the world. It is vewy simple. It is people. They are so tewwible. Oh, not you, not yet, you still haf time to become tewwible. Is that what you'd like, to become tewwible?"

"More than anything!"

"It is not a joke. Pwomise me, wight now, tell me that you will twy, not to become tewwible."

"What do you mean?"

"I mean—do not become someone who will do anything for money. Someone who does not wespect other people. Someone who tinks only of himself. A Nazi! An agent! A Wepublican!"

Helen was difficult and controlling and, God knows, secretive, but she was also genuinely moral. She not only helped her clients, sometimes with discreet loans which she knew would never be repaid, but she supported community-action groups and a heroin-addicted nephew and just about anyone else who came to her with a sufficiently dramatic hard-luck story. She was the sort of person you never wanted to disappoint.

"I will try," I promised her, "not to become tewwible."

"And now you are imitating me! Mocking me! You swine!"

I hadn't meant to imitate Helen, not to her face, but that "tewwible" had just popped out.

"I'm sorry!" I cried.

"Well," she said, "you should be. And now, do you know what I would like?" She'd turned wistful. "More than anything else in the world?"

"What?"

"An ice cweam cone." She paused and then shouted, "Go get me one! *Now!*"

2.

If Helen was a creature of shadowy Continental intrigue, Peter was an all-American loon. He was a gifted director, and one of Helen's clients, but his real genius was reserved for running toward friends or strangers on the street, with his arms outstretched, bellowing, "LAAAA!!!!" at the top of his lungs.

Peter was probably the gayest man I'd ever met, and that's saying something. Peter was, and I mean this as a compliment, scary gay. The first time I met Peter, I was at a party, and I felt a strange hand on my thigh. As it traveled upward I shoved the hand away. "Oh darling," Peter said, now coming into view, "I just wanted to say hi, and pleased-to-meetcha. You know, to your dick."

In a very still photograph, Peter wouldn't appear all that instantly, recognizably gay. He had the clear eyes, beaming smile, and perky outlook of someone in a TV commercial, an actor playing a friendly high school English teacher or a trustworthy young insurance agent. In reality, this wholesome, well-come-on-in package was wrapped around what one of Peter's many therapists had termed "a high-functioning polymorphous perverse personality."

Peter was always ebullient, with absolutely no sense of inappropriate behavior. I once asked him when he'd come out to his parents, and he said, "Probably when I was five. They were having a cocktail party with all of their friends and I wanted to entertain everybody. So I came down the stairs into the living room wearing a towel turban and lip-synching to an Eartha Kitt record." Peter's adolescence was pure porn: he'd actually had sex with half the guys on his high school's football team. When I asked him how he'd managed to do this, he said, "I was just really friendly, and most of the guys' girlfriends wouldn't have sex with them, or not often, and I would. What can I say, I was popular! Go, team!"

After having sex with probably everyone in his home state, Peter moved to New York. We would go out together, to parties and bars and clubs. Being with Peter was both wildly exhilarating and almost always embarrassing. On the one hand, he'd talk to anyone, which came in handy, for introductions. On the other hand, since Peter had no self-censoring mechanism, he'd say anything; if there was a lull in the conversation, Peter would grab the three nearest guys and say, "Okay, you, you, and you—let's all go home together, have sex, and then make popcorn!" If he was on the street and Peter saw an attractive man, he'd grin and growl, "Hey there, sailor boy!" and invite the guy back to his apartment. Peter would try this on young studs, rabbinical students, and tourists out sightseeing with their wives and children. Peter's glee was so spontaneous and untroubled that no one ever punched him, except his friends; his love objects would either run in the opposite direction or go home with him.

Once, Peter and I were invited for a weekend at a friend's woodsy country cabin, in the Catskills. Our rental car got stuck in a ditch at the beginning of the dirt road that led to the house. We hiked up to the front porch, and our host called the property's caretaker, a grizzled local in overalls, a plaid flannel shirt, and steel-toed work boots. He arrived promptly, along with his mulleted, teenaged, high school quarterback son. By the time they got our car moving and came up to the house, Peter was in the kitchen, wearing a flowered apron, because he was busily tossing a bowl of fruit salad. In his mind, Peter had become a fetching suburban housewife, and easy prey for the local roughnecks. Peter was having trouble unscrewing the lid to a jar of mayonnaise, so, with the glass salad bowl balanced on his hip, he held out the stubborn jar to the caretaker. "Why don't you try it," he whispered, with a Marilyn Monroe breathiness, *"Hercules?"* As the caretaker speedily opened the jar, the host and I ran from the house. Later, Peter asked us, "But why did you two take off like that?" "Because, Peter," I yelled, "you grew a VAGINA!" "Did I?" Peter giggled, tilting his head dreamily, now a winsome debutante awaiting her corsage.

From a certain perspective, Peter was perfectly well-adjusted: he saw the world as a happy, abundant place, and it was his job to sleep with everyone in it. He also lacked any form of urban gay elitism; he didn't have a specific physical "type" and went to bed with all ages, shapes, and races. Gender wasn't even an issue; one night a female friend of Peter's dropped by, distraught over a recent breakup. "So we had sex," Peter told me the next day. "I mean, she's such a great person, and I just hated seeing her so down about everything." "But she's a woman," I said. "I know," said Peter, "isn't that funny? The whole time we were doing it, I was having a great time, but I kept thinking, 'But you're a woman!'"

I only once caught Peter in a moment of cultural disdain. He was working on a new musical, and the book was being written by a fellow who lived on Staten Island, with his wife and children. Peter would return from his meetings and report, "Oh my God, I can't tell you what a pleasure it is to be around a normal, decent American family. Because, please, you know I love New York, but sometimes everything is too gay, gay, gay. And with Harold, I just bask in all of this amazing real life, with a mom and a dad and a lawn and a dog. Maybe you should try it." I finally met Harold when he came into the city; he couldn't have been nicer, but he was only five feet tall and had the tiniest hands. After asking around, I discovered a particularly relevant chapter from Harold's past, and I couldn't wait to tell Peter: "Darling," I said, "I thought Harold was just terrific, but don't you know—he's a transsexual. He used to be a woman. His wife was his girlfriend, and their kids are adopted." "I don't believe it!" Peter insisted, and then, "Oh, but he does have those little doll hands . . ."

As far as I know, Peter and Helen never had sex, but they were dear friends. Peter loved to mimic Helen's accent, referring to her as Hewen Mewwill, and since Peter's last name was Schifter, Helen called him Schifty. Like a large cat, Peter was always trying to coax people into scratching his neck or rubbing his shoulders. One night at Helen's apartment, I watched as Helen obliged, and Peter literally purred. "Mmmm..." he said, squirming luxuriantly, with his eyes closed, "I'm just Mister Sex Kitten."

Yes, Peter could be appalling, but there was also something pure about him: he was trusting, and he believed that life could be glorious. So when he got sick, he was at first uncomprehending, and then he became withdrawn, refusing to see friends or family members, but finally his lifelong optimism, his maniacally irrepressible style, reasserted itself. "I'm sick," he told me, "and I'm probably going to die, and it's all going to be unspeakably horrible, but do you know what? I don't know why, but I just don't believe it." This may have been heartbreaking, and an especially extreme form of denial, but it was also Peter at his giddy best.

His first hospitalization lasted many weeks. Christmas was coming, so Peter had six nurses pose around his bed, like Ziegfeld girls, and he had them photographed pointing to a bedsore on his undraped behind. He then used this full-color image on his Christmas card. As his illness progressed, Peter began to suffer from AIDS-related dementia, and one day I found him shoved into the far corner of his hospital bed. I asked him why he didn't stretch out, and he said that he couldn't, because there were people waiting outside his window who were planning to shoot him. I asked, "But who would ever want to shoot you?" Peter than looked at me, with the grandest, haughtiest outrage, and declared, as if he were standing at center stage, in an important gown, "Assassins!"

While Peter and Helen were close, she never went to see

him at the hospital. "I just can't," she told me, and at first I was shocked. But then, as I was dropping something off at her apartment, as I was leaving, she grabbed my elbow, hard. "How is Peter?" she asked. "How is he doing?"

"Not great," I said.

"Am I a tewwible person? Because I will not go to see him?"

"No. I mean, I told him you were thinking about him, and he's pretty out of it . . ."

"Stop," she said, interrupting my chatter. She sat down, shaking. "I can't, I cannot—see people like that. I cannot see them . . . when they are sick, and dying. That is not how I wish to wemember them. That is not who they are."

It occurred to me that Helen, more than anyone, and certainly more than Peter, was terrified of death, of any sort of faltering or shutting down. A fatal illness meant that there would be no more cigarettes or chocolate or fresh starts. And Helen desperately believed that escape was always an option, and that everyone was entitled to an unlimited number of new lives.

I didn't think that Helen was terrible; I thought that she was, despite her often rigid, tough-fräulein façade, completely human. She believed in compassion, and in behaving well under difficult circumstances, and when she couldn't live up to her own high standards, it was the closest she ever came to falling apart.

A few years later, when Helen developed emphysema, she was taken to the hospital, clutching her Xeroxed phone list; if she was still returning calls, she'd never die. The last time I saw her, she was still full of plans for new plays and new clients. "Oh, Wudnick," she said, "I have so much to do." She had planned for the future, however; her frugality had paid off, because she left an estate of almost four million dollars, stipulating that most of the money would be put in trust, to create an annual set of cash awards for up-and-coming playwrights.

At Peter's memorial, a friend remembered how Peter had once studied the grim, ultramodern set for some Shakespearean tragedy; the set was a sort of bleakly lit jungle gym of rusted iron bars. "Do you know what I would do with this set?" Peter had decided. "I'd tie big pink bows all over it." He was joking, and maybe this is an incredibly shallow thought, but still— which production would you rather see?

Sixty Seconds

When I was growing up, the family across the street had a rich uncle who worked as an art director on many movies and long-running TV shows. And every Christmas this uncle would ship his relatives what seemed like a truckload of gifts, wooden crates filled with professionally wrapped packages containing all the latest toys and games and clothing. I knew that deliveries from Hollywood were special, as if the boxes were packed with actual, napping movie stars and freeze-dried palm trees.

Years later, after my first play was produced Off-Broadway, to a resounding and completely justified lack of acclaim, I got a call from a Hollywood producer named Allan Carr. Allan had seen my show and wanted me to write the screenplay for a new, updated version of the sixties spring-break romp *Where the Boys Are*, a movie remembered mostly for its yearning title song—"Where the boys are, someone waits for me . . ."—as keened by Connie Francis. I was at a low ebb, but I wasn't sure if *Where the*

Boys Are was the antidote, so Allan offered to fly me down to Fort Lauderdale for some on-site convincing.

I was greeted at the airport by Allan, who was dressed in what can only loosely be called men's clothing: he was wearing picture-window-sized, white-framed sunglasses, white espadrilles, white capri pants, and a voluminous white silk blouse accessorized, at the breast, with a gleaming emerald brooch in the shape of a tortoise. He was standing, like Washington crossing the Delaware, in the backseat of an electric-cherry-red Rolls-Royce convertible with white leather upholstery; picture a hostessy polar bear bursting from the center of some enormous, heart-shaped satin candy box. The car was being chauffeured by a stunning, six-foot-tall, richly tanned blonde whose necklace spelled out her name in diamond chips: Starr. Starr was a superb driver, while wearing only a crocheted, powder blue string bikini and bronze, spike-heeled sandals. "Darling!" Allan yelped, tossing me into the backseat beside him. "This is just the Rolls—wait till you see Florida!"

Spring break had reached full capacity, and the streets of Fort Lauderdale were jammed with thousands of the sort of vivacious, platinum-fried coeds still tickled to be called coeds, being pursued by frat boys whose baseball caps came equipped with holsters for two cans of beer, attached to elaborate tubing leading to their mouths. Starr eased the convertible through this writhing, "Jen, over here!" mob, as if we were an ambassador's family fleeing the fall of some riot-torn republic. As Allan waved merrily, his blouse billowing and the sunlight bouncing off his emeralds, I was convinced that the college kids would torch the car, drag our pleading bodies from the flames, and then crucify us, before moving on to a wet T-shirt contest.

A note on my use of the term "blouse": I feel that any white silk garment that reaches the wearer's knees cannot really be called a shirt. "Blouse" has more grandeur. Years later, I witnessed a different, violently heterosexual movie producer wearing an even more Grecian white silk blouse as he entered a studio commissary in Los Angeles. Because his latest action blockbuster had grossed over 500 million worldwide, and because he was accompanied by Arnold Schwarzenegger, all of the executives abandoned their salads to claw their way toward the producer, assuring him, "Great look!" "Is that silk? I'm insane for silk!" and "Where can I get that? Tell me!"

Back in Florida, as I awaited certain dismemberment, the crowd surrounded the car, bringing us to a standstill, and a contingent of rowdy, shirtless guys in cargo shorts clambered onto the hood, like apes atop a downed fighter jet in the jungle. One dude approached Allan; "Man," he demanded, running a paw over the car's cherry red enamel, "whattya call this thing?" The crowd hushed and Allan replied, with not a little snobbery, "Expensive." As one, the kids roared their approval, and all the guys began high-fiving a jubilant Allan. The seas parted, and we soon reached our hotel.

Allan was riding high. He'd caught the showbiz bug early on, and by college he was already investing in Broadway revues. He'd managed the careers of such stars as Peter Sellers, Ann-Margret, and Marlo Thomas, and then escalated to producing, where his hits had included the movie version of *Grease* and the stage musical of *La Cage Aux Folles*. He'd bought Kim Novak's Hollywood estate and installed a neon-lit disco in the basement. His track record had allowed him free rein on his less lucrative projects, like the Village People musical *Can't Stop the Music*, which had starred a rollerskating Steve Guttenberg and Olympic champion Bruce Jenner, in a midriff-revealing sweatshirt. My friend Eric had worked as a production assistant on *Can't Stop the Music*, where his duties had included buying jockstraps for the near-naked, teasingly photographed locker-room number. Eric later worked for a Saudi prince, the one who'd acquired a Beverly Hills mansion where his landscaper had painted the pubic hair on all of the outdoor statuary an eye-catching tomato red. Eric had left that job after coming across a document that, in the event of an armed kidnapping attempt, listed the relative physical importance of all employees; Eric's job level had put him in the category of easily expendable human shield.

Once I'd unpacked at the hotel, I was told to find Allan on the beach, for his version of a script meeting. He'd changed into a resplendent linen caftan with a tropical print of palm fronds, pineapples, and toucans. He was leading an entourage that included at least twelve assistants, business associates, and an in-house drug dealer. As we strolled, Allan began discussing what he called "our movie": "I want it to be young and sexy and just wild! I want the hottest guys and the most gorgeous girls, climbing all over each other!" As he babbled, Allan would nod toward an actual hot guy playing volleyball or a gorgeous girl lounging on a nearby towel, and an assistant would race over and ask the young person if he or she wanted to come to a party and be in a movie. Phone numbers were acquired. Because we were on Earth, everyone said yes.

Allan wasn't clear on specific plot points, at least not yet, but he knew what he liked. He'd turn to an assistant and announce, "You know what this movie's gonna need? A whole pack of beautiful socialites, wonderful old stars, like June Allyson or Gloria DeHaven. In those gorgeous watercolor print chiffon garden-party dresses! And they'll be chic and dizzy and they could be spying on the kids! Gloria DeHaven, in a chiffon dress, climbing a ladder! I love that! That's the movie!" And the assistant would murmur, "Gloria DeHaven" into a mini Japanese tape recorder, as the other assistants debated whether Gloria was still alive, or, as they put it, "available."

Later that evening Allan and his crew gathered for a family-style dinner at our hotel's restaurant. Until this point, Allan had been nothing but effusive and embracing; he was like the tireless Grand Marshall of some personal Rose Bowl parade. Like everyone else, from the kids on the beach to the dads from Omaha snapping photos of the man in the dress, I couldn't wait to see what Allan would do or wear next. But then, around nine p.m., Allan began to sag alarmingly, and his celluloid-bright eyes dimmed. He also became increasingly vicious, not to me, but to his staff: "I said I needed to call the L.A. office, you fucking moron," he'd snarl. "What am I paying you for? Why don't you die?" This transformation was shockingly abrupt and quickly remedied, a few minutes later, by a drug delivery. Allan's joyous spirit returned, due to the largest rock of cocaine I have ever seen, hanging from his nose. Like everything else about Allan, even his substance abuse resembled a Christmas tree ornament.

The next morning began at an upscale marina, where a fast-food mogul was hosting a party aboard his yacht, to herald Allan's arrival in Fort Lauderdale, and to thank Allan for all the business he'd be bringing to the city. The dock overflowed with local politicians, newspaper photographers, and TV news crews. Allan posed happily with just about everyone, and then he headlocked both me and the owner of the yacht. As the flash-bulbs popped, he asked, "So, Paul, what do you think the caption to this picture should say?" "*Indicted*," I replied, and while Allan laughed, the yachtsman wasn't so sure.

I'd never been on a yacht, and the experience was everything I'd hoped for: appallingly ostentatious and irresistible luxury, like riding the waves while straddling enormous bales of cash. Yachts, like private planes, feel deliciously sinful, because they're so unnecessary. Nobody really needs a plane or a yacht, but once someone has far too much money, they start looking for trinkets to fly or to sail, telling themselves, "I've earned it," "You only live once," "It actually saves me time" and other such daily affirmations for billionaires. I imagined that poor people had been stored somewhere below, and could be jettisoned, as ballast. As we set out to sea, I found that the craft was stocked with bars, buffets, a helpful crew, and, mostly in swimwear, all of the male and female bodies which Allan had been picking up on the beach. They were being used, to their sometime confusion, as human decor. Allan was grouping them, beside railings and on deck chairs, for maximum effect: "Kimmie, stand next to Chad. Chad, put your arm around Savannah's waist. Perfect!"

I explored a blindingly polished mahogany hallway, and opened one of many doors. I peeked into a stateroom with

Wedgwood blue walls, cut crystal lamps with pleated silk shades, and a suite of antique French furniture, all of it bolted to the floor, in case of choppy waters. At the center of the room were Allan and a friend, on all fours, rooting around in the lush, cream-colored wall-to-wall carpeting. At first I assumed that someone had lost a contact lens, but then I saw that the two men had accidentally dropped some cocaine, and were snorting it directly out of the rug. Allan didn't stand up, or even rise to his knees. He simply rotated his head toward me and said, smiling, "If you ever write about this, I'll have you killed."

I withdrew and, a half-hour later, I was summoned to the rear deck of the yacht, where Allan was nestled on a built-in banquette upholstered in navy canvas. He was now wearing lime green harem pants, pointy-toed gold slippers, and a burnt-orange tunic embroidered with tiny Moroccan mirrors; he looked like a well-fed fortune-teller, or a special guest Mah-Jongg champion on *The Golden Girls*. Allan had always struggled with his weight, and he'd once had his mouth wired shut; I'd heard that he'd quickly wrenched out this apparatus himself, using pliers, because he craved éclairs and strawberry ice cream and because he couldn't stop talking. I sat beside him as the yacht glided past many impressive homes. As in Beverly Hills, the architecture of Fort Lauderdale called to mind a Hollywood back lot, with its careening mismatch of eras: there was a Roman villa, a Loire Valley château, and a sleek mid-century creation that resembled a private airline terminal. "So, what do you think of me?" Allan inquired, as he sipped from a large martini glass outfitted with a paper umbrella, a lemon wedge, and an orchid.

"I think you're . . . great," I replied automatically, because I was his guest.

"Fuck you," Allan said, still completely upbeat. "That's not what you think, not really. That's not what anybody thinks. So tell me, be completely honest, I'm a big boy—am I a clown? An asshole? Am I some ridiculous drug-crazed fatso Hollywood faggot?"

I hadn't been expecting this. Allan was, of course, all these things, but he was also extremely smart. "Look," he continued, "I'm from fucking Illinois. And I was a chubby little kid who wanted to be Mitzi Gaynor. And that ain't easy. But it ain't bad. And do you want to know my secret? Do you want to know why I live in a mansion, and why I'm worth God knows how many gazillions, and why when I call the head of any studio in the civilized world, they stop what they're doing and they take the call? And they say, 'Allan, do you know how much we love you?'"

"Why?"

"Because I wanted to be Mitzi Gaynor more than anyone else. Because I knew it was nuts and I didn't care. Because I said, I could give a shit if people laugh at me. But you know what? They didn't. Because I had an eye. Because I knew how to get things done. Because thanks to me, my high school had the hottest marching band with the most incredible uniforms, the biggest prom with the most silver and white balloons and an indoor waterfall, and a senior musical that got an offer to play in New York at the Winter Garden. And, no, I wasn't the star quarterback or the homecoming queen. But they were my best friends. I *represented* the star quarterback and the homecoming queen. So when I throw a bash, in Kim Novak's house, do you know who shows up?"

"Mitzi Gaynor?"

"And Streisand. Sean Connery. Nicholson. Every fucking star in the world. Because everyone wants to work. And, believe me, I was a manager for way too long, and I know how crazy these people are. How needy. The phone calls. 'Why did they cast her?' 'Should I get my eyes done?' 'Why didn't I see that script first?' But I love them. They're not Mitzi, nobody's Mitzi, but I love them."

I was feeling both excited and nervous, which is just how powerful people want everyone in their orbit to feel at all times, off-balance and therefore vulnerable. I still wasn't exactly sure what I was doing there. I wasn't attractive enough to serve as window dressing, and I knew that my play had been, at best, a nice try.

"Here's what I'm gonna do," said Allan, sizing me up. "I'm gonna make your wildest, filthiest dreams come true. Because I know who you are. I know who everyone is. So for the next sixty seconds, you can ask me anything, no matter how personal, about any star in Hollywood. Because I know all of them and I know everything. And you can ask about whatever you want, sex, money, murder, you name it. And I swear that, after you ask your questions, after the sixty seconds are up, I will tell you everything I know, in detail, and all of it. The God's honest truth. This is the opportunity of a lifetime, and you know it." He raised his forearm and stared at the massive diamond-and-ruby-encrusted platinum Cartier watch on his wrist. "Sixty seconds. Go."

I knew what I'd been offered. Allan had just worked with Travolta and Olivia Newton-John, he knew all the young hotshots and all the legendary names. And of course, Allan did know who I was: if I couldn't be Mitzi Gaynor, I sure as hell wanted to know whom she was fucking or who she'd had killed or whether she'd had anything lifted or tucked or sandblasted. As I groped for my first question, as my tabloid memory lurched from its starting blocks, I felt as if I were having a stroke and a heart attack and a divine vision, all at the same time. It wasn't that my mind went blank, it went convulsively white. Every little-boy-from-New-Jersey brain cell blasted into hyperdrive, and the harder I tried, the more I couldn't think of a single boldface name, replaceable body part, or mouth-watering scandal.

"Time's up!" Allan crowed, looking up from his wristwatch.

"But . . . but . . ." I blathered, begging the teacher for a few extra seconds on the pop quiz, pleading with the Reaper for an instant's reprieve.

"Sorry!"

I was so flabbergasted, so shakingly desperate that I didn't even think to ask if Allan played this insidious game all the time and if other, less amateur, contestants had come up with the goods.

"So," said Allan, "how about my movie? Have you thought about it? Whattya say?"

"I . . . well, I . . ." I was still spinning, from the whole experience, from the day and the sun and the boat and Allan. He laughed.

"I know," he said, "you're gonna tell me that you need to think about it just a little more, which means no. That always means no. And it's okay. Go write another little play. And when my movie's a smash, I'll call you every morning and laugh and hang up."

I was relieved that the decision had been made. I'd been wavering: I'd never written a movie before, the money would've been great, but while I liked Allan, and I found him fascinating, I didn't want to owe him anything. Because Allan wasn't just Mitzi Gaynor. He was Mitzi Gaynor with a coke habit and a bottomless hunger for constant movement, the brightest colors, and purchasable pleasure, and, when such things weren't available, blistering revenge. And I didn't want to be under contract when the coke ran out.

I didn't see Allan again until sixteen years later. His *Where the Boys Are* remake hadn't been a success, and his fortunes had nose-dived. He'd been especially reviled for producing the 1989 Academy Awards telecast, where he'd aimed to juice things up by having Rob Lowe duet on "Proud Mary" with an actress dressed as Snow White. Disney had sued for damage to Snow White's reputation.

It was July, and Allan was staying out at the Long Island beach house of a mutual friend. Allan had asked to see me, and I couldn't resist. He emerged from the house, in the heat, wearing the saddle shoes, the Kelly green corduroys, and the patchwork, crewneck shetland sweater of a freshman, or a chorus boy in a 1920s musical playing a freshman. He was using two canes, and he was also being supported by a much younger companion, someone in his twenties with questionably blond hair. Allan was in fragile health and would die, a few months later, of liver disease. But that afternoon he seemed as bouncy as ever, and even innocent.

"How are you?" he asked. "It's so wonderful to see you! But you should be tan!"

Allan sat, and I noticed that all of the outdoor chaises, and there were at least five, had been smoothly draped with beach towels printed with the *La Cage Aux Folles* logo. The towels looked brand-new, as if they'd been preserved in their original packaging since the show had closed, twelve years earlier. Allan was curious about my work, and he said that he was developing a new stage musical based on *Huckleberry Finn.* Raising his arms, he said, "Because I *am* Huckleberry Finn!"

"I thought you were Mitzi Gaynor," I recalled.

He grinned. "If Huckleberry Finn and Mitzi Gaynor had given birth to a very strange child, that would be me," he decided. That sounded about right: Allan was definitely the offspring of a movie star and a fictional character.

"Everyone thinks I'm dead," he continued, without rancor, "and sometimes even I think I'm dead, but not just yet."

"You're not dead!" worried his young friend. "I would know!"

"Kids," Allan murmured, gesturing to the boy and rolling his eyes. "But, you know," he remarked, turning his face to the sun, "for the first time in my life, at least I'm thin." At this last meeting, I was tempted to think of Allan as Norma Desmond, as a faded, demented diva, a relic of so many earlier Hollywoods and so much sequined excess. But unlike Norma Desmond, I bet Allan would've gotten the joke.

I Sh*u*dder:

An Excerpt from the Most Deeply Intimate and Personal Diary of One Elyot Vionnet

Yumbies

I don't know what possessed me. Oh, yes I do.

I was sitting up in bed on Tuesday morning, wearing my appealingly coarse white Irish linen nightshirt and nibbling on a slice of lightly browned and buttered whole-wheat toast, which had been presented to me on a tray by my imaginary manservant, Shabar. To avoid any issues of workplace discrimination, Shabar is of no particular race or creed, although I do change his skin tone to match my mood; this morning his face was an enigmatic cobalt blue, to accent the five brilliant yellow tulips sprouting from the miniature botanical garden atop his head, which also included a tiny koi pond and an almost invisible Shinto shrine. I used my remote to switch on the small television located inches from my feet.

I was expecting to watch the very latest incarnation of one of my true folk heroes, Martha Stewart. Since she was released from prison, Martha has been determined to reclaim her title as America's Headmistress. I worship Martha, because she actually stands for something, for doing it right, for taking the time, for doing your time, and for power-sanding vintage steel medical cabinets and then having them professionally spray painted with high-gloss auto enamel to exactly match your jadeite green forties mixing bowls and countertop appliances. Martha sets an example, and she doesn't care about being liked; she in fact discourages such easy chumminess. I model myself after Martha, as I'm tough yet fair.

And so I was looking forward to enjoying my toast and Martha, but she'd been bumped, for an entirely new program, some fresh lifestyle hour. The setting was not Martha's arctic Connecticut domain, but something more homey: a Great Room, that hideous American hybrid of sunny Tuscan kitchen, butcher-block tabled dining zone, and shapeless, over-wired, sectional sofa–ridden entertainment area. The Great Room neatly encapsulates all that is wrong with this country: it's a place for people wearing shin-length, untucked T-shirts and elasticized-waist sweatpants to gorge themselves while mesmerized by the largest possible, most wall-disfiguring flat-screen advance. I am convinced that morbidly obese people crave the most cavernous rooms and refrigerators in order to feel smaller, as a form of architectural dieting. This aimless sprawl was accessorized with grinning ceramic sunbursts, a roaring gas fireplace, and bookshelves "merchandised" with decorative obelisks, dried topiaries, and wooden bowls piled with useless spheres crafted from bark—anything but books. And then, exploding into all of this overlit, sumptuously banal, earth-toned hell came, as her announcer boomed, "someone just like you—hey, America, it's Abby McAdams!"

Abby, Google later informed me, had first been discovered as a college junior, when she'd participated in a reality show, rooming with several other kids in a loft in Denver. Abby had been extremely popular, applying her naturally exuberant outlook to extended chats with everyone, particularly a suicidal roommate given to cutting herself with a penknife. "Come on," Abby had counseled this morose young lady, "do you really want to spend the rest of your life wearing turtlenecks and long sleeves?" After graduation, Abby had founded a party-planning and catering service, specializing in bachelorette wingdings where the bride-to-be was served cupcakes iced with phrases listing her finest assets, such as "Your great big ol' heart!" and "Your rockin' boo-tay!" Abby's appearances on local morning shows had led to network attention, and now here she was, all but bursting from my television.

Everything about Abby seemed barely containable: her smile was a mile wide, flashing enough dental bonding to retile a subway stop, her jostling breasts threatened to leap from her skimpy tank top, vanquish her shrunken corduroy blazer, and wet-nurse the nation, and there was a boisterous band of pink flesh winking above the waistband of her shrink-to-fit, low-rise white jeans. When did this exposed sliver become an acceptable erogenous zone? Even on slimmer mortals it feels like a mistake, a swollen gall bladder marauding for its freedom.

"Hi there, hey there, what's up, you guys!" Abby exclaimed, acknowledging her studio audience's instantaneous standing ovation. Abby accepted this prolonged and lusty acclaim as her due, as if the obstetrician and nurses in attendance at her birth had been equally ecstatic: "Yay, it's Abby! Let's hear it! What a wonderful baby!" On the show, Abby eventually and reluctantly quieted her fans, and began her opening remarks: "Oh, man, are we gonna have fun today or what? First I'm gonna tell you all about my morning, and getting Max and Arabella off to school, and somehow making hubby Glen feel like I still love him best and the magic is still there—sometimes all it takes is a hug and a tiny little shopping bag from Victoria's Secret, am I right, ladies? And then we're gonna make some five-minute, I am not kidding you, five-minute angel hair pasta and peaches, yum-a-*lum*, and then we're gonna talk to Doctor Mike about seasonal depression, and why the heck February makes us all so gosh-darn ornery, I'm telling you, sometimes I just wanna tell Glen, hey, I know that it's Valentine's Day, but get off me, and then we're gonna have a very special visit from Cassandra Callahan, who plays Kelly on *Impossible Choices*, and who's here to tell us all about her skin-care collection for women who just don't have the time! Like you and like me, heck, look at my freakin' T-zone, I need spackle, I need sandpaper, I need Cassandra's totally miraculous Totally Miraculous Under-Eye Savior Gel! And I'm not sayin' that everyone in our audience is getting the entire Totally Miraculous Facesaver Plus Regimen Starter Kit, but yes, you are! Yay! Double yay! Let's get this party started!"

Something had to be done.

To make certain that I was responding rationally, I watched Abby's program again the next morning. She introduced her first guests: "Guys, I'd like you to meet two very special ladies, Candy Amberella and her daughter Kaitlyn, who both lost their husbands, who were firefighters, on 9/11. Can you imagine? I mean, I wasn't even in the city on that day, I was still busy plannin' parties out in freakin' San Diego, but I felt it. I knew it was bad. My heart was aching, I'm sure all of our hearts were aching, and maybe you were like me and you thought about the families and you thought, What could I make for them that would be both quick and easy, but also really yum-tastic? And that's when I came up with my idea for what I call Emergency Desserts, great-tasting, one-step, no-cooking treats that you can whip up when your neighbor's space heater explodes, or your sister's kids get into a highway pile-up after the prom, or when, God forbid, there's some sort of terrorist attack and we're all thrown together and we're crying and we're hugging and we're hungry. And I've asked Candy and Kaitlyn to sample my Lend-A-Hand Lemon Squares and to share their stories, about what they've been through, whether they've started dating again, and what they're cookin' for their families and maybe those hot new guys in their lives. Right after the break!"

I tried to determine exactly what appalled me the most, to the point where even seeing Abby's name in a newspaper listing caused an involuntary facial twitch. Was it her howitzer-level confidence, her use of the word "freakin'" as an expletive substitute, or the fact that when the focus wasn't entirely on her, I could literally see her mind wander, as her eyes glazed over and her head veered to one side. No, while all of these habits were certainly irritating, what truly disturbed me was her pride in her own lack of skills. She was a professional amateur; she had trademarked her own blundering. While Martha represented the rewards of research and practice, Abby embodied the triumph of the microwave attention span. "Shabar," I declared, "fetch my glen-plaid double-breasted suit, my Inverness cape, my homburg, and my walking stick. I'm going out."

Suitably attired, I began my trek across town, to a Barnes & Noble where Abby was holding a book signing, for the latest in a series which included *Abby McAdams' Sixty Second Entrees, Abby McAdams' Plan Your Wedding in a Weekend,* and *Abby McAdams' Have Your Baby Today!* As I strode along, Abby's face beamed at me from buses, billboards, and newsstands, which featured her signature magazine, *Abby Does It!,* with the cover lines "Six Great Vacations Without Leaving Home," "Twenty-Five Surefire Stressbusting No-Sew Slipcovers," and "From Zero to Orgasm Without Even Looking at Him." The city had become utterly ruled by Abby, from promos on JumboTron screens to window displays of Abbissima Almost Organic hair-care products, to sidewalk vendors offering bootlegs of Abby's *Sit-Snack-and-Lose* CD-ROMs. I felt Abby urging me on, toward our summit, our destiny, our Abby-tastic showdown.

I took my place at the end of a line over two blocks long, snaking out of the bookstore and into the street. The woman ahead of me was clutching the entire McAdams library. "Why do you love her so much?" I asked. "Because I watch her and I think, that really could be me!" the woman replied. "I never make any of her recipes or follow any of her advice, but I just think she's so cute and . . . and . . . she's a role model. She says, if you can't really do something, who cares?"

"And do you ever watch Martha Stewart?"

"Sometimes," the woman confessed, lowering her voice, "but she scares me."

"Why?"

"Because I know that if I didn't do everything just the way she says, she'd come to my apartment and slap me, really hard."

Hours passed, and I was finally in range. Abby was seated beside an enormous photo blow-up of herself holding a glistening version of what she had titled her Meatless-Mindless-Don't-Tell-Your-Mother Casserole. She was flanked by personal assistants, bodyguards, publicists, and giddy store representatives. In person, Abby was every bit as moistly nuclear as on television. As she signed the many McAdams volumes being offered by the woman in front of me, she squealed, "Thank you for coming! I love you!" "I love *you*!" the woman squealed in response, with that desperate yearning which is indistinguishable from an immediate need to urinate. As the handlers guided the woman away, I stepped forward. "Look at you!" Abby exclaimed, "It's Sherlock Holmes! It's Harry Potter!" Abby, like most Americans, was both astounded and perplexed at the sight of a man wearing a well-cut suit, a perfectly knotted tie, and a scrupulously tufted pocket square. "Do you have a book?" she asked me. "Would you like to buy one?"

As one of the store reps offered me a copy of *Abby McAdams' Clean Enough*, one of Abby's assistants handed her a cell phone. Abby held up an index finger, telling me, "Just a sec, hon." I waited patiently for her to finish her call, and then she told me, near tears, that, "Oh, my freakin' God, that was really amazing news. I just signed a deal to endorse an entire line of Abby-Approved Easy Meals. Pretty soon when you go to the supermarket, you'll see a whole bunch of stuff marked with my Double-A, Abby-Approved Seal. There's gonna be Stuffing-In-A-Jiff, Chicken-In-A-Tube, and Lo-Carb-Gag-On-The-Gallon-Mega-Yum-Ice-Cream-Alternative."

As always, I tried to be fair. I gazed deeply into the twin shiny black marbles that were Abby's eyes, and I said, "Abby, I'm begging you. Please offer me a single valid reason for your existence."

"Hon," she replied, with her warmest smile, as she took my hand, "dontcha get it? There is no reason. That's the whole deal. That's why everyone loves me. I'm just a person. And all I want to do is to let people know, that it's okay to just be you, and to never get any better at it. I just want to hug everyone in this whole dang world and tell 'em, 'Hey there, whatever it is, whether it's a lumpy salad dressing or a relationship-gone-wrong or your sister's degenerative heart disease, don't worry about it. Just give up, and you're gonna feel great.' Now, did you buy a book? Who should I sign it to?"

Before I could answer, someone had shoved one of Abby's books into my hand, while someone else had grabbed my wallet and removed $49.99. The next thing I knew, I was back out on the sidewalk. I opened the book in my hand, to see what Abby had scribbled on the title page. It said, "To that kooky old guy—You got gabby with Abby!!! Live and Love, Abby McA!!!" At first I allowed her a certain measure of respect, for resist-ing the preteen impulse to add tiny hearts or smiley faces to her signature, but then I saw the rubber-stamped addendum, in shimmery purple ink, reading "Yumbies 2 U!!!"

"Oh, Shabar," I said the next morning, as I sat up in bed, relishing my ice water and my bowl of Alpha-Bits. I consider Alpha-Bits to be a classic cereal, as the quarter-inch, sugar-drenched letters not only taste scrumptious but, arguably, provide most Americans with their primary reading material. "I wonder," I asked Shabar, "is this Abby phenomenon perhaps entirely acceptable? Is she simply a hardworking, unassuming, totally adorable great American, can-do success story?" Shabar thought this over, as the white tiger cub now perched on his shoulder playfully swatted Shabar's cheek with his paw. Shabar, whose face was now a vivid plaid, smiled with all of the unreachable allure of a worthwhile hallucination, and he handed me the remote.

My remote has at least thirty buttons, of different shapes and sizes, for changing channels, playing previously recorded programs, or muting that rollicking children's show about a young girl who's an ordinary high school student by day and a wholesome rock star in a heavy, cheap, blond wig by night. I turned on the set and watched as Abby began to demonstrate how to create her Sizzlin' Super Bowl Sunday Supermix, by taking a large plastic bowl and stirring together microwave popcorn, mini-Triscuits, Gummi worms, and tiny plastic footballs. As she grabbed a handful of this multitextured treat and opened her mouth Sizzlin' Superbowl Sunday wide, I pointed my remote at the screen, and just as I was about to eliminate Abby electronically, something extraordinary and deeply satisfying occurred.

Abby began choking on one of the tiny plastic footballs. After a suspiciously long moment, crew members rushed out onto the set and an assistant director tried to Heimlich Abby, followed by a cameraman giving her mouth-to-mouth. But they were too late. Abby lay inert on the laminate pine floor of her Tuscan kitchen, a wiggling Gummi worm dangling from her drooping lower lip. This Gummi worm lent Abby the stature of a long-rotting cadaver, as if the happiest, jewel-toned maggots had been munching on her for days.

Abby's death was the subject of a prime-time tribute special, a quickie paperback called *Abby: The People's Person*, a second investigative cable program called *Tiny Plastic Footballs: The Quiet Killer*, and, a year later, a made-for-TV biopic in which Abby was played by a has-been sitcom star, who told *TV Guide* that "I grew up on Abby. I ate Abby. I loved her."

But on the morning of the day after Abby's death, I was pleased to turn on my television and see the return of Martha Stewart's face, with her trademark barely disguised impatient sneer. I'm not completely certain, but I believe that during the closing credits Martha looked directly into the camera, right at me, and mouthed the words, "Thank you."

Good Enough to Eat

The strangest things can upset people, and I'm not talking about grinding poverty or global injustice, but about the mildest social behavior. I eat my breakfast cereal dry, with a spoon, without adding milk, and I sometimes empty sugar packets into the bowl as well, for a nice, sweet grit. This can cause public outrage. Total strangers have approached me in coffee shops and asked, "Aren't you going to put some milk on those Wheat Chex? How can you eat it like that? It's like eating dirt!" These food critics seem not only confounded, but angry, as if I've ruined their day or shattered some Judeo-Christian cereal commandment. I've never understood this response, so my answer is always, "Watch me."

An unlikely number of people, and particularly my family, have always been obsessed with my diet. This is because, since I was born, I have never had the slightest interest in eating any sort of meat, fish, poultry, or vegetable. I wasn't the sad-eyed victim of some childhood trauma; I was never frightened by a malevolent tube steak or a rampaging halibut. A greasy-haired stranger never lured me into his van and forced me to stroke an ear of corn, while he took photos. I don't have what daytime talk shows and the Healthy Living sections of newspapers call food issues. What I have is a sweet tooth which has spread to all of my other organs. I probably have a sweet appendix.

From earliest childhood, I refused to eat anything I didn't like, which meant just about everything. My parents were understandably distraught, especially regarding nutrition. They'd beg or coax or command me to nibble just an iota of hamburger or the slimmest slice of tomato, and, on extremely rare occasions, I might humor them, but then I'd immediately spit out the repellent cube of chicken or spinach that I'd briefly held on my tongue. I wasn't being perversely defiant and I wasn't the least bit concerned about slaughtering an innocent Elsie the cow or a blameless Sally the salmon. I just hated the stuff. Life would've been much easier if I'd pretended some moral high road and declared, "Until the American bald eagle is safe, and has been allowed to reproduce in sufficient quantities, I will only eat Mallomars."

My parents tried everything, from tucking shreds of cutlet deep within a layer cake, to holding me down and trying to shove potato salad down my throat. My Aunt Lil was more savvy, because she favored bribery, offering me five dollars for one mouthful of veal parmesan. I still refused, especially because her offers stayed in the single digits; I was always waiting for her to hold up a drumstick and her checkbook and say, "Let's make this interesting."

I was eventually sent to a child psychiatrist, who gave me toys to play with while he asked leading questions. He seemed to assume that while I was distracted by a miniature train or a five-piece jigsaw puzzle I'd blurt out some deeply buried neurosis. There was no breakthrough, although I did want to ask him why all of the toys he provided were very basic, blond-wood educational playthings, mostly just rounded blocks with holes for little cylindrical people. If he'd stocked anything plastic that required batteries I might at least have come up with a juicy lie: "A year ago, when no one else was home, My Little Pony cantered into my room and touched me."

As a result of watching far too many made-for-TV psycho-dramas, I did long for a repressed memory. In these TV movies, the heroine would lapse into a zombie-like state and hack someone to death, or a child would remain naggingly mute. An insightful therapist would usually hypnotize this leading character, who would then reveal multiple personalities, concocted because the character had once witnessed a human sacrifice, at an amusement park, or his mother having sex with his uncle. Once this memory was allowed to resurface, the character was cured. I didn't need to be cured of anything, but I loved the idea of having seen something so gruesome and warping that I'd forgotten all about it. I begged my parents to tell me what I'd been through, and they'd think about it and say, "Gee, nothing really comes to mind. We're sorry that your life is so boring." The child psychiatrist did ultimately tell them that, for all my weirdness, I was well-adjusted, and that they should probably just leave me alone and see what happened. "Like a time bomb," my mother later commented.

I was a physically healthy child, even on a diet of peanut butter and jelly sandwiches, milk, and brownies; these were my basic food groups, and pretty much all I ate. Even now, as an adult, when I tell people this, they often insist that I'm kidding. "You only ate Wonder Bread and candy corn? That's ridiculous, you must've eaten something else, your parents would never have let you live on crap. You're lying. You'd be dead."

There are two aspects of such a response that I find interesting and, at times, maddening. First off, the idea that I'm lying. Why would I lie about my diet? To nab a larger chunk of birthday cake? To seem more needy, or more accomplished, on Halloween? To irritate people as they slog through their yummy heaps of corned-beef hash? My imminent death is the other real conversation stopper. When I was in college, I developed a deep and lasting fondness for Pringles. I realize that such potato chips might, in a stretch, be considered a vegetable, but Pringles are made from some unholy partnership of potato derivatives and maybe even newsprint or styrofoam packing pellets, stamped into identical chiplike shapes that nestle conveniently inside the familiar cardboard cylinders. And, I'll confess, while I relish the searing chemical tang of Pringles, although never in the odious Pizza or Sour Cream and Chives flavorings, I also find the product to be aesthetically pleasing. Pringles are the snack equivalent of teakwood nesting tables, or low-cost modular housing. If a Danish architect had created Pringles, he'd have won international design awards. I've always tried to imagine the marketing prodigy who came up with the Pringles concept: "I know exactly what the world is waiting for—a food that stacks."

As an undergraduate, I not only consumed endless, tidy piles of Pringles, I also saved hundreds of the cardboard canisters and glued them together to form the base for a coffee table, and I dreamed of a World's Fair Home of Tomorrow built entirely of Pringles cans, especially the thronelike armchairs and the undulating headboards. Someone who saw my hoard of Pringles containers told me, quite seriously, "Paul, you've eaten so many Pringles that when you die, the mortician won't have to do anything, because you'll already be embalmed."

Pringles are one of those foodlike substances that offend high-minded people, but the treats that really bring out the frowns and the picket signs are another of my mainstays, the adorable Peeps. Peeps began as Easter-time, acid yellow baby chicks made of marshmallow, with sooty black eyes, and are now sold year-round in the forms of everything from thick, flat marshmallow jack-o'-lanterns to jolly, mint green marshmallow Christmas trees. Peeps are usually about three inches high, and they're available in families of six or eight, attached to their siblings in a Siamese-twin fashion. While billions of Peeps are sold annually, whenever I eat them, fresh from their cardboard-and-cellophane homes, onlookers will do everything but vomit, and transmit picture-phone images of me to their friends, accompanied by the text message "GROSS!!!"

Maybe this is because Peeps represent the purest, lumpiest, most unashamed form of refined white sugar, dusted with additional sugar crystals. When I eat Peeps, I'm telling the world, "Yes, that's right, I'm swallowing a hot pink marshmallow kitty, and I like it." There was a cable-TV program that documented how Peeps are made, and it showed unlimited hordes of Peeps bouncing merrily down a conveyor belt, right toward the camera. I came.

After I left college, nothing changed, neither my specialized food intake nor the reactions. I lived, and continue to flourish, on bagels, Kit Kat bars, Frosted Flakes, toast, cashews, Yodels, orange juice, Ritz crackers, Oreos, Hostess cupcakes, and waffles. And I know what you're thinking: Orange juice? That's disgusting! Yes, I occasionally allow a fruit selection to creep onto my menu, if it's been sufficiently depulped and artificially sweetened, and if it arrives in a clean, bright color, as if it were a melted and homogenized gardening clog.

A common question: Why aren't I hugely overweight? Probably because I exercise, and because I secretly believe that people only pack on the pounds if they mix foods. A pork chop and a Twinkie will bulk you right up, but the Twinkie alone is practically a vitamin supplement. I know that this theory sounds improbable, but it's no more deluded than the people who gorge only on dark chocolate because many years ago some obscure scientific study claimed that dark chocolate is slightly less fattening than milk chocolate, and that the darker variety is rich in antioxidants, or free radicals, or unregistered voters. This now mythic study is every lonely single woman's mantra.

A corollary concern: What about my teeth? While I've had plenty of dental work, so has everyone else in my family, none of whom are addicted to sugar. So, while we've all had root canals, I've also had every known Keebler product. I win.

Another question: What happens if I go out to eat at a restaurant, or to a dinner party at someone's home? The answer: I tend to have a perfectly nice time, while everyone else gets nervous. Eating out is a social occasion, and I enjoy the company and the conversation. But if a host or a dining companion doesn't know me, they can grow anxious. When I politely refuse her bouillabaisse, a hostess will usually ask me if I'm on a special diet and require something kosher, salt-free, or nonalcoholic. To save time, I usually just tell the truth and admit that I've already eaten, or I ask if the chef could prepare low-sodium Tootsie Pops or some Milky Ways blessed by an Orthodox rabbi. And while I can sympathize with a partygiver's wish to please a wayward guest, that partygiver really shouldn't worry about me. I'm fine, and I'm a cheap date.

At a restaurant, when I listen attentively as a waitperson recites the specials, and then I don't order them, that waitperson will often look wounded, so sometimes I'll say that I'm just having dessert, without adding, I'm just having dessert as a way of life.

Which brings us to gourmet treats. People who almost believe me, and who have begun to accept that I'll never be sampling the rump roast, sometimes imagine that I'm a candy connoisseur. They outdo themselves, buying me elaborately gold-foil-wrapped boxes of liqueur-filled truffles, or dense slices of flourless mousse. While I appreciate their efforts, they've still got it all wrong. I don't just like sweets; I demand crap. I like old-fashioned, carb-heavy, American milk chocolate, labeled Hershey's or Nestlé or Nabisco and packed with nothing more complicated than peanuts, caramel, and whatever is actually in nougat. Sometimes I feel like a hard-bitten gumshoe in a well-thumbed noir paperback, grunting, "Just the Three Musketeers bar, ma'am." A friend did once go too far in proving that she understood my taste buds. She frosted an aluminum pan of just-thawed Sara Lee brownies with an additional layer of canned frosting and rainbow sprinkles, draping the whole thing with a strand of artificial pearls. I loved the gesture, but even I experienced sugar shock. And, by the way, I only speak a single foreign phrase, but it's come in mighty handy: the Spanish for "rainbow sprinkles" is *chespitas de colores.*

My diet has led me to a certain knee-jerk empathy with other eccentrics. Whenever I hear the words "Oh, you're just being silly," or "Just try it," or "Everyone's staring," I feel an immediate bond with whoever's being picked on or pushed against their will, to dress more acceptably or calm down or play tennis. I can instantly side with any underdog, which sounds good-hearted until I hang around with people attacking Nixon or Lenin. I'll feel a perilous urge to say something like, "Excuse me, but you didn't even know John Wilkes Booth, so why are you judging him?"

My older brother, Evan, for example, was expelled from high school, in the sixties, for having shoulder-length hair. My parents didn't understand why he couldn't trim a few inches, just to get back to class and avoid all the controversy. I knew exactly why: it was his hair, and his business, and if long hair was also an effective "Fuck you" to a rigid high school principal, all the better. And when my folks tried to grab Evan in the living room and hack off his hair with a scissors, I was glad that he shoved them away. My parents weren't monsters; they just wanted their child back in school. But they were wrong, and years later I grew my own hair longer, as a show of solidarity. Sadly, I looked like a dateless sorority girl in desperate need of a makeover.

Being different is often seen as being stubborn, or even spoiled, and I do agree that parents should encourage their kids to try new experiences, and even strange, brown foods. But sometimes parents worry too much. After about the first six seconds of life, a child's personality is pretty much set, so a parent is off the hook. If your kid is going to grow up to be a criminal, like an arsonist or the vice president, it's already a done deal.

Even today, my mother still frets, over what I'm not eating and, even more bizarrely, over whether I need to use the bathroom. This latter concern may be a somewhat Jewish fetish, because the Cossacks were notorious for not letting Jews use the bathroom, or for only allowing them to use grimy Amoco station restrooms. My brother still has long hair, and I think that, deep in her soul, my mother still dreams that he might one day decide to head first to the barber, and then back to tenth grade. The first time she ever seemed a little more free was when, at some point in my early twenties, for some reason or other, my mother cursed at me, calling me a little shit. She's not especially prim, but in some new way, she sounded both tickled and relaxed. We were both pleased, because finally I could be a little shit, and maybe it wasn't all her fault.

And now, a beautiful story with the happiest ending. During my early days in New York I befriended someone who worked in a candy store. I asked him something that I'd always yearned to know: After Easter, what happens to the unsold chocolate bunnies? Maybe it's because, as a Jewish child, I was denied these delicacies, but I have always treasured these bunnies, especially the hollow variety, the bunnies that the boxes call

"Farmer Pete" or "Harvest Bob," the ones that grow bulging, hard-sugar eyes and hold a bright orange, hard-sugar carrot. My candy store connection told me that the suddenly out-of-season rabbits were given to foster kids and orphans, and while I loved them dearly, I instantly volunteered to kill my parents. The guy took pity, and that year, on the day after Easter, as proof that Jesus had indeed been resurrected, I received two large shopping bags filled with unwanted bunnies. I lined them up on the shelves in my refrigerator, which then resembled a shooting gallery, and, day after day, I ate them. I always started with their heads, so they wouldn't suffer.

If my feelings for chocolate bunnies seem near-erotic, I'm far from alone. I knew a woman who had nightmarish dating experiences, and she finally announced her engagement to a four-foot-tall bunny in the window of Li-Lac Chocolates, a Manhattan landmark. "Paul," she told me, because she knew I'd understand, "I have finally found the perfect man."

Enter Trembling

1.

As a timid person, as someone who apologizes for bumping into inanimate objects, I'm often drawn to large-scale personalities, to people who refuse to behave themselves. This certainly describes the producer Scott Rudin, whose many movies include *The Hours*, *The Truman Show*, *Clueless*, and *No Country for Old Men*. All of the stories you might have heard about him are true. For instance:

Scott was driving the two of us to a meeting in Los Angeles. As we sped along the expressway, Scott's phone buzzed. He answered it, and his face became a mask of rage. He yelled, "How did you get this number?" and hurled the phone at the windshield. "Who was it?" I asked. "My mother," he replied, instantly calm.

While he was president of production at Fox, the door that separated Scott's office from his main assistant's outer office was wired to a button on Scott's desk. When Scott pressed this button, the door would magically open, to admit visitors. There was a matching button on the assistant's desk. Whenever Scott or this assistant were furious with each other, they'd use their buttons to slam the door dramatically. When they were both angry at the same time, which was often, they'd both push their buttons, and the paralyzed door would vibrate helplessly. Another assistant in this office was legally blind. When Scott would fire him, which was often, this assistant would stand patiently out on the sidewalk, waiting for the handicapped van, at a bus stop in full view of Scott's office window. Watching this heart-tugging scene, Scott would always relent and send a lesser assistant out to rehire the blind one.

Scott once fired another assistant while they were both in Scott's car on the freeway. Scott made this assistant get out of the car in the middle of traffic, and left him there.

I once saw Scott glance at an assistant with such disdain that the assistant actually burst into flames.

Okay, that last story isn't true, but that's how rumors get started.

Here are some even more shocking stories about Scott:

He's relentlessly demanding and also amazingly generous. After he makes an employee work through a holiday weekend, he'll then send that employee on an all-expenses-paid two-week vacation to Hawaii.

No one works harder than Scott. He once tried to go on a

Hawaiian vacation himself. He got off the plane, sat on the beach with a pile of books for ten minutes, and then, bored to tears, got right back on a plane and flew home.

Scott's assistants know that if they can survive for six months, they'll be considered so well trained that they can move on to just about any other job they want in the entertainment industry. Or the Taliban.

Scott is secretly and genuinely caring. When any of his friends, his employees, or their family members are in real trouble, when someone gets sick, or a parent dies, or a writer or an actor or a director falls on hard times, Scott shows up and, very quietly, he offers everything: money, doctors, transportation, and hope. If people ever found out about this side of Scott, his reputation would be ruined. Because here's Scott's method: he knows that people are terrified of him, and he'll even encourage this image in the press. Because then, when a newcomer finally meets him, Scott pulls a fast one. The newbie will approach Scott fearfully, expecting an ogre, or at least a lethally aimed coffee mug. Instead, Scott will be devastatingly charming, funny, and open to ideas. This technique is completely disarming. And evil.

Scott often says that a producer's job is "to make people do what they don't want to do." When Scott hired me to rewrite *The First Wives Club*, the screenplay, which had already been revised by several other writers, was the fairly dark story of three women who were cruelly dumped by their arrogant husbands, who lusted for young bimbos. One of the wives, a WASPy matron, had a retarded daughter. I was asked to push the script toward comedy, and to make the daughter a lesbian instead. At first I proposed, of course, that we cover all our bases and make the daughter a retarded lesbian. This idea was rejected.

As I rewrote, and filming began, Scott saw that the interaction of the movie's three stars, Diane Keaton, Bette Midler, and Goldie Hawn, was really cooking, and so he asked me to write a scene where they all go to a lesbian bar. I asked, "But why do they go to a lesbian bar?"

"Diane needs to talk to her daughter," Scott explained. "Write the scene."

"And the daughter doesn't have a phone?" I protested.

"She left her phone at home. Write the scene."

"And without asking her, Diane somehow just knows that her daughter's at a lesbian bar. And Diane somehow knows exactly which lesbian bar."

"It's the daughter's favorite bar, she talks about it all the time. Write the scene."

"And Diane brings her two friends because . . ."

"Because she's nervous about going to a lesbian bar. Write the scene."

"And the friends agree to go with her because . . ."

"Because they're her friends, and because if you ask one more question I'm going to take you to a lesbian bar and ask all of the lesbians to kill you. Write the scene."

Very grudgingly, I wrote the scene; Diane found her daughter, while Goldie, who was playing an actress, danced happily with her lesbian fans, and Bette got propositioned. And Scott, as he almost always is, was right; it turned out to be one of the most popular, and least expected, scenes in the movie.

I first met Scott when we were both in our early twenties and Scott was working in Manhattan. He was tall and bearded, with a Talmudic intensity; when my aunts first met him, years later, they swooned.

"That is a very bright guy," said my Aunt Hilda.

"And he's so nice," said my Aunt Lil. "I thought he was supposed to be mean."

"Just like you," Hilda told Lil, then adding quickly, "I didn't say that."

Scott's weight has fluctuated over the years, but he's refused to age a day. It's not that there's a portrait somewhere, withering in an attic; I'm convinced that sometime around age twenty-three, Scott simply glanced toward heaven and barked, "Stop it!" Even God takes Scott's calls.

I worked with Scott on a few unproduced scripts, and then he had a meeting with the head of Paramount, where he pitched a big-screen version of *The Addams Family* by singing the first four notes of the familiar TV theme song and snapping his fingers twice.

Months later, Scott called me in to rewrite a draft of the movie's script by a team of other writers. The original Charles Addams cartoons featured America's most macabre clan: the wickedly smoldering Gomez and his swiveling, satanic wife, Morticia, who were doting parents to the pudgy, amoral Pugsley and his ghostly-pale, pigtailed child-demon sister, the unflappable Wednesday; Wednesday has remained my ultimate role model. These characters had been translated from single-panel delirium to a popular half-hour sitcom, but filling ninety minutes of screen time was another matter entirely.

Thanks to Scott, the film had been impeccably cast, with the dashing Raul Julia as Gomez, the winsomely vampish Anjelica Huston as his bride, and the fetchingly deranged Christopher Lloyd as that hapless, hulking man-island, Uncle Fester. The first-time director was Barry Sonnenfeld, who up until then had been an extremely sought-after cinematographer on movies like *When Harry Met Sally* and *Raising Arizona*. Hiring Barry had been Scott's inspiration, and he'd met his match.

Scott and Barry were, as their first names might suggest, both nice Jewish boys from New York, and were therefore perfectly suited to collaborate on a story of comic horror; they both insisted that, as some sort of barbaric childhood trauma, their fathers had sold their coin collections. Barry had also been humiliated when he was on a date, and the public-address system at an Earth Day concert had boomed, "BARRY SONNENFELD, CALL YOUR MOTHER."

Barry was the most talented, endearing and perverse three-year-old adult imaginable. He tested everyone on the movie, including me, by immediately sharing a tale of his early days as a cameraman, shooting porn. This was called the Double Penetration Story, and Barry would tell it, in his bubbly urban whine, as if it were *The Night Before Chanukah*: "Okay, so I'm shooting this porn flick, right, and there's this actress, and she's, okay, she's getting, you know, fucked, from both the front and the back, by these two guys. And I'm thinking, okay, fine, I need the money, but then, as the guy who's, you know, fucking her from behind, he pulls out, and I guess that the actress hadn't taken all of the proper precautions, because suddenly there's a fountain of human excrement, gushing right toward me. And I'm so upset that I run off the set and out into the street, where I vomit. And as I'm standing on the curb, vomiting, I look down at my shoe, and stuck to my toe, there's this little piece of shit. So I vomit all over again. Isn't that incredible?" Now picture Barry telling this story to Anjelica Huston, who, to her credit, didn't flinch. Like almost everyone else, she responded by smiling and saying, "Oh, Barry."

Barry also told of how, when shooting another studio film, he had wanted his crew to wear adult diapers under their clothes to cut down on bathroom breaks. Barry of course volunteered to test the diapers, in his shower. "Ya know, they don't really work that well," he recalled, sadly. "They're just designed for minor leakage."

Maybe as a result of these memories, Barry was phobic about cleanliness. He loved those breath-freshening strips that dissolve on your tongue, and he was a huge fan of Tucks, the premoistened pads used mostly by hemorrhoid sufferers. For all-purpose fun, Barry kept cases of Tucks in his office, filling every cabinet and desk drawer. As Scott would exit a meeting, Barry would leap to his feet, sliding packets of Tucks into Scott's pockets and begging, "Please, honey, just take a few. For me."

Scott and Barry would feud, but they enjoyed each other enormously. One morning Scott was furious at Barry over whatever, and he summoned me to the inquisition, as a witness. We were in a private, nondescript studio office. While Scott yelled at him, Barry methodically took apart a sectional sofa and used the cushions to build a fort in the middle of the room. Then he disappeared from view, crawling deep inside the fort. Scott was now haranguing a pile of foam rubber, which made him burst out laughing, as Barry's smiling head emerged. Barry was married to the loveliest, most unfazable woman alive, whom he worshiped and called Sweetie. "I asked Sweetie if I was juvenile," he proudly reported, "and she said no. She said—infantile!"

In addition to his unrestrained entertainment value, Barry's background in cinematography was a blessing. Barry not only understood comedy, but he could make the most complicated visual gag feel swooping and effortless, as he also proved later in the *Men in Black* films. The *Addams Family* script, however, remained challenging. As the movie opens, Uncle Fester has vanished for years, to points unknown. He returns, sopping wet, explaining that he's spent his lost decades in the Bermuda Triangle. The rest of the film tries to determine: Is this the real Fester, or a look-alike con artist after the Addams gold-doubloon fortune?

While I polished individual lines and scenes, no one could settle on an appropriate ending. Finally, the cast rebelled, and appointed Christina Ricci, the ten-year-old playing Wednesday as their spokesperson. Christina was then, and remains, an extraordinary actress. Most child performers have been signed up for way too many kiddie acting-and-tap classes, where they become adult-pleasing wind-up toys. Christina was the opposite: she had some inexplicable, direct bond with the ghoulish Wednesday, and she'd quickly and flawlessly mastered the necessary comic deadpan. When asked how the movie should end, Christina explained why the returning Fester had to be a true Addams for the story to be emotionally satisfying. We took her advice, and after the filming was over, Barry asked Christina how she'd understood the Addamses with such finesse. "Well," she replied, "it's because everyone in the whole family, we're all dead, right? So I just thought, well, how would a dead person act?"

The Addams Family was a hit, and so the studio demanded a sequel. I was delighted, because I revered Charles Addams and I was eager to work on the next movie from scratch. Barry had been offered many subsequent projects, so he wasn't sure about continuing the Addams cycle. Scott and I met Barry for dinner to persuade him, and because Scott was after something, he poured it on, telling Barry things like, "You look great!" and "I would love to have you do the movie, but if you can't, I will completely understand, with no hard feelings," until Barry looked at him and asked, "When does Scott get here?" Matters were settled only when Barry unrolled the blueprints for his dream home, to be built on many acres of prime Amagansett bayfront. The house was clearly going to be deluxe, and therefore expensive. As Barry pointed out the locations for the screening room and the many fireplaces, Scott smiled. "I *own* you," he told Barry.

The second film, *Addams Family Values*, was a pleasure to write, for two reasons: it was a big-budget studio offering which wasn't expected to be in any way wholesome or life-affirming, and, because the first movie had made money, we could get away with a lot more. For example, when Morticia gave birth, I christened the baby with the name that Charles Addams had originally intended for Pugsley, but which *The New Yorker*, the publisher of the Addams cartoons, had rejected. The forbidden name? Pubert. In the sequel, Pugsley and Wednesday hate and fear their new brother and try to kill him; as Barry told Sweetie in a gleeful call from the set, "Guess what, honey? Today we threw a baby off the roof!" Pubert was actually played by twin baby girls, with the addition of tiny, Gomez-like mustaches; female infants, I was told, were better behaved, and the use of twins extended the shooting day. The film's first cast returned, along with the heavenly addition of Joan Cusack as a black-widow killer.

Addams Family Values was my first unaltered script to be produced, which was sometimes unnerving. Alone in my apartment, I wrote the lyrics to a song for a summer camp Thanksgiving Day pageant, and then, months later, I arrived on the set to see a batch of flesh-and-blood children, dressed up as turkeys and pumpkin pies, singing, as the number was called, "Eat Me."

The movie's soundtrack was originally intended to include a dance track by Michael Jackson; Barry and Scott had met with the King of Pop at his Neverland Ranch, where he'd kept them waiting for hours, but had served them a bowl of M&Ms. As they waited, Barry also had the caretaker activate the full-size merry-go-round, and Barry and Scott both rode painted horses. While the movie was in production, the first of the alleged child-molestation scandals broke, and the Jackson tune was shelved, although His Oddness did shoot an extended video of the song, for release in Japan, in which Michael lives in a haunted mansion, where he's befriended by the neighborhood kids but hounded by grown-ups waving torches and pitchforks. There's an onscreen moment in *Addams Family Values* where Wednesday and Pugsley are imprisoned in the summer camp's Harmony Hut, to learn about friendship and decency; they spot a framed photo of Michael on the wall and shriek in terror.

While I'd written the joke prescandal, by the time the movie was released, audiences went berserk.

There were Addams-style auditions throughout the filming of both movies. The first film needed actors to play Gomez and Fester in flashbacks, as seven-year-olds and as teenagers. I sat in on the casting calls, particularly for the young Uncle Fester. The room was filled with hundreds of boys for whom looking like Uncle Fester was finally a plus. There was one twelve-year-old who finally couldn't be hired because he was just too disturbing, and Barry referred to him as "The Drooler."

Raul Julia was an expert, nimble, dementedly romantic Gomez. In life, Raul was equally irresistible, with his own point of view. I shared a car with him one morning, and on our way to the set he described the following event: "Paul, you will not believe this, but it is true! Last night I was at the bar, at my hotel. And I dropped a coin, and as I bent to pick it up, my eyeball fell out! And it rolled onto the floor! I was astounded! And before anyone could see, I plucked up my eye and I popped it back into my head. And it was fine! Tell me, is there any redness? Can you tell?" I couldn't, and as far as I know, Raul didn't have a glass eye.

2.

A few years later, Scott called me with another idea. When Tom Hanks won his Best Actor Academy Award for playing a lawyer dying of AIDS in *Philadelphia*, he thanked his high school drama teacher, calling him "a great gay American," and thereby outing the teacher on global television. Scott thought this incident might be the springboard for a movie.

At first I said no. By the time of the Oscars telecast, Tom Hanks's teacher, who was by all accounts a terrific man, was happily retired, and equally proud of Tom. I couldn't see where the story would go, after the initial outing. Then it occurred to me: Scott had never intended to base the movie on the real teacher's life, so what if our fictional guy was outed during the week when he was about to get married, to a woman?

Coming out has been seen as an essential gay rite of passage, and some people experience terrible rejection from unsympathetic friends and family members. I was lucky because, as a child, I was so appallingly egocentric that I assumed everyone was gay. I didn't divide the world into categories of straight and gay, but into people from New Jersey and people from New York. And while my parents were concerned about me, I was still encouraged to create elaborate Magic Marker drawings, to design and hand stitch a huge felt banner of the pharaoh's head for a junior high school production of *Joseph and the Amazing Technicolor Dreamcoat*, and to decorate my room, including the high-gloss wallpaper and the shag carpeting, in taxicab yellow and Sunkist orange. Years later, when we finally talked about it, my mother asked me, "So you're gay, right?" just to make sure she wasn't crazy.

My mother did have her revenge. After I'd left home, my parents moved from New Jersey to Philadelphia, where my mom went to work doing public relations for a dance company. One day she called me and asked if, since I was coming to Philly for a weekend visit, I could stop by a photographer's studio in Manhattan and pick up an envelope filled with photographs of the company's dancers. Then she just happened to mention, "I think that some of the pictures are nudes."

I picked up the large, packed manila envelope and I saw that it was sealed. Which meant that I had a two-hour train ride to either not look at the photos of hot, naked male dancers, or to try and figure out a way to open the envelope, look at the pictures, masturbate in public, and then somehow reseal the envelope. Or I could claim that the envelope was already open, and that the greasy fingerprints all over the pictures weren't mine.

Because I'm a hopeless coward, I did nothing and just sat on the train, cursing my mother, with the envelope on my lap. When I got to my parents' house, my mom asked casually, "Did you look at the pictures? I bet they're great." "No, I didn't look at the pictures," I snapped. "I hate dance."

My favorite coming-out story was told to me by a friend who was one of four gay siblings. After his oldest brother came out, their parents took some time to adjust, and then insisted that they were fine with everything, and that they loved their gay son. Then my friend Larry, the second-oldest, came out, and the parents were shell-shocked, but eventually came around, imagining that their acceptance duties were now over. When Larry's little sister came out, she took her even-younger brother, without consulting him, out with her, by blurting, "Mom and Dad, I'm gay, and so is Richard!" This was a variation on "Okay, so maybe I tried to flush a paperback down the toilet, but Richard stole a dollar from Grandma's wallet!"

While I was thinking about Scott's idea, I wondered if maybe coming out could be treated as a useful comic device, the way divorce and adultery were mainstays of the screwball comedies of the 1930s. What if, rather than writing another saga of tremulous gay heartache, I could pay screwball tribute to Howard Brackett, a small-town high school English teacher who loves his job, his family, Shakespeare, and Barbra Streisand?

And I know what you're thinking—Barbra Streisand? Isn't that a bit much, a trifle stereotypical, and not what the gay civil rights movement needs right now for the we're-just-like-you-and-all-we-want-is-a-little-quiet-dignity pamphlet? That's probably true, but I was once having a conversation with a beefy FedEx driver, and when I told him that he'd just delivered my ticket to see Barbra Streisand in her comeback tour, at Madison Square Garden, he melted instantly, asking, "Oh my God, do you think she'll do any of the early stuff, from *Color Me Barbra*?" When I got to the concert, I was most impressed by the traveling gift shop, where fans could purchase not just T-shirts and CDs, but also, for several hundred dollars, a large, ivory-colored silk scarf printed with an impressionistic collage of Barbra in all of her greatest film roles. I began wondering where a devoted man or woman would wear such a thing, and then I thought, oh, of course, to a Barbra Streisand concert.

The script went through countless drafts, as Scott and I tried to push Howard through as many comic hoops as possible. Scott encouraged me to invent Greenleaf, Indiana, the town that surrounds Howard, and to come up with a raft of characters who might have secrets of their own. A friend had once told me that limited minds sometimes think of sex as a matter of "in holes and out holes," and they condemn gay people because gays keep trying to insert the wrong things into the wrong places; I knew that such a learned discussion should find a home in my script, which was eventually called *In & Out*. The studio that was producing the movie remained pleased but wary, and whenever the script was threatening to become too gay, I'd get notes claiming it was "repetitive," until finally, at a studio meeting, I mentioned that, "some of us were born repetitive," and those particular notes dwindled.

Frank Oz agreed to direct and, like the fans who besieged him, I was in awe, because not only had he made such beloved films as *What About Bob?*, *Dirty Rotten Scoundrels*, and *Little Shop of Horrors*, he was also one of the creators of the Muppets and the voice of Miss Piggy; if this wasn't enough, he was also the voice of Yoda in the *Star Wars* movies. When starry-eyed strangers weren't gushing about his movies, they were demanding that Frank "do Miss Piggy" or "be Yoda." Being unnaturally decent, Frank would usually oblige, and the effect was mesmerizing. While technology and digital effects have transformed the movies, there's still nothing like hearing a tall, genial, bearded man instantly become a vain, flouncing sow or a centuries-old, cosmically wise dwarf.

Casting began, and Kevin Kline was set to play Howard Brackett. Kevin is the best sort of paradox, because he's a romantic leading man who's also a great classical actor and a baggy-pants burlesque clown. Kevin also proved to be the ideal choice because, as an actor, he'll do a fantastic job and then immediately doubt himself; Kevin can make anxiety, indecision, and dithering wonderfully real and funny.

Tom Selleck asked to read for the role of an openly gay journalist who comes to Greenleaf to report on the outing. Tom is one of the few stars who's even taller and more absurdly hand-some in person, and when he walked into the audition room, everyone, male and female, gay and straight, became a hope-lessly gibbering, lovestruck schoolgirl. Even Kevin, who's as straight as can be, got all dreamy-eyed and asked, "Tom, would you like some coffee?" And once we were shooting, my mom came to the set, and Tom kissed her, and, well, I just wanted to ask, "So who's happy to have a gay son now?"

Tom is also one of those actors who many gay men, especially online, like to claim as one of their own. I'd heard countless sto-ries of someone who knew someone whose ex-boyfriend's best friend had seen a Polaroid of Tom from twenty years earlier, in a Speedo, on someone's refrigerator, in a gay neighborhood. But here's what I always wonder: Why do these particular gossips never decide that any character actors are gay? Why don't they ever declare, "I know this guy in L.A. whose roommate went out with a flight attendant who went out with Wilford Brimley?"

Scott and Frank made sure that the entire cast of *In & Out* was first rate, and everyone fell in love with Joan Cusack, who played Emily, Howard's confused fiancée. Emily was inspired by the photos in the *New York Times* social pages, where, I'm con-vinced, like the gossips I've just condemned, that I can always tell when an unknowing woman is marrying an obviously clos-eted gay man. In these doomed marriages, the groom is always too thrilled at having his picture taken, as if he imagines the couple is on a movie poster. Of course, now the *Times* prints the announcements for same-sex couples as well, and these pairings are very brave, because their photos will be instantly dissected in gay chat rooms. "Oh, please," a typical comment will read, "the younger guy has horse teeth and the older guy should have his eyes done."

Before filming started, Scott and I gave Frank, who's straight, a "Gay Kit," filled with items like an original cast recording of *Gypsy*, some hardcore gay porn, a rainbow flag, and condoms. Frank was amused, because he insisted that the movie had to be, above all else, funny, because he wasn't interested in making a do-goody, gays-are-people-too, liberal Hollywood tract. At the first read-through of the script, Debbie Reynolds, who was playing Howard's wedding-obsessed mother, turned to me and said, "Paul, you're funny, and you know why? Because you're a Jew. Jews are funny, and I know, because I was married to a Jew." During the long days and nights of shooting, Debbie could be found either twisted into unbelievably limber yoga poses in a corner, or entertaining crowds of delighted extras, who roared as Debbie performed chunks of her nightclub act. Debbie also had an inspiringly raunchy vocabulary. During a scene toward the end of the movie, Debbie, in a wedding gown, tosses her bouquet into a mob of eager female guests. This activity had to be repeated many times, and Debbie revived the crowd by shouting, "All right, ladies! This time let's really feel it! Let's feel it in our *vaginas*!"

The filming of *In & Out* was a matter of creative substitution. Many of the movie's early scenes take place at the Oscars, but the exterior, paparazzi-infested red carpet mêlée was all shot in Manhattan, at a disguised Lincoln Center. Matt Dillon played Cameron, the movie star who innocently outs Howard, and clips from Cameron's Oscar-nominated role, as a gay war hero, were shown, and the bits set on a hellish, bomb-blasted

Vietnam battlefield were shot on a beach in Brooklyn. Most of the film takes place in the idyllic Greenleaf, which was faked on locations all over the tristate area, from Pompton Lakes, New Jersey, a town that had just settled a toxic-waste dumping scandal, to Northport, Long Island, where the cameras had to avoid catching a glimpse of the Atlantic Ocean. After we'd been shooting for months in a New Jersey high school, where real-life students were still attending classes, any glamour had dissipated, and a kid shouted, just before the cameras rolled, "MOVIES SUCK!"

Then there was the kiss. This was a major moment, about midway through the film, when Howard, with his wedding still scheduled, is falling to pieces. Tom Selleck's reporter tries to talk some sense into him, and coax him into coming out, and he finally just grabs Howard and kisses him. Howard succumbs and then freaks out even more. During the rehearsals for this scene, Kevin and Tom, in a room, held their scripts and marked the action—that is, when they arrived at the kiss, they both mumbled "kiss" and stayed a good few feet apart. The scene was shot days later, at a rural intersection in New Jersey, on a bucolic hillside surrounded by farmland and apple trees. Kevin and Tom began to kiss and, being smart actors, they really started to go for it, because the steamier the smooch, the more heartfelt and funny the scene became. The nearby roads had been closed for the day, but cars filled with onlookers kept circling, trying to see what was going on, and all I kept thinking was, if only they knew what Magnum, P.I., was up to.

Once the filming was completed, the studio released a trailer that gave the film's basic setup: a small-town teacher gets outed on the Oscars. Audiences were laughing, and as I watched this preview with an appreciative crowd, I could see that there was a titillation factor. Much of this audience, especially the straight guys, seemed to be assuming that the outing was a mistake, and that Howard was actually heterosexual. I began to wonder how audiences would react to a movie where the leading character was, in fact, gay, and by the end of the movie, quite happily so.

I found out. Frank put together an early cut of the movie, and the first test screening was held at a theater in midtown Manhattan. The audience for this screening had been recruited from a wide demographic, and included gay and straight people, teenagers, older couples, and a racial mix. All this audience knew was that they'd be getting a sneak peek at a new comedy. Scott and I sat in the back of the theater, across the aisle from Frank. Such screenings, while sometimes useful, are scary and suspenseful because, for the first time, the creative team finds out if their movie makes any sense at all, whether an audience will follow and like the story, and just how much work still needs to be done, in terms of further editing, musical scoring, and possible reshoots.

The movie was playing well, with the audience involved in the action, unsure of the outcome, and they were laughing. Then it happened: the kiss. The theater all but exploded: the audience began screaming and jabbering, and people stood up and talked back to the screen. The pandemonium didn't let up for many more scenes, as audience members began to discuss their reactions with one another, at the top of their lungs. I was sitting behind a straight teenage couple, and the guy shoved drinking straws into his ears, so he wouldn't have to hear another word of the movie. Scott and Frank and I stared at each other, because no one had anticipated this level of response. What was going on?

On our way out of the screening, Scott and I tried to eavesdrop on the moviegoers. We didn't have to strain, as everyone was still chattering away. As far as I could tell, some people, especially women, had enjoyed the movie. Some straight guys remained in shock. Scott and I stood behind two highly opinionated gay men on the escalator, who didn't see us, but one of them said to the other, "Well, if Scott Rudin and Paul Rudnick think they can get away with this horseshit, they have another thing coming!"

Frank and his editing team kept working on the movie, and there were more test screenings. Frank would take scenes that were unclear or too long or just not landing, he'd rework them, and suddenly they'd be funny. The screenings were now being held in suburban malls, and afterwards the audiences were asked to fill out questionnaires, to express their opinions. The favorable ratings kept rising, but there was one card that I cherished, and that I've kept to this day. In every category, this woman gave the movie the highest possible scores. She loved the actors and the story and the music, she thought the movie was the perfect length, and she couldn't stop listing her favorite scenes. Then came a final question: "Would you recommend this movie to a friend?" The woman's answer: "Absolutely not." The card inquired, "If you wouldn't recommend this movie, why not?" And the woman, who'd otherwise had the time of her life, had scribbled, "Against God's law."

The movie opened and did well, despite plenty of criticism from all over the political map. Some gay people liked the movie, while others found it unrealistic, particularly in that Howard had remained closeted for so long—this was before half of the country's married governors and senators were caught either propositioning undercover cops in public restrooms or appointing their secret boyfriends to government jobs. The reaction to the kiss held steady, as the crowds kept going haywire, with both applause and outrage. Making a mainstream gay movie is tricky, because what can seem tame in New York or Los Angeles can become incendiary in other parts of the country. The range of opinions was unnerving, but I was happy that people were laughing. Everyone loved Kevin, Joan got an Oscar nomination, and Scott and I told Frank that he was now officially gay. Politically, it was helpful that *In & Out* turned a profit, so the studios couldn't claim that gay subject matter was bad box office.

I've learned to almost relish the grand tradition of American hypocrisy. Americans will warmly embrace the Addamses, who are a family of murderers, graverobbers, and cannibals, but a guy-on-guy kiss can cause a near riot. After one of the Addams movies came out, a reporter from the *Jewish Daily Forward* asked me if the Addamses were Jewish. I answered, "Do you want them to be?" Even though there aren't any gay characters in the Addams movies, there's been online speculation about how the films have a gay sensibility. A gay reporter asked me why Howard Brackett loved Streisand, and I countered with, "Why don't you ask me why he loves Shakespeare?" Of course, secretly I was thinking, if I had to choose between watching the Royal Shakespeare Company performing *King Lear* and catching Barbra on cable in *Funny Lady*, there'd really be no competition. Because, as everyone knows, *Funny Lady* is Barbra's *King Lear*.

I Shudder:

An Excerpt from the Most Deeply Intimate and Personal Diary of One Elyot Vionnet

Intimacy—Why?

1.

Some people assume that I'm a homosexual, because of my superlative taste, my ability to dismiss another human being on the basis of his or her ponytail, and because my name is Elyot Vionnet. Others imagine that I'm heterosexual, due to my overwhelming sense of entitlement, my belief that God speaks to me directly, and my kneejerk hatred of any French film where the fine-boned heroine stares at the camera, wordlessly.

Everyone is wrong.

Like most people, I had my first sexual experience at the age of fourteen, with a married couple who lived in my neighborhood. This was in Deerling, Connecticut, where I was making pocket money by offering my services as a teen psychic. I would knock on doors, wearing a pale gray seersucker suit, with a third eye painted on my forehead, as a form of advertising. When someone opened their door, I would ask if they wanted information on their future, or that of their family. If a wife answered, she would usually announce that I was "too cute for words," and she'd summon her husband and children, as if I were promising a puppet show, or a series of bumbling card tricks. Meanwhile, I'd take the moment to assess the family's framed photos, furniture, and motor vehicles.

I first tried this on the McCrackens, whose last name appeared on a wrought-iron plaque dangling beneath the wrought-iron carriage lamp which was mounted on a Victorian-style lamppost at the end of their asphalt driveway. Tom and Laura McCracken gathered in their living room, with their two young sons. I sat on a mustard-colored, corduroy-upholstered wing chair, which I tried not to let touch my skin. I shut my eyes, extended my arms, and spoke in a ghostly, echoing drone.

"Tom and Laura McCracken! The Great Vionnini will see all and tell all! Tom, you will keep working at your family's pool-supply store and over the years, you will build the business into ten branches across the tri-state area. But even once he retires, your father will still refuse to praise you, or give you an ounce of credit for your success. You will spiral into a clinical depression, which you will self-medicate with alcohol, and you will begin gambling at a nearby Native American–owned casino and resort, where you will hire transsexual prostitutes, until late one night your Jeep Wagoneer will flip over on the Connecticut Turnpike, where you will be trapped inside for over forty-eight hours with a six-foot-two-inch person with linebacker shoulders and breast implants named Lady Ambrosia. Your left leg will be amputated."

Tom was now staring at me and starting to ball up his fists. I went on:

"Laura, you will continue to be a contented stay-at-home mom to your two boys, even as little Adam begins buying mushrooms from another boy in his third-grade class, and then starts selling even harder drugs, in order to buy himself the BMX bike which you promised him if he could maintain a C average and brush his teeth. Your other son, little Bradley, will seem to be perfect in every way, getting top grades and participating in every possible after-school activity, until during his freshman year at an Ivy League school he will decide to drop out and live in his van with his much older girlfriend, whose name is Sunrise and whose unshaven legs, high-pitched speaking voice, and nonironic use of the word 'communication' will make you physically ill."

By this juncture, Laura and the two boys were sobbing, and Tom offered me twenty dollars to please just shut up and leave, and when we settled on fifty, I did.

My forecasts weren't always as dire. One afternoon I approached a charming Cape Cod–style home, where the flower beds of hollyhocks and foxglove were bordered with cunningly angled whitewashed bricks, and where the door was opened by

Melissa Trimble, a wan, tremulous woman with bushy, plaintive hair. She brought me to her kitchen, where she'd hand-painted the stuccoed walls with a trompe l'oeil mural of ivy-covered trelliswork surrounding a rustic arched window opening onto an eighteenth-century French village. She poured us both tumblers of soy milk and set out items that contained bran, dried dates, and flaxseed, and which she insisted on calling cookies. In return, I provided the following predictions:

"Melissa Trimble! Within the next six months you will finally begin to accept the fact that your husband is not coming back and you will start to realize how secretly happy you are about this, and not just because he was cheating on you with that little whore from his office, although as a feminist you will try to refer to her as a victim of a society that objectifies women, even the little whores. A year from now you will use the cash from your divorce settlement to open a women's café and yarn shop, where the front window will feature a wall-hanging of a wide-hipped woman dancing joyously beside a waterfall with her own uterus. You will begin to teach seminars to help other women reach their full potentials as what you will call Self Weavin' Wimmin, who will not only create the rich, full tapestries of their own inner lives but who will also use their child-support checks to hire swarthy young landscape architects, or, as you will call them, Incan sun gods.

"Your café and yarn shop will go out of business and, in despair, you will embark on a journey of spiritual rebirth which will take you through India, the Italian countryside, and New Zealand, and you will achieve great wealth and fame by writing a guide to the cleanest restrooms in all of these places. Your next book will cover your relationship with your now grown daughter, and how you have learned to understand and even forgive her jealousy and hatred, and this book will be called *I Love You Anyway*, and its even more successful sequel will be called *I Love You Anyway Even Though You Sued Me.*

"You will ultimately find true fulfillment in commuting between your Paris apartment and your East Hampton beach house, with your twenty-five-years-younger Dominican lover, and then your thinly disguised novel will tell the story of how you found him in bed with your thirty-years-younger deaf lover. This book will become your biggest bestseller, and you will be played in the top-grossing film by a beautiful, aging star who will win an Oscar for the scene in which she tells the Dominican lover, in Spanish, that 'I was your poem,' after which she repeats the same line to the deaf lover, in sign language."

This forecast netted me $300 and, a few months later, a hand-knitted scarf and what tasted like a hand-knitted loaf of seven-grain bread. I was feeling cocky when I knocked on the door of Patti and Dave Mattison, who were the youngest couple in my neighborhood, and who were considered progressive, and even edgy, because their home was built after 1860 and because, at Halloween, they gave out little orange-and-black gift bags filled with phallic marzipan, buttons that read "Fight the Power," and diet pills.

Patti answered the door, in her loose, almost transparent, Mexican-embroidered beach cover-up and a miniskirt where the tie-dyed suede panels were stitched together with macramé.

"Hi, Elly," she said, in her scratchy, who-gives-a-damn voice. Until that moment, no one had ever called me Elly. No one had dared. "What's that thing on your forehead?" she asked. "Is that a third eye? You're kidding, right?"

Her husband, Dave, joined her. Dave had dark curly hair spilling onto the neck of his white T-shirt, which he wore with faded jeans and bare feet. This is how sexy Dave was: his sleepy eyes and his strong jaw actually allowed him to get away with wearing a silver and turquoise Navajo bracelet, a thumb ring, and no underwear. "Hey, El," said Dave, "we hear that you've been working the whole neighborhood. We've been waiting."

Patti laughed, and here's how sexy she was: she could laugh at a fourteen-year-old boy, and I felt both humiliated and aroused.

"Come on in," said Patti, and I followed the couple into their living room, which had no furniture but was almost completely filled with a single, gargantuan, overstuffed, mattress-like pillow, covered in a complicated batik print.

"Sit down," said Dave, as he and Patti eased themselves onto this mega-pillow. "We got this thing in Morocco. Once you get used to it, it's very comfortable."

"It's like a big bed," said Patti. "In fact, this whole house is just a big bed."

I hesitated, wondering if I should remove my grandfather's wing-tipped shoes. I didn't want them stolen.

"Take off your shoes," said Dave, "we want to see those argyle socks."

As I took off not only my shoes but my seersucker jacket, my sleeve garters, and my smart, summer-weight rattan fedora,

I knew, and I hoped, that I was being seduced. I decided that losing my virginity to a mixed couple would be highly efficient, in terms of finalizing any future gender preferences. It would be a form of one-stop shopping. I was thrilled and nervous and flattered, even as I wondered if the Mattisons ever dry-cleaned the batik covering on the mega-pillow.

"Would you like me to give you a psychic reading?" I asked the Mattisons, "or do you just want to have sex with me?"

"If you're really psychic," said Patti, "then you tell us."

A confession: at fourteen, I thought that this was a very sophisticated response.

"Do you want to have sex with me because I'm a fourteen-year-old virgin?" I asked, "Does that make me exotic?"

"Not at all," said Dave. "The bow tie makes you exotic."

That was when Patti kissed me, and lowered me onto my back. Dave followed suit, and soon we were all naked, in the darkened, Moroccan-themed living room of a suburban Connecticut home, having sex. I assumed that we were breaking, if not several Commandments, at least a zoning law.

Prior to having sex for the first time, I had read many books and magazines, pornographic and otherwise, and I'd developed certain expectations of intercourse. From paperback romances I expected to feel vaguely yet ecstatically ravished, as if, for the duration of the act, I would experience everything an ad for a drugstore cologne could ever promise. From more serious fiction, I assumed that I would be blasted with a torrent of conflicting emotions, flashbacks to my birth, a rough kinship with the natural world, perhaps a Booker Prize, and, ultimately, a sense of existential ennui. From mainstream movies, I hoped for a beautifully lit and choreographed series of thrusts and embraces, with my head thrown back, my eyes shut but not squinched, and my lips slightly but appealingly parted; I also felt that the sex might be edited, continually leaping forward in attractive bits and pieces, with only the dewiest bodily fluids. From porn, I trusted that sex would be alternately savage, degrading, pounding, and dull, and all of this sounded promising. From what my parents had told me, I knew that sex did not exist, and from what other schoolchildren had let on, I imagined that there was a real danger of getting stuck in one position or another, with the parties involved finally getting yanked apart in the emergency room.

None of this was true. While I was having sex for the first time, I felt exactly as I do when studying a Picasso or watching any program on public television: I was both interested and bored. All of the actions were, of course, primitive; despite the *Kama Sutra*, sex presents a limited inventory of limbs, organs, and procedures. I began to become crushingly disappointed: if this was sex, what was all the fuss about? Would it be better, or at least more engulfing, the next time? Should there be fewer people involved? More? As with any form of at-home entertaining, was it all about the guest list?

Just as I was about to stop paying attention entirely and to start mentally assembling an outfit for school the next day, I began to experience what I can only call a very Elyot Vionnet orgasm. I began to feel the rising, volcanic elation that I'd always known upon entering any stranger's home, or any public space. I began to come, because I began to observe.

I noticed, from the medicinal scent, that Patti, for all of her gypsy hauteur, used a dandruff shampoo. I saw that Dave, for all of his lanky, offhand ease, had lightly trimmed his chest hair. I realized that while Patti and Dave were both generous and skillful lovers, they were both a little too aware of, and pleased with, this fact. Looking up, I found that the massive, pierced tin Moroccan lighting fixture, with stained-glass inserts, which was hanging over our heads, was lit with a supermarket lightbulb that flickered to imitate candlelight, like the bulbs in apartment building lobby menorahs. I could tell that the afternoon's musk was wafting from a plug-in air freshener, in a variety called "Tantric Lovebreeze," and that a subtle wailing and sitar accompaniment was emanating from an eight-track cassette promising "Muslim Murmurs" from the Time-Life series "Restaurant Hubbub of Many Lands." Arching my back, I became aware that, from the Mattisons' proudly foreign, souk-purchased living room, I could glimpse a corner of a kitchen with antiqued Harvest Gold Formica cabinetry, and a vinyl wallcovering with a pattern of cartoon pepper mills waltzing with flirtatious salad tongs.

I'd always been obsessed with detail, but during sex I began to fully inhabit my powers. Just as Patti and Dave were pistoning, caressing, probing, and slurping, I reached an incomparably blinding climax, as I screamed, "Oh my God! There's a TV in the corner, but to make it look Moroccan you've draped it with one of those dorm-room Indian-print bedspreads! Your TV looks like it got stoned and thinks it's hiding!"

Needless to say, this outburst ended our group's activities.

"What did you say?" asked Patti.

"Who cares about our TV?" said Dave.

"But it's so interesting," I said. "You're being really strict about your theme."

"You know," said Patti, "everyone in this neighborhood thinks that we're weird."

"But, Jesus, Elyot," said Dave, "have they met you?"

2.

As I matured, I became a caring and attentive lover, although all of my relationships would crumble, with my partners asking things like, "Elyot, when we were kissing, were you looking over my shoulder at my grandmother's Lalique crystal decanter on the mantel?" "Elyot, when we were in bed, and we were watching that porn video, were you disgusted by the orgy scene, or by the purple-and-teal checkerboard sheets in the orgy scene?" "Elyot, when I told you that I loved you, did you actually say, under your breath, 'But you also love pleated khakis'?" One woman even told me that every time we made love, she began to wonder if I was a cat burglar, because I seemed to be casing her apartment.

I started to worry that I'd never find love. Could love even exist, in a world of grime-encrusted miniblinds and "Tiffany-style" lamps shaped like stained-glass roosters, and people who, while they were working out at the gym, would shut their eyes and boogie spastically to the music on their iPods? Could love possibly defeat such infamy? And yet I remained an impossible romantic. I fell in love every other minute, with the televised image of a polar bear cub stranded on an ice floe, with the carnal embrace of my favorite toffee-colored corduroy suit, and with the moment when I saw that, while I was at work, the scaffolding which had run the length of my building for over two years had finally vanished.

And then one afternoon, as I was substitute-teaching at an uptown middle school, a twelve-year-old student stabbed me in the shoulder with the blade of his father's sixteen-inch serrated hunting knife. I had been assigned to teach an English lesson, so of course I was instructing my students on the difference between English and Italian tailoring, and the fact that Englishmen need additional padding because most of them are born without chests or shoulders. It was then that the student rammed his blade through both my bottle green velvet smoking jacket and my flesh, because, as he later told the police, "I just wanted to see if that dude was for real."

An ambulance soon arrived, and that was how I met Lucy Wainscott, who was driving it. Lucy was lithe and alert, with a sensible yet buoyant haircut. Lucy always looked as if she'd just gone for a run, taken a quick plunge in some crystalline Alpine stream, and then arrived smiling and up for anything. As she was loading me, strapped to a gurney, into her ambulance, she was scrutinizing me with an intensely delighted curiosity.

"So you were trying to teach those kids about European tailoring?" she asked, securing the gurney and prepping an oxygen mask, with the speed and nonchalance of a first mate on some sleek schooner.

"Yes," I said, "because I believe that if a child learns to appreciate peaked lapels and working buttonholes, that child will be far less likely to inject heroin between his toes and hold up convenience stores."

When I say things like this, most people either laugh uncomfortably, because they're not sure if I'm being serious, or they move away from me.

"Oh my God," said Lucy, with complete sincerity, as she lowered the oxygen mask onto my face, "that is so fucking true."

Lucy and I began seeing each other, and I learned that she was from a distinguished if not especially wealthy Massachusetts family which had emphasized service above all. Lucy had dropped out of college after two weeks, and had then built roads in Zimbabwe, learned to pilot a helicopter, for making drops of food and medical supplies in the Sudan, and had briefly been taken hostage by a rebel faction in Colombia. "I could never figure out if the rebels were the good guys or the bad guys," she said. "I kept asking them to explain it, but they couldn't figure it out, either." After almost eight years abroad, she'd returned to New York, because, "I just missed it so much. But I still wanted to help out, so I decided, hey, there's plenty of guerrilla warfare and unknown fevers right here in midtown."

Lucy was the best sort of do-gooder, as she was driven equally by an almost Quaker decency and by a restless yen for adventure. "It's terrible to say it," she told me, "but people in trouble are just so interesting. Every time I pick up a junkie who's just overdosed and fallen off a bridge into a Dumpster, well, you know he's got a story to tell. And don't get me started on domestic disputes, like when he's late for dinner again and didn't call, and so she's decided to use the paella pan as a blunt instrument—I have the best job in the world!"

I loved hearing about Lucy's day, and, oddly, she couldn't get enough of mine. "So you were supposed to be teaching a math class," she'd say, "and you had the kids conduct an imaginary auction of their parents' art collections, from both before and after the last recession. That's so cool!" Like me, Lucy was ravenous for information, although unlike me, she was rarely critical. "So when you pick up someone who's almost castrated himself by masturbating with an industrial vacuum cleaner," I'd ask, "you're not allowed to giggle?"

Our mutual fascination became romance because, as Lucy said, "I have got to figure you out." When we made love, I wasn't distracted, because we both kept talking; the sex was pleasurable, but it was often exceeded by some wonderful anecdote about a woman who'd tried to hang herself with a jump rope, because she hated aerobic exercise, or by the story of my teaching a high school history class on the evolution of the handshake. Lucy and I were perfectly matched, because we had absolutely nothing in common, with each other or with anyone else on the planet.

As we fell in love, Lucy began allowing me to ride shotgun in her ambulance. While this was technically against the law, no one complained, least of all the sick or injured people, because I would always tell them something upbeat, like "Let's be honest—it's just a pinkie," or "Now you can have any nose you want!" Helping others, and careening through the city with the siren blaring, only brought Lucy and me closer. "We're perfect together," Lucy said, "because while I'm trying to get these people to a hospital and save their lives, you're reminding them to say thank you." One night as I climbed on board Lucy received an urgent summons to an address on 126th Street, where we climbed six flights to retrieve the broken bodies of a long-married couple.

Mr. Demetrios, it seemed, was ragingly jealous of his wife, even after twenty-eight years of marriage and seven children. Mrs. Demetrios was a still sensual if hefty woman in second-skin stretch denim cutoffs and a plunging electric pink leotard; she'd used iron-on letters to add the words "HAVE SOME" to her neckline, which contained the breasts that her husband adored and that were large enough to be declared as dependents on his income tax forms. While Mr. Demetrios, who was a musician, had been away for the weekend, playing at a mob wedding in the Adirondacks, Mrs. Demetrios had fallen into bed with his brother.

Mr. Demetrios came home early and caught the adulterers in the act, and he'd then used his saxophone to break his brother's arm, after which he'd attempted to strangle his wife with an extension cord. Mrs. Demetrios, breaking free, had slammed Mr. Demetrios in the head with an eight-slice toaster. When Lucy and I arrived, all of the parties involved were moaning, yelling, and clutching their mutilated body parts.

"How could you do this?" Mr. Demetrios demanded, as blood gushed from the toaster-sized crater above his dangling ear. "I love you so much!"

"And I love you!" the wife yowled, with the extension cord still draped, if more loosely, around her neck. "The only reason I slept with your brother is because he reminds me of you!"

"It's true!" said the brother, cradling his shattered arm. "The whole time we were doing it, she kept saying, 'You're not half as good as your brother! Or your dad'!"

"You really said that?" Mr. Demetrios, instantly remorseful, asked his wife.

"Of course," said Mrs. Demetrios. "When you're here, you're the only one I will ever love!"

"What have I done!" cried Mr. Demetrios, as he and Mrs. Demetrios fell into each other's arms. The brother tried to applaud, which caused him to scream.

"It's so romantic," said Lucy, as she prepared a plastic splint for the brother. "They've been together for so long, and they're still so passionate. All three of them."

As I placed Mr. Demetrios's ear, which had fallen off during the embrace, into a small Styrofoam cooler, I looked up, into Lucy's eyes. She was so lovely and so involved and so adept, that all I could say was, "Lucy?"

"Elyot?"

"Will you marry me?"

"Say yes!" urged Mrs. Demetrios, clutching her bosom; she'd now tied the extension cord into a decorative bow.

"Yes!" said Lucy.

3.

Lucy and I were both shocked, not just because, inspired by a scene of domestic gore, we were getting married, but because I had done something so spontaneous, and so epically out of character. And once I began, I couldn't stop. "Lucy," I said, in the ambulance, as we drove the now cooing Demetrios family to the hospital, "let's drop these folks off, and then keep going. Let's get married today!"

"Oh, yes!" said Mrs. Demetrios.

"You'll never regret it!" said Mr. Demetrios.

"Never!" said Mr. Demetrios's brother.

"What?" asked Mr. Demetrios, as his brother had spoken into his missing ear.

"Are you sure?" Lucy asked, "All of you? Because, Elyot, you know I love you, but we don't have to rush into this. It's so . . . not you."

"I know!" I said, "And that's what's so interesting. What if I actually broke free, and became someone else? What if I surrendered, to pure blissful anarchy? What if I . . . wore sneakers? Even—sneakers with Velcro straps? With the straps undone?"

"He's in love!" cried Mrs. Demetrios.

"Who are you?" Lucy asked me, laughing.

"I don't know!" I said, and for the first moment in my life, this didn't seem to matter. For once, I wasn't worrying about what I was wearing, or about what everyone else was wearing, or about how the world was going terribly wrong, and when and how I might point this out to everyone. I could barely remember my own name or my profession or my favorite shade of off-white: Was it parchment or eggshell or bone? Or even blanched almond? I didn't care!

For once I wanted nothing in my life to be cautiously measured, assiduously weighed, or painfully honed. I wanted to plunge in, to forge ahead, to flap my arms and chew with my mouth open and spend money heedlessly and then I wanted to declare bankruptcy and yet continue to spend, buying a home spa with fifteen pulsing underwater power jets! I wanted to be an American! At the hospital, I had Lucy arrange our blood tests, and then, with the siren at full blast, we raced downtown to City Hall, for our license and our ceremony.

"But, Elyot—City Hall?" Lucy asked, as we waited in the antechamber, with the other couples. "Is City Hall really you?"

"I don't know!" I said. "And I don't care! Look what you've done to me!"

"Elyot?"

"But, Lucy, what about you? I know you said yes, but is this what you want? Am I railroading you into all this?"

"Elyot, I've fallen out of a helicopter into a village where even the seven-year-olds have rocket launchers. I've paddled a bark canoe up the Amazon, where something the size of a pigeon turned out to be a mosquito. I've driven my ambulance into the middle of a gang war, where all of my windows got smashed by a guy who'd shot his cousin at point-blank range because the cousin had brushed against his leather jacket. But do you know why I want to marry you?"

"Why?"

"Because for the first time in my life, I'm scared."

The ceremony was brief and basic, as performed by a savvy, middle-aged female judge, with pleasingly honey-colored bouffant hair and the acid swirls of a Pucci blouse topping her black robes. She looked at Lucy and then at me, with a degree of doubt.

"Are you sure about this?" asked the judge.

"Yes," said Lucy, who was holding a bouquet of white Casablanca lilies, which we'd bought at a nearby Korean deli, and which she'd bundled with some tongue depressors and syringes from the ambulance supply.

"Yes," I said, with a Casablanca lily pinned to the lapel of my navy blazer, where the Demetrios family's blood had barely dried.

"You don't look like any of our usual couples," the judge commented. "And it's not because you're not pregnant, or drunk. But I've been marrying people for over thirty years, and I've never come across a couple quite like the two of you. And I mean this in the best possible way, but you look like a fairy tale where, instead of marrying the prince, the princess is marrying the wizard."

"I know," said Lucy, taking my hand, "but I would never marry a prince. That's too easy. That's just a crown and a castle."

"And you, Mr. Wizard, with that thing on your head . . ." She was staring at my derby, which I'd banded with yellow crime-scene tape. "Are you sure?"

I looked into Lucy's eyes, and she nodded, as if we were both standing at the edge of a cliff, with common sense and forethought and statistical probability running toward us, yelling, "Don't jump!"

"I'm sure," I said.

"I feel like a scientist, combining two volatile elements," said the judge. "I'm either going to cure cancer, or blow up the world."

"Either way," I said, "it's a big day."

4.

Our wedding night was euphoric, as we made love and ate ruffled potato chips and swigged orange juice and, most enchantingly, discussed all of the other couples that we'd met at City Hall. "I loved those two eighty-five-year-olds," said Lucy, "because they'd been high school sweethearts, but then they'd broken up and they'd both married other people and had kids, but then both of their spouses died and they'd found each other again at their fiftieth high school reunion. And whenever the clerk used the words 'husband' or 'wife,' one of them would always ask, 'Wait, you mean this one or the dead one?'"

"My favorite was the blind couple," I said, "because they were so devoted, and because the husband took me aside and whispered, 'So she's pretty, right? Really pretty? And she says she's twenty-eight, what do you think?'"

We finally fell asleep, rapturously exhausted, in each other's arms. The problems only began at eleven a.m. the next day, when we woke up. As I opened my eyes, I saw Lucy, still asleep. And I thought, she's beautiful and I love her and I'm so transported, and yet . . . she's in my apartment. I tried to banish such a selfish and petty train of thought, as Lucy yawned and opened her eyes.

"Good morning, you," she said, stretching in the sunlight.

"Good morning," I said, trying to keep the discomfort out of my tone.

"I love you," she said, still not moving from the bed.

"And I love you," I replied, "and I have a wonderful idea. Let's get out of bed, and pick up our clothes. Off the floor."

Of course, I was being polite, since before I'd fallen asleep I'd stowed the remaining orange juice in the refrigerator, and tossed the empty potato chip bags down the incinerator chute in the hall. Then I'd smoothed my shirt and my suit with a hand steamer, placed both garments on wooden hangers, and returned them to my closet. I'd inserted cedar trees into my shoes, which were then slipped into individual clean white linen drawstring bags and stored in their original box, and then I'd draped my necktie with the other members of its color family on the rack attached to the back of my closet door. My cuff links, watch fob, collar stays, and suspenders were then deposited in their labeled compartments in my great-grandfather's gold-embossed Florentine kidskin accessories caddy, my socks were hand laundered, matched, rolled, and filed in their drawer, and my wallet and loose coins were symmetrically arranged atop my bedside table, beside my crystal carafe of ice water, my bud vase containing a single unopened white tea rose, and my Bible, by which I mean Emily Post's original etiquette manual, the edition aimed at families with at least five servants.

Lucy's clothing had been flung carelessly over my single chair and her shoes were strewn haphazardly beneath it. This is the chair carved to resemble a human skeleton, and even in death, it looked outraged.

Lucy gradually roused herself and slipped into my best dressing gown, the one in a Black Watch woolen plaid with quilted satin lapels and a tasseled belt. As I was trying to surreptitiously de-rumple the sheets, Lucy sprawled back onto my campaign bed, munching my new favorite breakfast cereal, a muesli of steel-cut oats, walnut clusters, and honey-roasted crickets. She was eating this cereal with her hand, right from the box.

"Lucy," I said evenly, "I love you, but I don't love crumbs."

"I'm sorry," she said, "and oh my God, I've finished the whole box. Elyot, I'm so sorry."

"It's . . . fine," I said, trying to ignore the fact that she was now holding the box upside down and shaking it, allowing the cereal dust to fall onto my great-grandmother's matchlessly threadbare Oushak rug.

After Lucy bathed, I went into my bathroom, which has not been updated since the building was constructed in 1870, and which therefore boasts white subway tile with narrow black tile accents, nickel and porcelain fixtures, a clawfoot tub, and a floor of small, octagonal black and white tiles. My grooming products are arranged, by size, in a row of frosted, ribbed glass jars with nickel-plated lids, and my towels are the thickest, whitest Egyptian cotton, with a black embroidered border and my monogram. A person's bathroom, I believe, is the only three-dimensional expression of their soul.

Lucy had used a towel as a bath mat, and she'd run my tortoise shell comb through her hair, and had then left the comb dangling precariously over the edge of the sink. There were small dabs of my English tooth powder on the etched and beveled mirror over the sink. Lucy had also soaked a washcloth and left it dripping over the lip of the tub. As you can imagine, I was having trouble breathing.

"So, Elyot," said Lucy, as I left the bathroom and noticed that, while she'd made a half-hearted attempt at straightening the sheets and bedcoverings on the campaign bed, she'd also rearranged the matching cushions so that they made no sense at all. It was like Chernobyl. "Elyot," she wondered, "do you think we should live here or at my place, or should we find a bigger place of our own?"

I tried to smile, or at least to inhabit the body and lips of someone who, at some point in the future, would be able to reclaim his smiling muscles. My brain was in shreds. Lucy lived in a one-bedroom in a white-brick high-rise in Murray Hill, an apartment which she was subletting from a nurse who was taking a year off to visit her five sisters, each of whom lived in a different midwestern state. Lucy's sublet included commemorative plastic plates, purchased at highway rest stops, picturing the official flower, bird, and nickname of each sister's home state, hanging on the wall of the breakfast nook and arranged around a large, full-color photograph, draped in black polyester crepe, of the nurse's dead Siamese cat.

I considered finding a new apartment, for Lucy and myself. This would be an apartment where I would have to respect Lucy's belongings, and where she would, on occasion, undoubtedly touch or use or sit on mine. It would be an apartment where, even if, for a split second, I could place everything harmoniously, it would never remain so, or not for very long. It would be an apartment, maybe even a roomy and desirable apartment, perhaps with a river view and central air conditioning, but, above all else, it would be an apartment and a life which I would be expected to share. For better or for worse, I know myself. And every day, I try desperately to improve the world, to reach out and to devote myself to helping others. Although of course I fall hideously short, but I aspire, as we all must, to a form of Gandhi-like largesse. But there are restrictions and amendments and codicils to my agreement with humanity. And this was the deal breaker: I don't share.

I looked at Lucy, who was still fresh and winning and altogether sensational, and who deserved only the utmost happiness. Then I looked at my apartment, where, at that time, I'd already lived for twenty years. I looked at the unassailable dimensions of my single room, at the furniture chosen with more care than any nation selects its leaders, at a life distilled to an essence of pristine, limitless, impossible elegance. Between this marvelous woman and this flawless studio apartment, I had never been so gut-wrenchingly torn.

"This isn't going to work, is it?" asked Lucy, without even a hint of accusation. She'd been watching me, in my agony. She knew me, better than anyone ever had. And she loved me, not despite my majestic lunacy but because of it.

"I'm so sorry," I whispered, and, for a moment, I almost wished I was someone else, someone normal, someone who wasn't anguished by the single white porcelain plate, lightly smeared with jam, which Lucy had left tilted in the sink. Smeared. *Tilted.*

"Oh, Elyot," said Lucy, "I think that the very best marriages never last more than a day."

"Really?"

"I think I knew that we could never really be together. But I just wanted to be able, at least for a day, to call myself Mrs. Elyot Vionnet. Just to see the expression on people's faces."

"I will always love you," I swore, and I meant every word. "Now get out."

In Pieces

When some people are asleep they look like little angels. When Candida is sleeping, she looks like she's listening patiently, as the angels plead their case and explain why they're necessary, right before Candida begins grabbing each angel by the throat and ripping its wings off.

While Candida's natural facial expression, even in repose, is one of bitingly intelligent fury, she's also compassionate. She was a religious studies major in college, and she'd be a great minister or rabbi if only, as she puts it, "all of the major religions weren't so incredibly fucked." Candida is someone who, if a homeless crackhead tried to mug her, would tell the crackhead, "Look, we both know why you're doing this, and why it's the drug cartels and the mob and ultimately the current administration who are profiting from your misery. And if you'd like, I can try and get you into a treatment program, and then I'd have you take an aptitude test, because your street skills could most likely be translated into a decent career. And you probably don't have any place to live, so we can work on that, and please don't be offended, but a shower isn't going to kill you. So what do you say?" By this point the crackhead would have forgotten that he was trying to rob Candida and he'd be gratefully holding her backpack while she got her mail.

Candida is small and wiry, and her short dark curls sometimes get her mistaken for a sexy Greek delivery boy. I first met her at a party, and as we spoke, we kept being interrupted by a spindly guy who wanted us to follow him into another room, where he was going to play his flute. When he intruded once too often, Candida turned to him and said forcefully, but without raising her voice, "We're trying to have a conversation, which you are welcome to join, but if you don't stop bothering us, and everyone else, I'm going to shove that flute so far up your ass that it's going to come out your mouth."

Candida was raised in a well-to-do family on Central Park West. She once showed me a short promotional film in which, as a five-year-old, she'd been asked, by friends of her parents, to play with a new doll. In the film, the very young Candida has pink satin bows in her hair and wears a ruffled pink party dress. She holds a doll, dressed in an identical outfit, in her fist, at arm's length; Candida stares at the doll with revulsion and pity, as if she can't decide whether to yank its head off or send it to a gulag for reeducation.

Because she believes in common sense and justice, Candida is fearless. The only time I ever saw her quaver was when, as a favor to her mother, she'd agreed to wear a dress to a family wedding. I've seen a photo of Candida in what ended up as an embroidered black velvet bolero and matching skirt ensemble: she looks like there are rifles being pointed at her, just off camera. Before she'd gone to this wedding, she'd asked me to accompany her, for moral support, to buy the appropriate women's shoes. It took me at least forty-five minutes to coax Candida from the street and into the shoe store, and another half hour to calm her into taking a seat and trying on a one-inch heel. "I can't, I can't, I can't!" she wailed, as a small crowd of salespeople tried to soothe her. "Why are you torturing me?"

For such a forceful personality, Candida never prejudges anyone. She actually listens, and she can be sympathetic to the most unlikely causes. For a hard-core liberal, she's never knee-jerk or doctrinaire, and her sense of humor can surprise people. She was once part of a feminist discussion group where the women decided to rename their genitalia, since so much of the standard nomenclature has been coined by men. "Womynflower" and "herzone" were mentioned as more sensitive possibilities, and then Candida said, "You know, I've always kind of liked 'gash.'"

For a time, Candida was roommates with Kelly, a conceptual artist who used their small apartment, without asking, as her personal gallery. Kelly had used black spray paint to stencil the words "In the refrigerator . . ." on the front door of that appliance; and inside, scotch-taped to the vegetable crisper, was a sheet of notebook paper typed with the words, " . . . there is no confusion." Kelly had placed a chocolate chip cookie with a bite out of it on top of the toilet seat, and, after using the commode, guests were told to put the cookie back on the toilet seat, because the entire process was "a piece." Or, as I like to think of it, "a peece."

It helped enormously that Kelly was very pretty, with the flawless, lightly freckled skin and the spiky, naturally blond hair of a four-year-old. Kelly had many things in common with a four-year-old.

Candida enjoyed Kelly's antics. "I'm not sure if she's a genius or a doorknob," she told me, "but she might be on to something, and she's fun to watch." One evening Kelly draped a floor lamp with a saffron-colored scarf, to filter the light, and she filled a large tin washtub with water. Then she directed Candida and me to kneel beside the washtub with our hands behind our backs, as she dumped fifty tea bags into the tub. We weren't allowed to speak, and Kelly watched us intently for an hour, as the tea spread through the tepid water. Then, with a knowing smile, she left us alone. The instant we heard Kelly shut her bedroom door, Candida and I plunged our hands into the washtub and furiously ripped all of the tea bags to shreds.

"Yay!" we both yelled.

"The tea is dead!" I shouted.

"We killed the tea!" said Candida.

"What are you doing?" asked Kelly, returning, horrified. "I can't believe you!"

"The tea kept looking at us," Candida explained.

"The tea was asking for it," I agreed.

"I'm so disappointed, in both of you," said Kelly, with disgust, shaking her head. "If you hadn't given in, if you'd resisted your urge to destroy the tea bags, you would've kept that tension for the rest of your lives. You would have felt a balance, between chaos and desire. But because you were so weak, you ruined the whole piece. I hope you're happy."

Candida and I knew that we should be deeply ashamed. We looked down at our damp, tea-stained hands.

"Actually, I feel pretty good," Candida concluded.

"I feel great!" I said.

Kelly soon became a member of a therapy cult that mandated that its members blame everything bad that had ever happened to them, or to the world, on their parents. The appeal of this strategy was obvious. If Kelly was caught outside in the rain, she'd turn to the sky and mutter, in all seriousness, "Thanks, *Dad*." If she ran out of milk, she'd shove the empty carton into the trash, griping, "My fucking *mother*." Kelly also became affiliated with a sort of theater company that was linked to Robert Wilson, the gilded emperor of all things conceptual.

Wilson was world famous for creating theatrical events, usually onstage at the opera house of the Brooklyn Academy of Music, and these shows could last up to twelve hours and beyond. And right now, I just have to say something: Nothing, no matter how pleasurable, should ever last for twelve hours. Sex shouldn't last for twelve hours. A car trip through the south of France shouldn't last for twelve hours. Even a family-sized bag of peanut M&Ms couldn't possibly last for twelve hours. Here's the rule: art should never require more than one bathroom break. Ever.

Still, everyone said that Wilson was a genius, and I wanted to keep an open mind, so I bought a ticket for one of his silent operas, or futurist epics, or whatever the critics and graduate students were calling them. I took my seat and saw an empty stage with a foggy gray and purple backdrop. After a while, a woman in a long skirt appeared, and she began to move, with deliberate, painstaking slowness, from one side of the stage to the other. After fifteen minutes, she'd moved about twelve inches. After half an hour, she'd gone about a yard. After an hour and forty-five minutes, she'd hit mid-stage. This struck me as an achievement only for someone in a nursing home. I wanted to run down the aisle, jump onto the stage, grab the woman by the elbow and scream, "GET GOING ALREADY! LET'S SEE SOME HUSTLE!"

The evening went on for many, many more hours, as a few more people did things like sit on a chair, or spin in a circle, sometimes to the accompaniment of an electronic thump, but all at dead-tortoise speed. At one of the several intermissions, I overheard people saying things like, "It's hypnotic," "It's mesmerizing," and "It's so moving." I wanted to yank these people and shake them and say, "Maybe it's moving, but it's not moving anywhere FAST."

I was never clear on exactly how Kelly's friends were associated with Robert Wilson, but most of them were working on a variety of his projects, and they all worshiped him. They were like the Jonestown Drama Club. One morning, Kelly told Candida and me that she pitied us, "because you're both so aesthetically unaware." To help us improve, she asked us to participate in a conceptual dinner party that her group was holding in Brooklyn. I don't know why so many conceptual events take place in Brooklyn; maybe it's a form of quarantine. Kelly's dinner party was going to commemorate the Russian Revolution, and she told us that "During the dinner, all of the guests have to change their gender and their social class at least twice. Do you understand?"

"Will there be a pony?" I asked.

"Or a clown?" asked Candida.

"You have to take this seriously," said Kelly, "or you can't come."

"Will there be a Russian pony?" I asked, as Kelly practiced her yoga breathing, to stop herself from hitting me.

Candida and I decided that this party sounded, at the very least, entertaining, so we started making plans. Our friend William, who was both a monarchist and a theater designer, supplied us with costumes, although he warned us, "I hope that you're not going to make fun of the Tsar. He was doing just fine until the Communists ruined everything."

"But weren't the Communists trying to help people," I asked, "at least in the beginning?"

"Excuse me," said William, "under Communism, everyone's supposed to share everything, which means that everyone gets to be dirty and smelly and have a potato. Communists don't really want freedom and equality, they just want ugly brick walls and folding chairs."

On the night of the party, Candida and I bundled all of our preparations into garment bags and pillowcases and took the subway to Brooklyn. The party was being held in a spacious, raw loft, and by the time Candida and I arrived, things were already under way. There were about thirty guests, all wearing jeans or gauzy skirts with vague historical touches, like striped, double-breasted vests, ear-flapped fur hats, or scraps of battered military gear. Candida and I went into a side room and put on our costumes for our first incarnations. Candida emerged first, wearing a bustled, purple moire satin gown with a hoopskirt, black lace, elbow-length gloves, dangling, jet earrings, and a towering wig that resembled a prizewinning pumpkin made of human hair. Candida had no problem donning even these elaborate women's clothes, as long as people knew she was in costume. Candida and I had sketched out our dialogue on paper before the party, so the following re-creation is pretty much verbatim. And remember that both Candida and I were amateurs, and idiots.

"Gudt evenink!" Candida exclaimed, to the other guests. "I am de Grand Duchess Olga Maria Despolenta! Andt zis ees my dewoted ladies maid, pliss velcome—Babushka!"

I entered behind Candida, groveling. I was of the peasant class, in a full burlap skirt and a rough linen blouse, packed with soccer ball breasts, with my head swathed in a humble turban made from a brown corduroy bedspread.

"Tank ju, my meestress," I said, on my hands and knees, kissing the hem of Candida's gown.

"Pliss do not feed her," Candida cautioned the guests, regarding me.

"Um, what are you doing?" asked one of the guests, a hippie-ish looking man wearing a black, all-purpose cape.

"Tell dem!" I insisted, to Candida, "Tell of jour voe!"

"My vat?" asked Candida.

"Jour voe!"

Candida then strode to the head of the long dinner table and slammed her fists onto the tabletop, rattling everyone's china and glassware, as I scuttled behind her.

"De Cossacks!" Candida howled, now pounding her bosom. "Dey are comink, andt dey are takink everytink! Dey are takink my home, andt my aneemals, andt dey are takink my cheeldrens to be solchers!"

"Her cheeldrens!" I repeated, weeping.

"Dey are takink my dotter, Anna Constancia Magdalena," Candida continued, "andt my son, Mikhail Horacio Diploma, andt my babee, my leetle Tina Irina Farina Margarina!"

As Candida sobbed loudly, I comforted her with a lurching hug. "Eet veel be alright, my meestress!" I assured her. "I am lyink," I whispered to the other guests.

"I cannot tell de story!" Candida said, "I cannot go on!"

"But ju must!" I thundered. "Ju must tell of jour hardsheep!"

"I still haf sheep?" Candida asked, perking up.

"Hardsheep," I corrected.

"But, vhy are my sheep hard?"

"Tell dem!"

We went on like this, sharing the sweeping epic of how the Grand Duchess fell in love with and married an American fighter pilot named Bud Dorn, and then moved, along with Babushka, to a suburban ranch home in Bel-Air, California. The tale ended with Candida proclaiming, "I am no longer de Grand Duchess Olga. Nyet. My name ees ... Meesus Bud Dorn!"

With that, Candida collapsed, with her head in the salad bowl, as I wrapped my bulky, devoted frame around her. Raising my head, I saw that everyone at the table was staring at us, in horror, shock, and confusion. They had all been making mild remarks about the Red Army and the Tsar's Winter Palace, and there'd been bursts of recorded gunfire from speakers near the windows. But the Grand Duchess and her Babushka seemed, well, beyond conceptual.

Candida and I had a history of misguided public behavior. Candida once had a yen for a girl who was attending music school, an oboist. Candida wanted my opinion, so she invited me to her crush's end-of-term recital. Some of the students, including Candida's favorite, were very talented, but then a guy came onstage with his guitar. He was musically cutting edge, so he never tuned or even strummed his instrument. He hit it. He sat on a chair, repeatedly smacking the wooden body of his guitar with the open palm of his hand, harder and harder, as if the guitar had misbehaved and he was spanking it. As he kept slapping away, for quite some time, I turned to Candida and whispered, "Bad guitar. BAD guitar!" Then we couldn't stop laughing and had to run out into the front hallway, to pull ourselves together, so we could later tell Candida's soon-to-be-girlfriend that she was terrific and that her fellow students were "so interesting, really."

Back at the Brooklyn loft, Candida and I would not be daunted. After appearing as the Grand Duchess and her staff, we retreated to a side room and changed our clothes. Candida then returned to the dinner party, calling out, "Bonjour! Bonjour, mes aimés!" She had now waved and center-parted her own dark hair, which was complemented by a sprightly, waxed, and curlicued stick-on mustache. Her black velvet jacket, with braided frog closures, matched her black velvet knickers, her black silk hose, and her Cuban-heeled dancing shoes.

"Bonjour!" she trilled, with a valiant French accent. "I am Monsieur Serge-Pierre DuFlessix! And I 'ave come all ze way from Paree, to become ze dancing instructor, to His Royal Highness, ze twelve-year-old Crown Prince of All Ze Russias, please welcome—Tsarevitch Nikolai Alexandrovitch Romanov!"

I entered, proudly, a royal vision in a Prussian blue tunic bisected diagonally, from shoulder to waist, with a heavy pink satin sash, pinned with medallions, commemorative brooches, and rhinestone crosses. My white trousers were tucked into my gleaming, thigh-high black boots, and I clicked my heels with military precision.

"Good evenink, everybody!" I cried as I gave a royal wave. "Good evenink to all my devoted pipple. Excuse me a moment."

I then dabbed at my nose with a white lace hanky, which was instantly drenched in blood, because, as any student of Russian history knows, the little prince was a hemophiliac. Candida and I had mixed up buckets of stage blood, using red food coloring and Karo syrup, to fill small plastic bags, which we'd tucked inside my royal attire. As I surreptitiously stabbed myself with a fork, the blood now oozed from my collar, and spread across my sash.

"Mais non!" Candida yipped, as I swooned, teetered, and gradually collapsed onto the floor. She knelt beside me and cradled my head.

"Ze leetle prince is dying," Candida told the appalled party-goers. "And do you know why? Because not enough people, zey do not believe in princes."

We had based this part of our routine on the second act of *Peter Pan*, when Tinkerbell's twinkling light goes all but dark. "What ees wrong wiz zees world?" Candida pleaded. "Why can we not believe? Look! Wiz every breath, ze leetle prince, he grows weaker!"

As I struggled to stay alive, Candida shoved her hand inside my tunic, and pulled out a medium-sized, blood-soaked satin pillow in the shape of a heart. As I gurgled, she held the heart aloft, and made it throb. "Eet ees his heart! Eet ees almost silent. He weel die. Unless . . ."

Through slitted eyes, I checked out the room. Against all of their better judgment, the guests were now riveted.

"Unless what?" someone asked.

"Unless we all show heem zat we believe!" said Candida. "You know, maybe, just maybe, eef we can all put our hands togezzer, he weel hear us. Please, I am begging you, eef only everyone who believes in ze leetle prince weel clap zere hands, zen maybe ze leetle prince does not have to die!"

The guy in the cape began to clap. Then another guest joined in, and another, until pretty soon the whole conceptual collective was stomping its feet, whistling, cheering, and applauding wildly.

I raised myself up on one elbow, just a few inches off the floor, and I tried to open my eyes. I fell back. The ovation quadrupled.

"Oui! Oui! Eet ees working!" said Candida. "Because you believe in ze leetle prince, he LIVES!"

Candida always encouraged me to do potentially humiliating things, so I'd meet many different sorts of people. She once had us wear matching shiny red polyester satin shirts with knitted waistbands, which she thought were festive, and she took me out dancing, at an after-hours club in midtown. The DJ was playing some of the lushest, most seriously throbbing music I'd ever heard, and the place was packed. As we danced it dawned on me that I was the only white person there; people often think Candida is a Latina, so she didn't count. As an extremely Caucasian idiot in a ridiculous shirt, I started to get nervous, but then Candida shot me a don't-be-an-asshole look, and I ended up having a wonderful time.

Sadly, Kelly hadn't been able to attend the Russian Revolution event, but she'd heard all about it. "I still don't think that the two of you really understand our process," she sniffed.

To this day, Candida's process remains very much her own. She's become, among other things, a major political activist, an event planner, and a drug counselor, but she still loves adventure. Once we were both invited to a formal dinner party at the home of a very WASPy fellow, and there were framed hunting prints on the deep green walls. After dessert, Candida corraled me and insisted that we investigate our host's bedroom. We were awestruck by his closets, which were inhumanly tidy, and I cherish the image of Candida staring at the apartment-owner's many belts, which included a few with tiny embroidered whales, and which were hanging full length in perfect rows, from a wooden rack. "Look at his belts," Candida said. "You can tell that, in just a few years, he's going to kill someone."

I Hit Hamlet

The ad in the *Times* real estate listings said "medieval duplex," which was tantalizing, unless "medieval" referred to the plumbing. I was apartment hunting, so I arranged to meet the broker at a brownstone just off Washington Square. The apartment was four steep flights up, and the walls of the final landing were a rough stucco, with an oddly shaped, high niche, for a candle or a skull, just outside a rounded, rough-hewn door with elaborate ornamental hinges.

The apartment consisted of the full, narrow top floor, and I was smitten. The theatrical plasterwork continued throughout, and there was a bay window with a window seat, flanked by additional portholes of thick, leaded, Mediterranean blue stained glass, all overlooking the leafy corner of Washington Square Park where fanatics play chess. There was a micro-kitchen, one tiny closet, and a cramped, 1970s-vintage bathroom, but none of this mattered, thanks to a vaulted skylight, a fireplace, assorted archways, and a hidden winding staircase. The stairs led to the roof, where I found a deck, with a six-foot-high, sun-bleached oak ship's wheel, leaning against the outer wall of a hobbit-scale, one-room cottage, with a beamed ceiling. The broker was delightfully old-school and chatty, and she mentioned that the apartment had once been the home of John Barrymore.

Here's how long ago this was: I didn't fearfully snap up the place on contact but told the broker that I'd phone her the next morning. That night, I called my agent, Helen Merrill, and told her about the apartment. She remarked, in her German accent, "Perhaps you vill find my hairpins." It seemed that Helen, thirty years earlier, had conducted an adulterous affair on the premises with Barrymore's son-in-law, an erstwhile actor married to the troubled Diana Barrymore, whose mother was a poetess aptly named Michael Strange. Helen recalled the apartment, if not the son-in-law, in fond detail, and the karma became overwhelming. The next day I met with Winston Kulok, the charming and affable owner of the town house, who occupied the first two floors with his family, and the lease on the Barrymore place was mine.

As I settled in, I researched my new home. Barrymore had taken up residence in 1917, just before he began performing his legendary Hamlet uptown. His film career at that point was limited to locally shot silent movies, including an early take on *Moby-Dick*, which may have been the source of the ship's wheel. Barrymore had remodeled the apartment as a gothic retreat, christening it the Alchemist's Corner. He had installed all the false beams, monastery-inspired ironwork, and stained glass, which made his lair resemble a stage set for an Agatha Christie whodunit in summer stock. The rooftop had been his master-piece, and had at one time included a garden, with cedar trees, a slate walkway, and a reflecting pool. Tons of soil had to be hoisted up by pulley, and eventually caused a collapse into the rooms below. Of Barrymore's vision, only the cottage remained; he'd likened it to a roost overlooking the spires of Paris.

I read up on Barrymore's life, particularly in his entirely fraudulent, ghostwritten autobiography and in *Good Night, Sweet Prince*, an equally fanciful work devised soon after the star's death by his close friend Gene Fowler. There was a story that, after his demise, Barrymore's poker buddies had snatched his body from the morgue and propped it upright at their club-house table, for one last hand.

Barrymore was born into an illustrious family of American performers, which included his sister Ethel and his brother Lionel, and John had been nicknamed The Great Profile for his beauty, and acclaimed as a classical actor of extraordinary per-sonal magnetism and range. He was later drawn to Hollywood, appearing as Katharine Hepburn's wayward father in *A Bill of Divorcement*, a mature Mercutio in an all-star *Romeo and Juliet*, and, most uproariously, as a bulging-eyed, fire-breathing pro-ducer, opposite Carole Lombard, in the screwball gem *Twenti-eth Century*. Perhaps his signature role was that of a handsome, dissolute jewel thief, redeemed by his brief, ethereal passion for Greta Garbo in the sumptuous MGM melodrama *Grand Hotel*. This film exemplified the public perception of Barry-more as a gifted, doomed wastrel. The more I absorbed, and the more months I spent under Barrymore's bastard Jacobean roof, the more I felt required to write something set at the address. Someone or something had led me to these quarters and would not be denied. I began a novel about a character named Andrew Rally, the young star of *L.A. Medical*, a fatuous network gold mine. Andrew moves into the Barrymore apartment just as he's about to play Hamlet at Shakespeare in the Park. He gets apprehensive about returning to the stage, and he's ready to flee to Los Angeles when the ghost of Barrymore appears. I soon realized that the material would make a better play than a novel, as it took place primarily in a single location and was overrun with theatrical types. I surrendered, to God or Satan or the will of Barrymore, and completed a draft of a two-act comedy called *I Hate Hamlet*.

An out-of-town workshop in Saratoga went well, and a group of producers decided to bring the play to Broadway. The characters by then included Deirdre, Andrew's love interest and an ardent twenty-nine-year-old virgin; Gary Peter Lefkowitz, Andrew's pal and writer-producer-director, who's given to remarks like "You don't *do* art, you *buy* it"; Felicia, a gregarious real-estate broker; and Andrew's agent, Lillian, a flinty German émigrée, a tribute to Helen Merrill. In an early scene, Lillian asks her companions if she might smoke, and Deirdre implores her not to because it's such an unhealthy addiction. Lillian replies, "I know, I really must stop." Deirdre asks, "Smoking?" and Lillian says, "No—asking."

Most of the cast were New York stage actors, including Evan Handler as Andrew and the whiskey-voiced Caroline Aaron as Felicia. Lillian was to be played by Celeste Holm, who'd won an Academy Award for *Gentleman's Agreement* and who was practically the sole surviving cast member of both *All About Eve* and the original Broadway production of *Oklahoma!*. Celeste was wry and glamorous, and Helen was gruffly pleased. The supremely funny Adam Arkin would be Gary, and he later won my heart when, during a particularly trying and self-indulgent rehearsal, I noticed that Adam was calmly making a completely appropriate, masturbatory motion at his crotch.

Our great challenge was in casting the role of John Barry-more—ghost, thespian, and lecher. If you've written a star, you need a star. From Fanny Brice to Ray Charles, the imperson-ator must reignite the legend. The audience needed to believe that whoever played Barrymore, from the instant he stepped onstage, was an Olympian Hamlet, a devastating seducer, and everyone's favorite scoundrel. *I Hate Hamlet* was a romantic comedy by an unknown playwright being directed by the very young Michael Engler, so it wasn't easy to find, persuade, and sign a Barrymore.

The search finally arrived at Nicol Williamson, a Scotsman who'd achieved fame several decades earlier as a self-loathing solicitor in John Osborne's *Inadmissible Evidence*. Nicol had played a savage Hamlet in London and New York, and he'd become a reliable character presence in such films as *Robin and Marian* and *Excalibur*; in the latter, he'd been a memorably baroque Merlin. Onstage, Nicol was notorious. At a curtain call during the Broadway run of the musical *Rex*, in which Nicol was Henry VIII, he'd slapped a fellow actor whom Nicol felt was drawing focus. Our casting director had heard countless tales of similar misbehavior and advised us to acquire Nicol's services "only over my dead body." We didn't listen.

Nicol accepted the role, and an introductory lunch at a midtown restaurant was arranged between our Barrymore, the producing team, the director, and me. Like any decent star, Nicol arrived last. He was a tall, shambling man, with a bald pate bookended by buttresses of reddish curls, clinging to his head for dear life. His eyes were doleful and piercing, as if he'd seen far too much, enjoyed most of it, and had somehow managed to avoid arrest. His basso voice was gorgeously Shakespearean.

"Hallo, mates!" he boomed, and we all grinned and exchanged delighted glances, because Nicol was, if nothing else, everything an American wants a reprobate, Continental stage personality to be. He beguiled everyone with tales of beautiful women, show business, and air travel. He was an incipient tyrant, an Amin or Evita, caught at an early stage, when charm was of the essence in crafting a grateful, adoring cult. Clearly, here was Barrymore. After many hours, as the group departed, Nicol slung a long arm over my shoulders and said, "Dear fellow, I know you've heard tattle, but don't believe a word. I'm in top fighting form. And I haven't touched a drop in over a year."

I chose to believe it, despite a quick backward glance at the table, which held a brandy snifter, a wine bottle, and a beer mug, all of which had been recently emptied into Nicol.

The early rehearsal period was, as early rehearsal periods often are, a promising Eden. Nicol embraced every company member, and everyone seemed happy with the play. Celeste provided delectable anecdotes. In 1949, she was costarring with Loretta Young in the uplifting film *Come to the Stable*, in which the pair appeared as radiant, tennis-playing nuns, founding a children's hospital in Bethlehem, Connecticut. In reality, years earlier, Loretta had secretly given birth to Clark Gable's illegitimate daughter. For publicity purposes, she'd then contrived to remain virginal by adopting her own child. All of this subterfuge had made Loretta an even more devout Catholic, and during the filming, whenever anyone used profanity, or took the Lord's name in vain, she had the person drop a nickel into a cuss box, with the proceeds shipped to Vatican-related charities. One afternoon, Ethel Merman visited the set and was told of the cuss box. She yanked a bill from her wallet, located Celeste's costar, and brayed, "Here's ten bucks, Loretta. Go fuck yourself."

In our second week, Nicol invited me to his small, bare Hell's Kitchen pied-à-terre, where he hunched over a rec-room quality Hohner organ and played and bleated a song cycle that he'd composed, based on his open-wound divorce. Each number was devoted to a militant, usually obscene hatred of his ex-wife and assorted female members of her family. After each ditty excoriating another ungrateful bitch who'd charbroiled his soul, Nicol would turn to me eagerly, for an opinion. "Wow," I kept repeating, "she sounds awful."

"Yes!" Nicol thundered each time. "That's exactly right!"

Early in the play, the real estate agent suggests that Andrew hold a seance to contact the ghost of Barrymore. An attempt is made, which, though apparently unsuccessful, later results in the great man's return to earth. "Am I dead?" the ghost inquires. "Or just incredibly drunk?" To prepare for this scene, the cast decided to hold an actual seance in my apartment. We hired a psychic, a frazzled woman with a matching perm, who, I suspected, owned more than one cat and far more than one scented candle.

In my apartment everyone gathered around a massive oak library table. I'd furnished the place in the Barrymore manner, with burnished leather couches, heavily carved and gilded thrones, the sort of antique coats of arms found in any suburban steak house, and a tarnished, tilting brass candelabra. Hosting on a budget, I served reasonably priced wine, microwave popcorn, and Pepperidge Farm Milanos. Our psychic offered each cast member a brief, sketchy reading, identifying the invisible spirit guide that stood just behind each person's chair.

Some of the actors had angelic, Victorian child guides, or Native American shamans with names like Sunshaker or Windclimber, which sounded like recreational vehicles. The psychic made a foolish mistake in contacting Celeste's spirit guide, a gentle Navajo who warned Celeste against wearing fur. Celeste prided herself on upgrading her mink every few years, so she graciously wondered if she could fire her spirit guide. The meter was running, so I encouraged the medium to aim for a direct hit on Barrymore. We all clasped hands and she shut her eyes, clanged her finger cymbals, and began a rhythmic moaning that was either a trance state or a belated Kaddish for my grandmother. She directed us to concentrate our spiritual energy on the door that opened on the stairs to the rooftop. Nicol, who'd cornered the reasonably priced wine, staggered to his feet and, in a sepulchral wail worthy of any character on a *Simpsons* Halloween special, bellowed, "Come!"

Nothing. We all sat up straighter and glared even more aggressively at the door. "COME!" Nicol bellowed again, raising his arms in Dionysian welcome.

Still nothing. We were all quivering with ecstatic, ectoplasmic yearning, and Nicol howled "COOOME!!!" with such ferocity that I feared for his sexual partners.

The door moved a fraction of an inch. It didn't swing open, and Nicol had certainly been producing some Hindenburg-quality hot air, but who knows? I've often wondered if everything that followed was the result of that seance, if just maybe we'd actually unleashed some cackling, uproar-seeking, heedless Barrymore imp. We waited, but nothing else happened, except for the psychic reminding us that her rates doubled after the first hour. Nicol pronounced the evening "a fantastical success!" I switched on the lights, and everyone went home, with Nicol cradling the last unopened jug of reasonably priced wine. Celeste couldn't have been more well-mannered, even as she offered the psychic a slightly frosty, "Thank you, dear."

I continued to rewrite the play, but with each passing week Nicol grew more paranoid. His complaint was essentially that he was being asked to appear onstage with other people. He took to calling me at three a.m., always opening with a solicitous "I didn't wake you, did I?" He'd had a brainstorm: What would I think if Evan left the show and Nicol played the parts of both Andrew and Barrymore simultaneously? I couldn't even begin to formulate a response, since not only was Evan first rate, but the characters had many scenes together, including a ripsnorting duel that climaxed the first act. As I sputtered,

Nicol jumped in: "Oh, I know just what you're thinking. Of course I could play both parts easily, but Andrew is intended to be, what, twenty-six-years-old? And you're wondering, will the audience accept me as twenty-six? It might be a concern, but it's not a film—from the stage there'd be no problem at all!" Nicol was then fifty-two.

Our preview performances began. The set, by Tony Straiges, was a grander approximation of my apartment, resembling the great hall of some fantasy castle, with tapestries, a large oil portrait of Nicol as Barrymore, and, on a wooden stand, an enormous parchment-covered globe that, in the early moments of Act II, opened to reveal a wet bar.

Nicol was sensational. In a luxuriant wig and sculpted black tunic and tights, he was utterly persuasive as a dashing, brutally comic Barrymore. He commanded the stage, and seemed to be having the time of his life. He was possessed by Barrymore, both in the play's more burlesque moments and in his speeches from *Hamlet*, which he delivered with eloquence and simplicity, as a lesson to Andrew and the rest of us. It was too good to last.

After the first few shows, Nicol embarked on a self-destructive binge. He repeatedly propositioned the stage manager, and when she resisted his groping advances, he called the management and demanded that she be fired. This didn't happen, but the atmosphere backstage became poisonous. The cast posed for a raft of promotional photographs, and Nicol tried to block the release of any picture in which he appeared with another actor. Then he began murmuring directions, while onstage, to other cast members: "Is that what you're doing?" "God, that's awful," and worse. During scenes in which the script called for him to hover, as a ghost, and eavesdrop on the action, he would leave the stage. He gradually and deliberately alienated almost everyone, until the production became a war zone. One night, I stopped by his dressing room to make a final attempt to repair our relationship. When I entered, he took a wobbly swing at me, aimed at my head and connecting with my shoulder. I was more surprised than hurt; it was like being assaulted by a sleeping bag. Further revisions to the script became impossible.

During the opening-night performance at the Walter Kerr Theatre, I sat crouched on the carpeted steps at the rear of the balcony. Like any opening-night crowd, the audience was appreciative and vocal. As I watched, I thought, *My play is opening tonight on Broadway.* This was a glorious and yet conventional dream, and that was the problem. Conventional dreams, such as Broadway openings, weddings, and elections, aren't about joy; they're about expectations, pressure, and blind panic.

The cast party was at Tavern on the Green. Everyone's friends and family were in attendance, and Nicol ruled the night. He still wasn't speaking to just about anybody, but there he was, in a white dinner jacket, grabbing the microphone and forcing the band to back him on assorted Tom Jones hits. It was like attending the coronation of a sadistic, self-proclaimed emperor, with toasts encouraged by armed guards. I longed for Nicol to be a caddish yet magnetic rogue and win everyone back. But he couldn't. Owing to drink and bitterness and rage, he needed to be loathed by friends and adored by strangers.

The reviews were mixed. "Mixed reviews" is a phrase like "creative differences," or "of unknown origin"; it's what the government tells the widow. Nicol was accused of genius, slumming, and everything in between. Reports of his bad behavior had been rampant, so his notices were like bulletins from the front, hoping to make sense of a battle still in progress.

Now that we had opened, the fun truly began. During the first act, Barrymore's ghost arrives to coax and browbeat Andrew into playing Hamlet. Andrew is ambivalent and wary. While he hates playing opposite a hand puppet in his lucrative ads for Trailburst Nuggets breakfast cereal, he's terrified of the stage, the tights, and the Bard. His friend Gary backs him up: "I mean, it's not even dinner theater. They sell whole-wheat brownies and little bags of nuts and raisins. It's snack theater. It's Shakespeare for squirrels."

Barrymore scoffs, asking Andrew, "Can you possibly believe that every prospective Hamlet did not tremble and pale and bolt? Hamlet will change you, Andrew, make no mistake. What are you to be—artist, or lunchbox?"

"Get out!" Andrew wails.

"En garde!" cries Barrymore, now brandishing a dangerously gleaming sword.

I wasn't there on the Thursday night, a month or so after the opening, when Nicol went for broke. I had gone to see another show, and at a restaurant afterward a friend rushed over to my table, asking, "Oh my God! Have you heard anything? Is he really hurt? Is he okay?"

"Who? What are you talking about?" I asked.

"Tonight! At your play! Nicol Williamson stabbed Evan Handler!"

During the swordplay scene, Nicol, it seemed, had actually

struck his costar. Evan, quite wisely, had left the stage, the performance, and, ultimately, the production. His understudy had finished the show that night.

Later that evening, another friend came running up to me. "Oh my God," he said, "it's so tragic!"

"Nicol?" I asked. "And my play?"

"No! Jerzy Kosinski! He's dead!" Kosinski, the acclaimed, controversial, Polish-born author of such works as *The Painted Bird*, had committed suicide in his bathtub. The next day, Kosinski's grisly end shared billing with the *I Hate Hamlet* tumult on the front page of the *Times*. In the *Post*'s weekend edition, a photograph of the duel filled the entire front page, under the headline "I HIT HAMLET! ACTOR STORMS OFF STAGE AFTER CO-STAR WHACKS HIM IN BUTT." There was coverage all over the world, and TV news crews stood outside the theater, every night. I learned to say "No comment" in many languages.

Evan Handler wanted to bring Nicol and the production up on charges. A meeting was called, and the producers and I tried to determine a course of action. Should Nicol be fired? We realized that he'd been brilliantly, maliciously sly; because of all the publicity, he now *was* the show, and no other star in his right mind would step into the role. The situation was impossible. At an earlier meeting, two of our producers, the gentlest and most well-intentioned men, became so frustrated that a fistfight broke out. The brawl ended within seconds, with instant apologies all around. Even when he wasn't in the room, Nicol was winning.

Evan's understudy took over, and the show wobbled along for a few more weeks. Nicol was in clover. He began leading the audiences in singalongs of "Happy Days Are Here Again," and, at the curtain calls, he liked to instruct the crowd to "Head home and enjoy a nice juicy slice of sexual intercourse!" The Tony Award nominations were announced around this time, and while Adam Arkin received a nod, Nicol did not. He was livid, and took to haranguing the nominating committee from the stage.

I attended the closing-night performance, and afterward I went backstage. On a small table outside Nicol's dressing room was a bottle containing his blood-pressure medication. I considered replacing the pills with—what? Arsenic? Rat poison? What could possibly kill him?

I had never spent time around a world-class, drain-the-keg madman before. Nicol belonged to a boisterous, selfish, elite cadre of mostly British actors, the Angry Young Men of the 1950s and sixties. They were the working-class blokes who'd banished the decorum of Gielgud and Olivier; they were brawlers who went for birds and lager and, at least onstage, a grittier realism. This reckless brotherhood included Richard Burton, Richard Harris, and Peter O'Toole, all of whom binged their way to the top. But Nicol had been denied the leading-man screen stardom, and the eventual knighthood, that his peers had won, and this can't have pleased him.

Nicol believed, I think, that if he could just get to the theater, if he could only step onstage, he'd be fine. Some nights, he'd saunter in at five, even ten minutes after eight, knowing that we'd hold the curtain. But there was one performance when he'd overslept, or passed out in his apartment, and his understudy had gone on. Although we hadn't spoken in weeks, the next day Nicol called me, assuring me that everything was fine, and that he'd be on that evening. Then he abruptly hung up. For the first time, he'd sounded shaken.

After the final performance, I had no intention of talking to Nicol. I was still too angry. As I was heading upstairs, to bid farewell to the more lucid actors, the door to Nicol's dressing room swung open. He stood there, a soused, lunatic, fifty-two-year-old Hamlet. We stared at each other as if we were miles apart and might wave. Nicol finally spoke, and his tone was both kind and accusing. He said, "You knew this was going to happen." And then he smiled and shut the door.

I Shudder:

An Excerpt from the Most Deeply Intimate and Personal Diary of One Elyot Vionnet

Good and Evil

1.

I have known a goodness so radiantly pure that it has literally transported me, and I have witnessed the most malignant evil, a dark force of such soul-churning horror that it can only be called Susan Marie Henkelman.

How have I experienced these two most opposite poles of the known moral universe? Like all towering, indisputable truths, the answer is simple: I take cabs.

As a substitute teacher, I subsist on the most laughable and precariously meager income. I have lived in the same rent-controlled studio apartment for my entire adult life, and I haven't purchased an item of clothing in almost as long, although happily, my wardrobe is of such an enduring quality that only minor repairs have been necessary. And because, as a reader of low and explicit interests, you're wondering about my underwear, I will explain: my intimate apparel is manufactured from a Swiss cotton of such whisper-soft resilience that it is normally used only to wrap the painfully sensitive faces of the world's wealthiest women as they recuperate from their acid peels in private clinics. Unlike these women's jowls and brow-lines, however, my undergarments require mending only once per decade, when I mail them to a Long Island convent, where the nuns compete to gently darn and patch my private attire, because, as Sister Herbert Elizabeth once wrote to me, in her own blood, "Mr. Vionnet, your boxer shorts and undershirts do not merely speak to me. They sing."

And so I continue in borderline poverty, save for my one indulgence, no, my single absolute necessity: I take cabs. Yes, on occasion, when I wish to see what people with unpleasant skin conditions are wearing, I do take the subway. I have never, I am proud to say, taken the bus, because people who take the bus have given up. They have said, I am nothing, I will never know a second's joy or even the most minuscule accomplishment, I am a rotting fleshbag rolling toward my squalid garden apartment in one of those fictional neighborhoods, such as Inwood or Yorkville. I am not living, I am simply waiting to be recycled;

instead of a soul, I own a Naugahyde briefcase or a clear plastic rain bonnet, I am God's mucus, and therefore—I take the bus.

But a taxi! I leave my home, and for a moment I am lost, disoriented, unsure of my destination, my purpose, my next breath, and then—a cab appears! And behind the wheel—an angel! God has provided these holy messengers, and crowned them with turbans and tweed caps and the most superbly pet-rified hairpieces, toupees which resemble nothing so much as some ancient seagull trapped forever in an Alaskan oil spill, and dusted with volcanic ash. God has anointed these charioteers, He has commanded His minions to travel the earth, assisting His human creations, He has said, ferry Mr. Vionnet, cushion him, swaddle him in pine-scented, Plexiglas-partitioned, limited-leg-room love!

I'll come clean, in case anyone is unsure of the true reason I hoard my pennies and often dine for weeks at a time on only saltines and Hershey's Kisses, to underwrite my taxi habit. I take cabs because, when I board the subway, I'm off to work; but when I hail a cab, I can picture any destination, from the Bowery to the Seychelles to a Romanian bakery to Vatican City for the election of a new pope—I always like to yell "NOPE!" at the losers. Cabs promise glamour and fantasy, along with a certain solitude, which are all I ask of any religious experi-ence. Mass transit is a constant reminder of a crowded, halting, sloppy existence, reeking of a fellow passenger's take-out taco or teen-stud body spray. A cab, to a truly unfettered imagina-tion, is a time machine or a spaceship or a chauffeured buttery yellow Bentley. A cab can go anywhere.

Certainly, there have been squabbles, the occasional cab-related misstep. For a time, as the meter clicked on, the recorded voice of a local celebrity urged the rider to use his or her seat belt. This irritating reminder not only caused every passenger to defiantly ignore all forms of safety, but eventually an angry mob tracked down these celebrities, forced them to kneel in a public square and apologize, and then all of these celebrities were hanged, using seat-belt webbing, from sturdy lampposts in Times Square, as the mob chanted, "Buckle up! It's the law!"

The latest taxi deformity is the touch screen, a computerized video panel which allows riders to laboriously pay the fare using a credit card. People who use credit cards in cabs, or to purchase small plastic packages of breath mints in drug stores, such people are lower than Judas. They are, in fact, Satan's army, and I can prove it. When standing behind someone using their credit card to pay for an item under ten dollars, use this test while you're waiting: take a match or a cigarette lighter, and set the person using the credit card on fire. I guarantee that such demonic cretins will relish the flames, they will bask in them, as they idly pluck a tabloid from a nearby wire rack and scan the cover story, titled "Best Celebrity Beach Bodies—and the Worst!"

Lower than even those who use credit cards in cabs are undoubtedly the newscasters who appear in the video clips on the backseat screens, underscored with pounding Action News theme music. If a rider acts instantly, he or she can halt these mini-newscasts and weather updates, by touching an always difficult to locate, microscopic video dot, but this is not always possible. Sometimes the off button is broken, and the babbling newsperson joins you, unbidden, unwanted, and unstoppable, for the duration of your journey.

This happened to me just last week. I entered a cab, and lunged to jab at the microdot before a chubby, bright-smiled weatherperson could begin his forecast for the Texas panhandle. It was no use, as the more I jabbed, the louder and more repellent the forecast became. I asked my driver, "But can't something be done? Can't we get rid of these touch screens, and this blathering weather shill?" The driver, my companion in misery, gestured helplessly, and together we hatched a remedy.

The driver brought me to the midtown TV studio where the weatherman's morning news show was under way. A customary, adoring crowd was gathered in the street outside the studio, watching the broadcast through a bulletproof plate-glass window. I left the cab, carrying a hefty chunk of ragged cinderblock which I'd acquired from a nearby construction site. As I heard the weatherman begin to ask one of the show's pathologically upbeat cohosts about her plans for the weekend, I shouldered my cinderblock and heaved it high over the mob and through the massive barrier window, which was blessedly not Vionnet-proof. As I headed back toward my cab, I heard the glass shatter and the weatherman scream and fall to the studio floor, his neck completely severed, with his now decapitated head rolling across the studio floor, directly onto the left foot of a cohost, who shrieked because her shoes were both open-toed and brand-new. The fans cheered and rushed even closer to the TV cameras, raising their homemade placards, which read "Hi From Ohio!" and "I'm 41 Today and I'm Standing Outside Watching a TV Show!!!"

Back in my taxi, the touch screen had gone black, and the grateful driver promised me that, upon my death, I would be greeted in the next world not by a measly thousand dark-eyed virgins but by a billion applauding cabdrivers.

My communion with this driver is only one example of the divinity, and the ethereal goodness of the Manhattan taxi. Which brings us to its opposite, to the unspeakable, and to the woman who can only be called Satan's less-attractive sister.

Susan Marie Henkelman had moved into my building earlier this year, and I first encountered her a few days later, on the sidewalk outside our building's front entrance. It was Sunday, and I was en route to St. Patrick's Cathedral, where I like to linger in a rear pew, on the aisle, and suggest possible prayers to other parishioners on their way to take Communion. I offer thoughts like, "Ask the Lord about that ketchup stain," "Beg Jesus to forgive you for imagining that you are one of the three people on the planet who can wear a beret" and "Tell God that you're sorry about having sex with your cousin, on his wedding day, and, by the way, everyone knows."

I was eager to arrive at the cathedral, so I raised my hand to heaven, in the familiar cab-hailing Manhattan salute. After fifteen seconds, I heard a voice which was both petulant and abrasive, insisting, "Excuse me! Excuse me! I get the first cab!"

Have you ever noticed that when the words "Excuse me!" are shouted, they no longer serve as a form of polite behavior but as a threat?

I turned to see what I can only call a raging asparagus. Susan Marie Henkelman was tall and rangy, with angry, sticklike, thrashing arms, a face squeezed into an accordion of feverish self-importance, topped by a hairdo of rigidly stalklike shafts frosted with quivering curls; her hair was like a mushroom cloud, or the cacophony of drunken bluebirds and wobbly exclamation points which hovers over the cranium of a comic-strip drunk. Susan looked to be somewhere in her thirties, which is not a good neighborhood for a single mom in Manhattan, and her sleeves and slacks seemed too short and too tight, as if her limbs were expanding with ire, and sprouting with vengeance. Her shoes were square and cheap and sensible, like something a pilgrim would buy on sale, and she was carrying a baby across her body in a Norwegian-designed, Chinese-manufactured, and American-discounted sling.

"I get the first cab!" Susan repeated, her body coming to a halt mere inches from my own, as if her leash had been fortuitously yanked.

"I beg your pardon," I said, not wishing for a squabble, "but I was here first."

"I have a sick baby!" said Susan, thrusting out her chest, causing her infant to lurch toward me.

"Prove it," I said.

"What is wrong with you, my baby is very sick!" said Susan, as the baby began to squall obligingly.

"Stop twisting that baby's ankle," I suggested.

"I'm not twisting it. I'm massaging it."

"Then why is the baby crying and trying to pull its leg away?"

"She has . . . an ankle rash!"

"Is that even really your baby? Or do you just keep it stashed with the extra umbrellas behind the front desk, and use it to hail cabs?"

"How dare you! I am a mother with a sick child!"

"I'll give you five dollars, for the baby and the first cab."

"What?" said Susan, with unparalleled outrage, and a smidgen of interest; I could sense her calculating an instantaneous list of pros and cons, with the "pros" list beginning, "I could probably talk him up to ten, and I'm still young, I can have another baby." "No!" she decided. "You are disgusting! And I am taking my baby . . . to the baby hospital!"

It was then that a cab pulled up, only a few feet from our fracas.

"That's my cab! My cab!" shouted Susan, trying to shove past me. As the cab honked, to encourage a decision, Susan grabbed her baby and held the child out in front of her, like a talisman, or a bargaining chip.

"Tell my baby," said Susan, "tell him to his face that you won't let us go to the baby hospital."

"I thought your baby was a girl."

"She is, but I'm not going to label her. Tell her!"

I placed my hands over Susan's, so that we were now both holding the baby, and I spoke to the infant with a firm tenderness.

"Baby," I said, "I realize that you're only an innocent pawn, but your mother is not only a bully and a hysteric, she is a criminal."

The baby gave a tiny snort, as if replying, "Tell me something I don't know."

"Cabs are sacred sedans," I continued. "A cab must be earned and deserved. A cab should never become a battleground for petty feuds. And your mother has betrayed the bounty of God, because your mother . . ."

I raised my chin an eighth of an inch, and the baby raised hers.

"Your mother—is a *cab jumper*."

As the baby's eyes widened, and her innocence fell away, I heard a whoosh, as if someone had used a razor to slice cleanly through a sheet of paper, or had broken the sound barrier. I stepped back. Susan had somehow moved past me, and was now seated in the backseat of the cab, as if she'd mastered the art of time travel, or had become a vapor. The baby looked at me helplessly, imprisoned on her mother's chest.

"The Lovely Lady Nail Salon and Day Spa, at Forty-fifth and Madison," Susan hissed to the driver as the cab sped away.

2.

Our next confrontation occurred two days later. I stepped from my building, headed for the Forty-second Street Library, where I like to leave detailed, bogus, and therefore delectably frustrating treasure maps in the pages of dusty atlases. As I raised my arm, I heard, "Excuse me! Excuse me!"

I turned, as Susan came hurtling down the street toward me, pushing a double stroller the size of a tank, only far more destructive and less visually distinguished. The stroller held two infants, and was piled with a canvas tote, a clutch of plastic grocery bags, a quilted vinyl duffel, and a net sack bulging with grimy, neon-colored toys, a Tupperware container filled with crackers shaped like tiny, eyeless fish, a jar of what was either organic baby food or raw sewage, and at least five of those miniature bottles of vodka found in hotel room refrigerators.

"That's my cab! Don't take my cab!" Susan bellowed, heading right toward me, her open beige trench coat exposing her beige safari-style pantsuit and her beige imitation-python fanny pack. Susan was dressed for an expedition, as if seeking a Mommy & Me gymnastics class somewhere on the Serengeti.

"I get the first cab!" Susan declared. "We've already established the pecking order! Don't give me any trouble!"

"I beg your pardon," I said evenly, "but I was here first. And this time you're not getting past me."

"He's trying to steal my babies!" Susan now announced, rotating so that everyone passing by, on either side of the street, could hear her plaintive wail. "This man is trying to kidnap my babies! Help, please, somebody, help!"

A suspicious crowd began to form around us.

"What's the problem?" asked an older man, the operator of a nearby newsstand.

"Do you need help?" a woman asked Susan, a woman who looked and sounded almost exactly like Susan. "I have a great pediatrician, and a killer divorce lawyer."

"Is this joker bothering you?" asked a younger man, whose hugely muscled forearms and glassy eyes indicated that he'd just been tossed out of the police academy, before lunch, on his first day.

"I'm not bothering her," I explained patiently. "I was simply standing here, attempting to hail a cab, when this woman came running toward me, claiming for some absurd reason that she deserved the cab more than me. This woman . . ."

I stood tall, and used my hailing arm as if it were a dowsing rod, pointing not to subterranean water but to unmitigated gall.

"This woman," I said, my rigid index finger now an inch from Susan's vibrating button nose, "this woman is a *cab jumper!*"

There was a collective gasp, and Susan's face twitched, as she rethought her game plan. Her shoulders slumped, her chin drooped, and her gait became pigeon-toed. "I'm sorry," she said, in a whispery, bedraggled voice, to the crowd. "I should never have asked for the cab. I'm just . . . another, totally average, out-of-my-mind working mom. No, it's fine. No special favors. It's just, oh, I shouldn't be bothering you, any of you, with my ridiculous problems, especially not such an older and well-dressed fellow, like this fine gentleman."

She gestured to me, and continued: "But, you see, my husband dumped me, an hour ago. And he said, 'Susan, I'm leaving you, and I'm leaving you with nothing, except for two kids, a mortgage, and a mountain of bills.' And then he shoved a full-color picture in my face, of his new twenty-two-year-old girlfriend in a string bikini, and she was holding a picture of me, and she'd drawn a Ghostbusters symbol over my face, and she was laughing. But when I heard our front door slam, I fell to my knees, and I raised my fist and I swore to Our Lord that I would keep going, that I would work double shifts, that I would do whatever I have to, just to take care of my babies, just so that Eliza and Trad can have at least one hot meal per week and a roof over their heads. And even if I have to sell my body, or pieces of it, well, that's what I'm going to do. And just now I was bringing my babies to our local shelter for homeless families, because that's the only place where we can all stay together. But no, please, really, I'm fine."

She turned to me and said, "Please, I insist. You take the first cab."

As one, the crowd shifted its penetrating, accusatory glare to me as a cab pulled up to the curb, and I fought the most insistent urge I'd ever known, to blurt out, "*Trad?* You named your baby *Trad?*"

"Buddy, do you really need this cab?" the police academy reject asked me, raising a fist.

"I only wish that after this cab takes you and your babies to the shelter," said the woman who looked like Susan, "that it could run over your filthy ex-husband's head. I wish it could run over the heads of every filthy ex-husband in this city!"

By now someone else had helpfully opened the cab's rear door, and the newsstand operator had folded up the double stroller and was carefully placing it in the cab's trunk.

"No, really," Susan told me, "you take the cab. You were here first."

"No," I said, still suppressing every just and honest impulse. "You take it, by all means."

"Well . . ." said Susan, daring to add a slight, pretubercular cough.

"You have to," said Susan's near-twin, helping Susan into the cab, and shoving the $263 which she'd collected from the crowd into Susan's fanny pack.

"Do it for your kids," said the police academy psycho, passing the first baby, little Eliza, into Susan's arms.

"Here you go," said the newsstand operator, but as he was about to hand Susan her second child, Susan had already slammed the cab's door and screeched, "Saks Fifth Avenue! The Forty-ninth Street entrance, near the fur department!"

"But your baby!" the newsstand operator called out.

"Little Trad!" said the muscle-bound lug.

"I have a suggestion for little Trad," I said, as the pilly, powder blue rayon blanket in which Trad was swaddled fell away, revealing a large zucchini, on which Susan had used nail polish to paint a crude pair of wide eyes, one leaking a painted teardrop.

"Instead of bringing Trad to the homeless shelter," I advised, as Susan's raucous cackle could still be heard, even though her cab was already many blocks away, "let's think about a salad."

3.

That night I sat in my apartment, in my skeleton-shaped chair. I had found this chair lying in bony, cherrywood pieces, in a dusty shop at the end of an alley in Venice, many years ago. Like any piece of important furniture, it frightened me. Purchasing this chair meant living with a constant reminder of the meaninglessness of life, and the inevitability of death. Every morning when I awake, this chair beckons, asking, "Is today the day? How many days do you have left? Let's think about it. I dare you. Take a seat."

When I wish to center my thoughts, and to consider the most profound matters, before I sit in my skeleton chair, I first put on a fresh white cotton undershirt, starched white boxer shorts, and purple cashmere socks. Over this I add a 3,000-year-old kimono from the Han Dynasty, a garment richly embroidered with the massacre of a picnicking peasant family by a flock of rabid herons. This kimono was commissioned by the emperor Kulatsu, who had thirty wives, all of whom complained about money, over a thousand concubines, all of whom felt neglected, and easily 1,200 children, none of whom ever amounted to anything.

The emperor decreed that every day, while he was out ruling the empire from his royal offices, his bedchamber would be repainted a different color. In this manner, he hoped that each morning would represent a rebirth, and thus he would become immortal. He lived until the age of 103, when he awoke one morning to find that his bedchamber had been painted a vivid hot pink with lime green moldings, which was so Palm-Beach-cabana-kerchief that he died of embarrassment.

Arranging the emperor's kimono around myself in graceful yet imposing folds, I contemplated Susan Marie Henkelman, and I tried to define good and evil. Good, I decided, is when another person agrees with me in every respect and gratefully bows to my will. Of course, this gives rise to questions like, "Well, what if Hitler agreed with you in every respect, would that make him good?" I have learned to ignore theoretical, dorm-room debate analogies involving Hitler, because they always leads to propositions like, "What if all of the major critics thought that your first novel was sketchy and derivative, but Hitler thought that it was winningly quirky and a breath of fresh air?" or "What if it was the day before the prom, and because you didn't have a date you'd told everyone that you despised the whole idea of proms, because they were pure social fascism, but what would you do then if Hitler called and said that Eva Braun had a stomach thing and would you be his date? Would you go with him? Would you go with him but still tell everyone that you were just friends and that you were only going to goof on the whole idea of a prom?"

Goodness is also the passionate belief in anything pure and worthwhile—like taxis, or nonviolent protest, or a more violent protest when the thing that you're protesting gets in the revolving door with you, as if that were a cute thing to do. Being good means assessing any given situation and determining how you can offer the most benefit while causing the least harm. For example: if a friend asks your opinion of her new haircut, you could say, "It's just awful and unflattering, and it exposes your completely deluded vision of yourself as a hot teenaged blonde." This would be cruel, and would only serve your own probably equally deluded sense of superiority. A good person would say, "I love your new haircut, and I especially love that it makes you so happy, and someday it will grow out, and then you can get another, maybe slightly different haircut, just for fun, and you can feel even happier."

Another example: you're walking down the street and you pass an irate man belittling his long-suffering wife by telling her that she's slow and stupid. You could punch this lout and tell him he's small-minded and most likely small-penised, and then you could ask the wife if she'd like you to call someone. If you accomplish all this, the husband will most likely stab you, and as you lie bleeding to death on the pavement, his wife will kick you in the ribs and snort, "Mind your own business, asswipe! I love Dwayne!" The correct response, a product of goodness, would be to watch the couple and then tell the wife, casually, that, "You know, when Dwayne and I were together, he used to treat me exactly the same way. Isn't that funny?" As you depart, the couple will now be on a far more equal footing, and will most likely begin an entirely new, and more provocative conversation.

Goodness requires performing acts of both local and global

charity. Let's say that I'm in an elevator, and a couple with their rambunctious, undisciplined children join me, and the children begin screeching and demanding to be taken to certain pricey restaurants and fed certain extravagant pastas. I could tell the parents that, "You should be sterilized, without anesthesia" and I could inform the children that, "Even gourmet pasta will not save you from your parents' genetic cesspool." But instead I could behave more charitably, by imagining how difficult and exhausting it must be to raise children; by enjoying the harmless horseplay of toddlers; and by using my mental abilities to teleport the entire ear-splitting clan to an isolated airport during a blizzard, where all of the flights have been canceled and all of the vending machines emptied.

On a global level, I will contribute whatever I can to organizations that battle international hunger and disease, and I will proudly use the adhesive-backed mailing labels, printed with my name and address and a photo of a puppy wearing a Santa hat, which these organizations will send me in return. When I watch TV news footage of any horror, bloodshed, or starvation, I will weep, I will praise and support those aid workers who travel selflessly to stricken lands, I will curse the negligent or barbaric governments involved, and I will even more fully appreciate my own cozy studio apartment. I will in fact wish that every human being on earth could possess not only decent nutrition and effective sanitation, but a perfectly proportioned studio apartment, although I suspect that somewhere there's a famished, legless Third World child who would take one look at my place and sneer, "But why doesn't the bathroom have double sinks?"

Which brings us to evil. Evil is often far more appealing, and even more delicious, than good. Yet evil is essentially lazy. Evil is amassing mountainous wealth, and then purchasing many homes where the televisions are mounted over the mantels and disguised by priceless oil paintings. A Matisse should never mechanically vanish to reveal a sitcom where the characters rely on the rejoinders "Hell-*o*!" "I don't think so!" and "Maybe on your planet!"

Evil is imagining that an apology erases a sin, as in "I'm so sorry that my dog leapt on you with his feces-covered paws—what can I say, he's a jumper!" or "I know that my country has caused at least two world wars, but we're terribly sorry and we enjoy American films and miniseries related to the Holocaust" or "I'm sorry that I abandoned you as a child, but I was only a child myself, and if I had it to do all over again, I'd remember that you needed *two* ice skates."

Evil bespeaks a contempt for the highest, greatest good, which is common courtesy. If everyone on earth demonstrated the most basic good manners, evil would cease to exist. Warlords and tyrants and dictators are just people who've never learned, or who refuse, to write thank-you notes by hand, and to never take what doesn't belong to them, such as, for example, Poland. Evil is monopolizing both armrests on an airplane, or at a movie theater; evil is not using a handkerchief when sneezing in a small, enclosed space; and evil is a lack of compassion for other people, with the exception of those other people who stop dead in the middle of a busy sidewalk, blocking traffic in both directions, in order to hug and babble with a friend whom they haven't seen for almost fifteen minutes.

Some feel that a sociopath is a person born without a moral compass, or any empathy whatsoever. There is a test that psychiatrists offer to imprisoned serial killers, in which these criminals are asked if they delight in harming small animals, if they have no problem with physical violence, and if they believe that their hapless victims get what they deserve. I feel that, in order to save valuable taxpayer dollars, this test could be condensed into a single question, so that the psychiatrists could ask only: "Are you Susan Marie Henkelman?"

By defining good and evil, I saw that I had a choice. While I have always been thoughtful and caring, particularly toward those without an ounce of flair, I don't think I've done enough. So that evening, in my kimono, I decided to not merely trot toward goodness at a fine, healthy pace, but to hurtle upwards, onto God's shoulder. I set my life's goal: I would become a saint. Was this near-psychotic egomania? Or a divine calling? Is there a difference? Perhaps a saint is just someone who can say, with confidence, I know better and I can help you. So please stop chewing on your hair and then asking your stylist why you have split ends. Please stop asking everyone on line behind you at the supermarket if we'd mind waiting just a sec while you run to fetch those forgotten Portuguese flatbread crisps, because the answer is this: No, of course we don't mind, if you don't mind all of us spitting in your sixteen yogurts. Please don't run for president, just because you can't hold a real job.

I stood, sweeping my kimono around me. I raised my eyes, seeking God's approval, which I have always found in my choice of chandelier. I went to my single window, which looks out onto the corners of several undistinguished buildings, down at a battered and ordinary sidewalk, and, if I crane my neck, at a sliver of Gramercy Park. Gramercy Park resembles, in many ways, the Kingdom of Heaven. It is cramped, tiny, and locked, and a personal key is required for entrance. The park is administered by a ragtag committee, led, I believe, by a psychologically unstable, paranoid, social-climbing woman of uncertain background. And yet on a sunlit day, the park is incomparably lovely, and someday I hope to be admitted, and to sit on a bench in the balmy April air, beside a drooling invalid's disgruntled Honduran nurse.

To achieve such entry, to know God, and to embark upon sainthood, I decided to treat Susan Marie Henkelman, and all of the Susan Marie Henkelmans, not as my enemies, but as my targets. Targets for my piercing arrows of kindness, transformation, and love. I would embrace, teach, and bombard these wayward figures with a gale-force benevolence, with a village-flattening typhoon of caring, until they were plastered against the jagged, mighty cliff of my goodness, screaming, "Thank you, Mr. Vionnet! You are so right, about everything!"

The next day, I was called to substitute-teach at a private preschool in SoHo. I gathered the children around me, seated on their miniature chairs, which, since this was SoHo, were midget replicas of bentwood Austrian classics. I divided the group into the children who were well-behaved because they were on scholarships, and the children who were well-behaved because they were on Ritalin. "All right, children," I said, "who would like to hear a wonderful story?"

I was deeply touched as a roomful of hands shot into the air, my own included. Look at all of these shining, untroubled faces,

I thought, even six-year-old Easton Schwab, who was allowed to wear her flannel bunny pajamas to school because she was being tested for allergies to all other fibers.

"Once upon a time," I began, "there was a little girl named Talisa, who lived with her original parents, her nanny, the housekeeper, and the cook, in a thoughtfully but not reverentially restored townhouse on East Tenth Street, with five working fireplaces and a lap pool."

"Oooo," said all of the children, except for young Gareth, who raised his hand and commented, "My father is an architect, and he says that lap pools always leak and mean nothing in terms of resale."

"And that's why your father only designs warehouses with aluminum siding in Pennsylvania," I explained sweetly. "But Talisa was so happy, going to school and playing with her friends and taking French and ballet and cello lessons, so that she would become well-rounded and someday get into an Ivy League school, or at least a rich kids' party school."

All the children nodded approvingly.

"But then one morning, Talisa's mother was feeling stressed out and refused to give the cook a half-day off so she could go to the dogtrack. And so the cook put an evil spell on Talisa's entire family, and she said, 'From this day forward, all of you will lead fabulous, successful lives, but you will always wonder if something is missing. There will always be an asterisk.' And with that, the cook vanished into thin air!"

"Our nanny vanished once," said Gareth's twin brother, Plein. "But then the police caught her in L.A. with my daddy's camcorder and all of my mommy's credit cards. So my mommy had to cancel them."

"All of them?" asked Easton, more than a little frightened.

"*All of them*," said Plein, and Easton curled into a ball on the floor.

"And from that very day," I continued, "all sorts of nice things happened to Talisa's family, but there were always nagging questions. Her daddy made partner and handled billion-dollar contracts for a media conglomerate, but he started to wonder, what if he'd followed his boyhood dreams and opened a string of boutique hotels in Central Asia? Talisa's mommy wrote a screenplay that was optioned by a major studio and then made into a commercial blockbuster, but an insistent voice in Talisa's mommy's head kept asking, but what if you'd found the funding and made the movie independently, using more offbeat actors and a soundtrack featuring morose ballads by a dead English folk-rock legend, then wouldn't you feel less like a whore?"

Some of the children, despite their many medications, were now starting to feel anxious, and were hugging themselves and rocking back and forth.

"And then Talisa trained very hard and made the Olympic team in cross-country skiing."

"Yay!" said little Copely Westin-Blatt, whose two mommies had each taken her aside and asked to be secretly called Mommy #1.

"As an alternate," I said. "So Talisa never got on the Olympic slopes."

Copely took a deep breath and began mechanically stroking the two matching stuffed pandas that her mommies had given her, although one of the mommies claimed that her panda was part of a signed and numbered limited edition.

"And then, Talisa volunteered for a program which cleaned up vacant lots and created more green space for inner-city kids-at-risk, and she also went to theater camp, where she played Juliet and a supporting role in the head counselor's musical about his father's drinking problem, and then Talisa's parents hired a tutor to prepare Talisa for her SATs, and she did very well and she got into Harvard!"

The children all looked at me, holding their breath.

"Waiting list," I told them, and I watched all of their little faces crumple. "But another girl who'd been accepted got kicked out, because the admissions committee discovered that she'd lied on her transcript about having her pilot's license, so Talisa got in! But to this day, even after she graduated summa cum laude, and went on to Harvard Law School and became a senator with credible presidential aspirations, Talisa still wonders—why was I waiting-listed? Does any of my life, or do any of my achievements, really count? What if that other girl hadn't lied, or if my mother hadn't made that anonymous phone call to the secretary of the Admissions Committee? Is my whole life really just a first-runner-up lie? Have I been permanently waiting-listed for any real happiness?"

With savage abandon, all of the children began to moan and tear at their flesh, using safety scissors and the most expensive colored pencils, which included such hues as Powdered Olive and Uncertain Ochre. As they all began hurling themselves against the classroom walls, Susan Marie Henkelman walked into the room and clapped her hands briskly. The children froze, and then instantly sat in a circle, with their heads lowered.

"What is going on in here?" Susan demanded.

"We were having story time," I explained.

"I see," said Susan, fixing her gaze on me. "I know you. You live in my building. You tried to assault me."

"I am Mr. Vionnet. And you have stolen my taxis, and undoubtedly those of many others. But rather than seek an emotionally immature revenge, I have pictured you drowning in a sludge-filled swamp of your own evil. Yet as your head is about to be submerged for a final time in the thick, rotting morass of your venal behavior, I reach out a hand of salvation and forgiveness. You grasp my hand, and while it's still too late, and you choke to death on the muck of your own bottomless sin, you perish, thanks to me, in a state of grace. Isn't that good news, children?"

The terrified children refused to raise their heads.

"But what are you doing here?" I asked Susan.

"I work for the Internal Review Board of the State Commission on Faculty Performance," she said, with a glimmering satisfaction. "I'm sent to schools throughout the city to evaluate all substitute teachers. I file reports and make recommendations. I have the authority to hire and fire any nontenured personnel."

4.

Later that day, I stood in a particularly airless subway car, squeezed in between five high-decibel teenage girls having a vicious slap fight over who stole someone's nose ring and boyfriend named T-Poke; a family of tourists sharing what looked and smelled like a barbecued skunk; and a woman wearing a hairnet over her face who wouldn't stop howling that she was having the mayor's baby. As all of these people's sweating bodies became molded to mine, I pondered why my fate lay in the grasping talons of Susan Marie Henkelman. Then, just before my stop, the train ground to a halt, and remained stalled between stations, with the passengers stranded in darkness for the next two hours. After we finally got moving and I left that malarial petri dish on wheels, I trudged toward my building, where I saw Susan stepping blithely out of a cab. "Oh, hello," she said. "You look terrible."

"I took the subway."

"Really. I've just had dinner at this great new French bistro, and then I did some shopping, for just a few fun things. Isn't it lovely out, and there are cabs everywhere."

I focused all of my abilities on trying to make her head explode, into a billion glistening particles of painfully bleeding goodness, but it was no use.

"Sweet dreams!" she trilled, shoving her way past me and into our building. As I reached the elevator, the doors were just closing, with Susan inside, performing a thoroughly unconvincing mime of trying to locate the button which would keep the doors open for a few seconds longer.

"Oopsie!" said Susan, as the doors hissed shut. "Sorry 'bout that, Ellen!"

Life and Death and New Jersey

1.

Whenever I stumble over my own feet, or blurt out a thought that makes no sense at all, or leave the house wearing one pattern too many, I always think, It's okay, I'm from New Jersey. I love New Jersey, because it's not just an all-purpose punch line, but probably a handy legal defense, as in, "Yes, I shot my wife because I thought she was Bigfoot, but I'm from New Jersey."

New Jersey never disappoints. The paper placemats at Jersey diners are often printed with factoids about the Garden State, but they rarely mention that, as of this writing, the last three New Jersey governors have all broken their legs while in office. Among those on this disabled list was ex-governor McGreevey, who stepped down after coming out as a proud Gay American, having appointed his Israeli mancrush as the State Director of Homeland Security. McGreevey and his understandably peeved ex-wife then published dueling memoirs, and Jim later crowed that Dina's book hadn't sold well due to "her awful appearance" on *Oprah*, "in an inappropriate and ill-fitting ball gown with a plunging neckline." Jim is now studying to become an Episcopal priest.

I was raised in the suburb of Piscataway, where the Chamber of Commerce sponsored a promotional billboard picturing two cartoon Native Americans, in feathers and striped war paint. One of these braves was shading his eyes with his hand and scanning the horizon, above the caption, "They went Piscataway!" Piscataway is also the home to many industrial parks, where gracefully landscaped acreage surrounds the buildings that market bath towels, silicone breast implants, and napalm. There's a nearby complex that manufactures the contraceptive Orthocreme, and the site is so large that it contains a road named Ortho Drive. There also used to be a majestic grove of evergreens along the highway, enhancing a sign that advertised feminine hygiene products, with mammoth, lustrously lit scripted letters reading, "Modess . . . because." As a child, this sign enticed and confused me. Because why?

My high school was a standard cluster of low brick buildings that housed students from varied social and economic backgrounds. The school once hired a mediator to run a student discussion group, to figure out ways to improve the school's performance. I was part of this group, and as we all brainstormed about class size and additional after-school activities, one student politely raised his hand and asked to be excused for a bathroom break. He returned to the room a while later, after having used a screwdriver to yank a few tape decks out of parked cars, and he was carrying the tape decks with him, with their slashed wires dangling.

The school's female population could be rambunctious. I knew two girls, Sherry and Barasella, who were best friends, until Barasella refused to return a certain red-and-purple-striped tube top that she'd borrowed. As revenge, a righteous Sherry snuck into the principal's office and grabbed the microphone for the school's public address system, and then everyone in the classrooms and hallways listened as Sherry chanted, accurately, "Barasella had an abortion yesterday! Barasella had an abortion yesterday!"

LaDonna Racyk was always stomping around, on sturdy, shapely legs, with her mane of untamed, ragged hair flying out behind her. She was sexy, as a sort of white, teenaged Tina Turner, and while she could be violent, she wasn't unreachable. During homeroom she once threatened my friend Jean Anne with a knife, but Jean Anne just sighed and said, "Oh, LaDonna, put that knife away," and LaDonna did. One morning LaDonna appeared, uncharacteristically, in a short, filmy, flowered dress. When I asked her why she'd chosen this outfit, she said, "Because this afternoon I have to fucking get married."

Some of the teachers had a grim, defeated air, but others were quirky and helpful. Nina Denning was an art teacher, and indisputably cool, as she had short black hair, a bemused squint, and she drove a convertible. She'd encourage her students' creativity, and she tried not to laugh at the results. My best friend James, with a sculpture deadline upon him, inflated a long, narrow red balloon, and tied it to a coat hanger, accompanied on either side by two smaller, round red balloons, as a penis mobile. Ms. Denning took a look and said, "Baby, I like where you're going, but you're not there yet."

Later that year Ms. Denning was assigned Ken Schatzke, an ultraliberal, committed young student teacher, who made the fatal mistake of trying to be buddies with his students. We instantly caught on to his ferrety, moist earnestness, and declared war. After he'd left early one day, we all made crappy clay vases and then loaded them into the art-room kiln, rigged so that the next morning, when Mr. Schatzke opened the kiln door, all the vases would cascade onto the floor and shatter. When this in fact happened, we all pretended to be devastated, sobbing and staggering around, clutching the shards of our broken vases. "But, Mr. Schatzke," James moaned, "this was a gift for my mother!" "Everyone, I'm so sorry, this is all my fault," said Mr. Schatzke, who was horribly guilty and upset. "And, Mr. Schatzke," said James, "she's *sick*."

Ms. Denning knew just what was going on, and could barely control her laughter. After a few months of this teen torture, Mr. Schatzke left the school and told us sadly that he didn't know if teaching was really "my thing." My art class baked him a going-away cake, and we bought some of those small tubes of neon, gel-like frosting at the supermarket, and wrote across the top of the cake: "Have You Learned Nothing From This Experience?" Ms. Denning scolded us, and then offered everyone, although not Mr. Schatzke, a ride in her convertible.

One of the first people I ever knew who died went to my high school. I'd heard about people dying before this, including all of my grandparents, but I'd been too young to have these deaths really register. But Mike Berwin's death made an impression. Mike was a few years ahead of me, and I'd only met him once or twice, but in Piscataway he was famous. He was an alcoholic and a drug addict, and he'd dropped out of school. After hitting bottom, he'd turned his life around, and he'd become a motivational speaker. One morning, he came to our school to talk to the student body, in the auditorium, about his life. He wore a tan polyester suit and his hair was moussed and slicked back; he was trim and good-looking, like a battered quarterback-turned-Toyota-dealer. He was still only in his early twenties, and he told us, "Take a look at my life. Learn from it. I was just like all of you. I was a kid. And then I got into drinking and drugs, until I was stealing from my mother's purse to get high, and hot-wiring cars and waking up in the gutter, covered in my own vomit."

This got our attention; and it had also gotten us out of biology.

"But do you think I was happy? Okay, sure, sometimes it was exciting, and I didn't have to do homework and I met a lot of girls, but was I happy? No. I thought I was happy, I thought I was doing great, but I wasn't. I was an accident waiting to happen."

By this time, my friends and I were all pointing to each other and whispering, "That sounds just like you," "He's talking about you," and "What does heroin taste like?"

Drugs, at least back then, were New Jersey's state hobby. If you opened any garage door, clouds of pot smoke would billow out. A friend of mine had a plastic bag of pot stolen from his locker and he asked me, quite seriously, if he should call the police, because, "Man, somebody stole my stash." Later, during our graduation ceremony, out on the football field, a prim, studious girl named Teri climbed the stairs to the plywood dais to receive her diploma, in her cap and gown. Since kindergarten, Teri had always carried a round, hatbox-like black patent-leather purse. I was sitting near a group of raunchier students, and as the principal handed Teri her certificate, one of the bad girls yelled, "Yo, Teri! Whatchoo got in that purse? Co-*caine*?"

But Mike didn't approve. "You think that drugs are cool," he told us. "You think that getting high will solve all of your problems. And that's just what I used to think. And that's how I almost lost everything—my health and my family and my future. Because one morning, I got so stoned on smack that I ran right off the road, hit a tree and totaled my car, and almost lost the use of my legs."

Now everyone was riveted because, to a pack of New Jersey high school students, getting injured wasn't so frightening, but losing the use of your car would be an unthinkable tragedy.

"I wonder what he was driving?" whispered someone behind me.

"I totaled my dad's car, but we still used it for parts," said someone else.

I was thinking about the tree involved. The poet Joyce Kilmer was a New Jersey native, and in elementary school I'd been required to memorize his poem "Trees," which begins with the lines "I think that I shall never see / A poem as lovely as a tree." Kilmer had allegedly written this poem about an actual tree, a white oak that had grown a few miles from Piscataway. After providing many decades of shade and leafy splendor, this tree had become diseased, and after much civic debate the town council had chopped it down. I was glad that Joyce Kilmer was dead by this time, so he wouldn't have to come up with a rhyme for "ugly stump."

"The judge gave me a choice," said Mike. "He said, 'Young man, you can either go to jail, or you can get clean. I'll give you one last chance.' And I took that chance, and I turned my life around, and now here I am, I'm still young, I'm healthy, and I've got my life back. And I'm trying to help others, I'm trying to help you, before you make all of my same mistakes. Any questions?"

There was a pause, as we all shuffled our feet and whispered to each other, things like, "Ask him where to buy acid," "Ask him if he ever has cool flashbacks," and "Ask him if he as a girl-friend," a remark that was followed by, "Sherry, shut *up*, I can't believe you, you are so horny!"

Finally a teacher raised his hand and said, "Mike, first of all, thank you so much for being here today, and I'm sure we'd all like to know: Was there any one person who made the biggest difference in your getting clean and sober?"

"Absolutely," said Mike, "and I'm glad you asked, because that would be my girlfriend, Debbie, who, and God only knows why, but she stuck by me, even when I was using, even when I was treating her like garbage. But she believed in me, and she always told me that, deep down, I was still a good person, and today, she's my wife. I owe everything to that judge, and to Debbie."

Led by the teacher, we all applauded, because Mike seemed

like a good guy, because he had dared to try to talk some sense into a horde of snickering New Jersey teenagers, and because "Debbie" is pretty much the state name.

"See, he's got a wife," Sherry told Barasella, during the applause.

"So what, he's still hot," said Barasella.

"So hot," agreed Sherry.

"I would so do him, even if he was still doing heroin," said Barasella.

Two weeks later, Mike was killed in a car accident that didn't involve a drunk driver, just a flatbed truck and an icy stretch of highway. This death shocked me, because I'd just listened to Mike in the auditorium, and because I couldn't figure out if his death offered any moral lesson. Why bother getting clean and sober if you're just going to die at twenty-three? Or did Mike's life still have value, because he'd died a happier man? And, after all of her patience and hard work and understanding, how did Debbie feel? But I think I was shocked mostly because, as a teenager, it hadn't occurred to me that either celebrities or young people could ever die.

2.

Years later, after I'd moved to New York, the first person I knew who died from AIDS, or, more correctly, from complications related to AIDS, was a lawyer in his early forties named Steve. This was before the disease had a name, or an acronym, so Steve was just a man who died very young and shockingly fast of what was then seen as a particularly virulent form of pneumonia. No one knew what to make of Steve's death, which seemed freakish, an anomaly. I had often met up with friends at Steve's Upper West Side apartment, before heading out to bars or clubs. I was living in a downtown hovel, so it was especially fun to visit a duplex with leather couches and nice sheets, where there was real art on the walls and the lights were set on dimmers. I loved New York because of this mix: the poor and barely employed could mingle with all sorts of people, and critique their imported Italian brass lamps and potted orchids.

Gradually, other people began to get inexplicably sick and then die, often in agony. There was no preparation. It wasn't like a war, where the soldiers leave home and perish on a battlefield in a foreign country. A plague happens down the hall, or on the next block, right where everything had seemed just fine the day before. Suddenly a friendly waiter was in the hospital, or an up-and-coming actor's neck and arm were covered with crusting purple lesions. No one knew what was happening, or why, and no one had the slightest idea of what to do about it, other than panic. Rumors were all anyone had to go by; only a very few people, who were genetically susceptible, would get it. For some reason, porn stars and hustlers were immune. Some people would contract only the mildest case, and recover completely. Everyone, gay and straight alike, was going to get it, and everyone was going to die. Any facts were so unknown that, in those early days, I wondered if AIDS was being spread over the phone.

I'd met Chris at college, where he was a graduate student in set design. He'd come north from Virginia, with his best friend Eric, who was studying to be a stage manager. Chris and Eric were a revelation: they were both great-looking guys who could slip effortlessly from the most raucous, masculine behavior, to the most flamboyant, hey-girlfriend carrying on. Chris and Eric were the opposite of political correctness.

Political correctness predicts that in the future, once gay people have attained full legal equality, they will abandon urban ghettos and in-crowd mannerisms and psychologically crippling, effeminate hijinks. Chris and Eric, when they were bored, would sometimes "walk in heels." When they were, say, waiting for the light to change, they'd raise their heels a few inches off the ground, and cross the street with a hip-swinging grandeur, as if they were aloof, highly paid runway models. Chris once left my apartment, and I heard him simulate a terrible fall on the steps, as he cursed, "Dammit! Broke a heel!" Eric was once asked by a security guard to leave a public library for walking in heels.

Political correctness insists that, as discrimination ends, gay people will flourish everywhere, and their lives will become indistinguishable from those of straight people, whom political correctness somehow assumes are indistinguishable from each other. Gay people will marry and raise families in the suburbs and small towns of the world, where a housewife will be heard to remark, "Wait, are Bob and Jim both gay men? You know, I really didn't notice. I just don't see gender preference anymore."

While Chris and Eric were comfortable everywhere, they thrived in New York. Gay people move to New York for the same reasons straight people do: sex, money, opportunity, and the chance to visit the giant Christmas tree that looms over Rockefeller Center, and to cruise the nearby ice skaters. And anyone who imagines that social and legal equality will erase a certain gay style, well, they just haven't been watching the twenty-something contestants on *Project Runway*, who aren't afraid of asymmetrical haircuts or making eloquent snap judgments with their eyebrows.

No, all gay people aren't witty and sophisticated, especially not the ones who think they are. But as I watched Chris and Eric, I decided that, among other things, being gay could be like knowing a second language, a banter composed of equal parts irony, healthy self-deprecation, and full-blooded swagger. I once saw Eric, on the street, as he spotted an especially hunky UPS deliveryman, in his snug brown uniform. Eric stopped dead in his tracks, admired the deliveryman from any number of angles, and finally growled, "Que *hombre*!"

When Eric got sick, Chris took care of him. Chris and Eric shared an apartment with two other guys, and Chris eventually looked after all of them, bringing them to the doctor, making sure they took their medication, comforting them, and, when necessary, changing their sheets and their diapers. Chris never abandoned his trademark perspective: "Oh, my dear," he told me, as his apartment became a ward, "it's just like running a daycare center. After you finally get one of them to take a nap, another one starts spitting up."

At this time there were no effective treatments for people with AIDS. Almost nothing was known about the disease, so some hospitals refused to admit patients with AIDS, and some doctors and nurses refused to touch them. When Eric, who had no money and probably no health insurance, became seriously ill, he was put into an ambulance and ferried to a suspiciously deluxe hospital suite on the Upper East Side. Chris explained it: "They gave Eric this gorgeous room because last week the hospital had an AIDS patient who jumped off the roof, so they're not taking any chances. And they've posted an armed guard outside his door, just in case. It's fabulous, they're treating him just like Sunny von Bülow."

My friend William and I went to visit Eric, and at the reception desk we were issued surgical gloves and face masks, and told to put them on before entering Eric's room. This seemed unnecessarily cautious, so we carried the gloves and face masks as if they were dance cards and feather fans and we were attending a Mayfair ball. I hadn't seen Eric in a few weeks, and the disease had progressed. The effect was unnervingly theatrical, because Eric now looked like a handsome young actor who'd been artificially aged for a role, with heavy makeup and spray-on hair coloring. His skin was gray, his cheeks were hollow, and he'd lost half of his usual body weight. "How do I look?" he asked, and then, "Don't answer that."

"You look better," said William.

"Oh, please," said Eric, "but do you know what I love about being sick? I take these walks, dragging my IV pole, and I smoke in the hallway. And these nurses keep coming over, and just as they're about to tell me there's no smoking, I glare at them. And they *scoot.*"

Eric was not a Hallmark Hall of Fame model patient, and who could blame him? AIDS had given him all sorts of horrifically uncomfortable ailments, with names that sounded like an English law firm: hives and shingles and thrush. He was emaciated, but he had no appetite, and his sores and aching bones made every position, in and out of bed, pure torture. And all of this made him cranky: "I told that idiot nurse that I wanted a Fresca, and she brought me a Sprite. Then I told her that I wanted cherry Jell-O and she brought me lime Jell-O, and I just said 'Listen, bitch, if you bring me lime Jell-O one more time you're gonna leave this room wearing it.'"

"The nurses love Eric," said Chris. "They're going to buy him a puppy."

"My dears," said Eric, "this place is a hellhole. The doctors don't want to come anywhere near me, and the wallpaper looks like projectile diarrhea, which, by the way, I have."

"Good to know," said Chris.

"And it takes forever to get anyone to change my gown. I told her, Nurse-whatever-your-ass-is, I'm just asking for another clean, hideous mint green smock, not a fucking Dior for dinner at the White House. And I need lozenges and some decent slippers, and maybe a nice robe. William, can't you get me a decent robe, maybe cashmere, in camel, it's not like I'm hard to fit, and some nonsurgical shampoo, and some lotion, and on your way out could you tell that nurse that I'd like some ice cream and a sponge bath and a Valium, if she's not too busy microwaving her fucking NACHOS!"

After an hour or so, William and I left the hospital and threw ourselves onto a nearby park bench. "Now, you know I love Eric dearly," said William, "and I will do anything for him, and I know that he's dying in torment . . ."

"But he's such a *pain*," I agreed, and we became hysterical with laughter, because New York was overrun with smart, enraged men, who if they couldn't get a cure, or a pillow, or a second's recognition from any politician, or even a phone call from their parents, well, at least someone could bring them a pint of Ben and Jerry's Rocky Road and a copy of the *Architectural Digest* with Cher's latest beachfront estate on the cover. "We will bring Eric anything and everything he wants," William decreed, "and then we'll *slap* him."

I went to see a highly publicized New Age preacher at Town Hall. She was an attractive, boisterously spunky woman in her thirties, and I wasn't surprised to hear that she'd once been an actress and an aspiring nightclub chanteuse, as she did everything but sip a highball and fling the microphone cord over her shoulder. "Welcome," she began, to the packed house. "How are ya? And what are we gonna do about this world, am I right?"

She went on: "We've got disease and war and crime, and some days, I'm tellin' ya, I don't even wanna get out of bed. Because on top of all that, what about my hair?" She paused, and the crowd laughed appreciatively, at the woman's folksy, what-the-hell-do-I-know bonhomie. "And I'm not saying that I've got any answers—no way, José—but you know, you can feel better. We can all feel better. We can feel blessed.

"But it's all about your attitude, people," she added, a bit later, now using a drill-sergeant, tough-love, kwitcher-bitchin' vigor. "If you have a negative attitude, well, then, my friend, you're gonna attract a negative energy. You're gonna attract bad hair days. Fights with your significant other. Illness. That's what I'm talkin' about, kiddos!" This last thought bothered me, because she seemed to be blaming people for getting sick, as if a sunny outlook was your best antibiotic.

Still, she was doing her self-actualizing rah-rah best, and if I was being honest, I'd really gone to see her because I'd been told that she had a large following among both male and female models. It was true: as I checked out the crowd, I saw a definite abundance of intimidatingly gorgeous people with long, employable legs and tiny little Prada backpacks, which I was pretty sure they'd received as gifts from the designer. As I watched one knockout thoughtfully and carefully writing down everything the preacher said, in a little Prada notebook, it occurred to me that maybe I shouldn't rely on models, at least not as moral guideposts, because I'd only end up asking myself: what would Jesus wear?

I wasn't satisfied, so I started going to ACT-UP meetings. ACT-UP was a guerrilla group that was using aggressive tactics to force the government into acknowledging the AIDS crisis, and into funding and fast-tracking medical research. ACT-UP was known for its zaps, which were high-profile, media-friendly demonstrations where ACT-UP members would chain themselves to the front doors of drug companies, or toss fliers from a balcony overlooking the floor of the New York Stock Exchange, while wearing black T-shirts with the ACT-UP logo in hot pink, reading "SILENCE = DEATH." The group's meetings were held in a low-ceilinged hall on Thirteenth Street, and they were jammed with doctors and lawyers and dog-walkers and colorists, with all sorts of people who were scared and pissed off and fed up with being ignored. These meetings were exciting, both for the rhetoric, and for the many cute guys wearing plaid flannel shirts with the sleeves hacked off, to expose their angry, tattooed, gym-hardened biceps. Most of the guys with the biceps and the trucker caps and the biker wallets were really design assistants and publicists, but that was fine, because that way you'd get the snarling ex-con fantasy without the smell.

These meetings were led by elected facilitators, and the first night I attended, one of them was a young, sideburned guy wearing a faded gray, fashionably corroded T-shirt and a drab black denim skirt fastened up the front with tarnished industrial snaps, as if he were in serious-minded, neo-Stalinist drag. He was adamant about following *Robert's Rules of Order*, which meant that anyone who had signed up before the meeting was allowed to speak.

"Okay," said the facilitator, consulting his clipboard, and trying to quiet the room, "first up, we've got representatives from the United American Socialist Party."

Five men and women, all with an unwashed, forlorn air, instantly leapt to their feet and began passing out Xeroxed pamphlets while shouting, "Capitalism causes AIDS!" "The U.S. government is making you sick!" and "AIDS equals oil!" It turned out that these people went to every meeting of every political organization in the city, regardless of the cause, and always took up a lot of everyone's time.

"SHUT UP!!!" shouted the ACT-UP regulars, and the Socialists sat back down; they seemed extremely used to this response.

"Julie Felder?" asked the facilitator, and a frantic woman with rippling, Amnesty International hair jumped up and began screaming, "I've just returned from a small village in El Salvador where the lesbian community has no access to dental dams or any other form of safe sex! We must buy dental dams for the lesbians of El Salvador! Where is our humanity?" As Julie made her plea, I began wondering, just how big is the lesbian community of a small village in El Salvador? Would maybe one box of dental dams pretty much cover it? Would it be cheaper to just fly the lesbians here and let them shop?

Other, more practical-minded people began to speak. An oncologist asked about finding money for three more beds in an AIDS unit, and someone else needed the loan of a van, for delivering posters. Then the leader of one of the many ACT-UP committees stood up and talked about a project his group had been planning: Jesse Helms, the North Carolina senator, had been a vociferous foe of any AIDS funding, and had blamed gay men for the disease, so "We tracked down his home address, and next week we're going to drop this huge condom over his whole house, and we need volunteers." There were cheers, and while I didn't participate, ACT-UP actually did this, using industrial plastic to create a Mount Rushmore–scale rubber, and the event got airtime on just about every news show in the country, and probably allowed a lot of frat boys to insist, "Yeah, that's the size I use."

People were dying in droves, and the effect became unreal, and impossible to process. There was a young, wickedly talented novelist named Christopher Coe, who had the air of a whimsical, slightly scattered classics professor. I'd see him on the street, in a flapping tweed overcoat, with an Oxford don–style scarf trailing behind him, and our gossip would range from Aeschylus to deciding exactly how painful it would be to get your balls tattooed. After Christopher got sick and I didn't run into him for over a year, I assumed the worst. Then one day

I was in my local supermarket, and he came sauntering around the corner of a pyramid of Cheerios boxes. My jaw dropped and he smiled, asking, "You thought I was a ghost, didn't you? Haunting the cereal aisle!"

He died a few months later. When I was little, I'd hated hospitals, with their toxic smells and waxy linoleum and hallways piled with pastel metal equipment that always looked exhausted and out of date, beaten down by inflating one collapsed lung too many. Now I was at ease in hospitals, and I'd glide through these buildings, telling strangers that you followed the green line on the floor to get to Radiology, and that the purple line led to Outpatient Care.

3.

As AIDS prowled its way through Manhattan, and everywhere else, my father was diagnosed with lung cancer. While this was terrible news, it was bizarrely unsurprising, since illness was everywhere.

My father was a Depression baby, raised in a Jewish family in Middle Village, Queens. He had two strong-minded sisters, the older being Lizzie, who never married and had spent much of her life working in a necktie factory, and who wore black lace dresses and heavy white rice-powder makeup, with scarlet lipstick, as if she were always about to attend a bar mitzvah in a kabuki drama. Lizzie, unlike her sister Pimmie, always seemed to be enjoying herself. Pimmie was a birdlike worrier who instinctively sought the tsunami lurking just behind the sunshine. Pimmie was often bedridden, and my mother continually tried to cheer her up, mostly for sport. When my mother congratulated Pimmie on the birth of a grandchild, Pimmie sighed heavily and said, "I'm sure it's a very nice baby, but I'm too weak to pick it up."

My father married into a clan of even stronger women, and his choice became a battleground. From the time I was about four years old, Pimmie would phone me and ask, as if she were ready to dial 911, "How is your mother treating you? Are you all right?" When I'd tell her I was fine, she'd always sound disappointed, so one day I whispered, "I don't know if I can take it here. Last night my mother bought a gun and started waving it around." "Really?" said Pimmie, with triumphant interest, until I told her I was joking. "Oh," she said, "but if she ever did buy a gun, you would tell me, wouldn't you?"

"Pimmie is really lovely, and I know she's only concerned with everyone's well-being," my mother would tell my father, "I just think she needs a little fresh air."

My father became an ace diplomat, refusing to take sides and soothing all wounded egos. He'd been a math whiz, in both college and graduate school, and he'd become a physicist. Because, especially in these areas, I was hopeless, we didn't have all that much in common, but because my father was so devoted, and because he believed in the mystical power of continuing education, he kept trying to help his little moron.

I knew that I was supposed to study and work hard, in order to get into college and not embarrass all of the Jews all over the world, who were not only monitoring me every second but who were eternally poised to call my parents and cluck, "So we heard that Paul got a C on his geometry quiz. Maybe it's time to start thinking about putting him in a group home." Jews, I was taught, excelled in all academic fields, but had little aptitude for sports, except for Sandy Koufax, the saintly Dodgers pitcher who refused to play on Yom Kippur, and Jews did not, under any circumstances, drink, practice adultery, or commit crimes, which were all activities that Gentiles customarily pursued, while jotting down fresh ways of persecuting the Jews. When I was in college, I came across a newspaper story about a distant cousin of mine, a teacher who'd been arrested for selling Quaaludes to his students in the high school parking lot. "And he's Jewish!" I yelped gleefully. "He's a Jewish criminal!" My father laughed, and my mother said, "You don't know, maybe he's only half Jewish. Maybe it was the Protestant half that was selling drugs. Or maybe he's innocent. And why do you think it's so funny? Do you want to sell drugs in a parking lot?"

"As long as you stay in school," said my father, and my mother swatted him.

My father tried to teach me math. We'd sit at the kitchen table, with my textbooks open and some freshly sharpened pencils and a pad of graph paper nearby. My dad was an excellent and sympathetic teacher, carefully and scrupulously explaining things like tetrahedrons and variables and how to use a protractor to outline a proof. I would stare at him and try to focus, the way a dog looks at his master, hearing only nonsense syllables and hoping for a biscuit and a walk.

"So x equals y, with the triple coordinates of z, w, and t," my father would say, as gently as possible, as if by his speaking slowly and distinctly, my dormant brain cells would burst into intellectual flower. "Do you understand?"

"Yes!" I would answer blankly, wagging my tail.

"You didn't understand a word I just said, did you?"

"Yes!" I would say. "I understood the words 'the' and 'you.'"

"I wonder if it would help," my mother would suggest, in passing, "if you hit him in the head with a hammer. Maybe just a tap."

I looked at my father eagerly, because this hammer deal sounded much more promising than all of those numerals and squiggles in the math books.

"Don't listen to your mother," my father said. "I know you can do this. We just have to figure out a way for you to hook into it."

"What if I ate the pages?"

My father stared at me with Vulcan determination; he did everything but grab my hand and use his index finger to write the equations on my palm, while shouting, "It's called algebra, Helen! It has a name!" But he was too nice to confront me with what we both knew: "You are not my son! You are a hubcap!"

Things only got worse when my father tried to teach me to drive. I did fine on the written test, and received my learner's permit. I then sat behind the wheel, in our driveway, with my father beside me, in the front seat of our mustard-colored Olds-mobile sedan.

"Okay, what's the first thing we do?" my father asked.

"Change places."

"What's the first thing we do?"

"Call a taxi."

"Paul?"

"The first thing we do is . . . to put on our seat belt."

"Very good!"

"And then we start screaming uncontrollably."

"Paul?"

"And then . . ." I tried to stumble my way through the thick fog of my total disinterest and ineptitude. "And then we . . . put the key in the ignition?" I was just guessing, from having watched cartoon characters drive cars.

"You're close, you're getting very close . . ."

"We . . . adjust our mirrors?"

"Yes! Excellent! And why do we adjust our mirrors?"

I resisted the urge to answer "To check our lipstick," or "To smooth our bangs," and simply replied, "So that we can aim at people?"

I got the car started, and with the engine humming I asked, "Isn't this enough for today? I don't want to overlearn. I want to grow into driving."

"That's not a problem," said my dad. "But I tell you what, I'll make you a deal. We'll just drive around the block once, just for starters, and that's all we'll do for today. How does that sound?"

"What if a deer jumps out at us?"

"There are no deer in this neighborhood."

"What if a foreign government has tampered with the brake linings?" I had no idea what brake linings were; perhaps they came in coordinated fabrics or fur.

"The brakes are fine."

"What if I lose control of my vehicle and plummet into a ravine?"

"What if you check your mirrors again, release the brake, and put the car in gear?"

"ARE YOU INSANE?"

Somehow my father managed to coax me and the car out of the driveway and onto our deserted neighborhood street. I drove incredibly slowly, with a death grip on the steering wheel, as if I were a dangerously shrunken senior citizen whose gnarled head could barely clear the dashboard. I drove the way I bowled. At our local alley, I would use both hands to send my ball rolling very slowly, as if in arthritic torment, down the lane, with a lulling, repeated thump. I had a system, as I was convinced that the ball's torpor would force it to stay on course, and slowly but surely get the job done. Instead, the ball would meander into the gutter, or politely tap an unresponsive bowling pin, and then, acting as if nothing had happened, roll meekly away.

"You're doing great!" insisted my dad, as I inched down the street. "Do you see that mailbox?"

"What mailbox?"

"Turn! Turn the wheel! No, *the other way*!"

After many more attempts, even my aberrantly patient father agreed that maybe someone else should give teaching me a shot. Many people tried, including friends and other family members, all of whom ended up screaming at me and then apologizing and running away. My high school driving instructor didn't fare much better, but he had other things on his mind, as, during their one-on-one sessions, he'd been driving his more attractive female students to a nearby motel, and offering them a different sort of lesson.

I ultimately took my driving test six times, under all possible conditions, including amid regular traffic, on a closed track, and in a few neighboring counties. Each time, when I came home, my father would give me a big smile and ask, "So how'd it go?" Here's why he was so understanding: he wasn't asking if I'd passed, only if I'd failed less completely. He wasn't embarrassed by having a son who couldn't drive, merely puzzled, as if he couldn't decide which piece of my brain was missing, and where I'd left it.

The last time I took the test I was doing pretty well, until the official from the Motor Vehicles Bureau, who was sitting in the front seat beside me, asked me to parallel park between four orange rubber highway safety cones. As I eased the car between these cones, I nudged one of them with my rear tire.

"You just killed a child," the official said.

"I did not," I protested. "I just killed a rubber cone."

"Get out of the car."

When I limped home from this final defeat, I felt almost vindicated—you see, I told you I couldn't drive! I told you I had no business being on the road! What do I have to do, plow into a busload of schoolchildren? Then will you people believe me? My father saw that I was unexpectedly happy, and this confused him. "What happened?" he asked.

"I almost passed, I swear I did. But the guy giving me the test was anti-Semitic."

Here's why I loved my father: he agreed with me.

By the time his cancer was diagnosed, my father had already had a heart attack and a bypass operation, interspersed with brief periods of relative health. He remained stoic and uncomplaining, as he began to cough up blood. Each cough seemed to surprise him, as if his body was refusing to play fair.

After my brother and I left home, my parents had moved to Philadelphia, where they could enjoy city walks and restaurants, instead of suburban sprawl. They were having a good time with new jobs and new friends, so my father's illness seemed especially cruel. At first my mother was desperate to keep my dad at home. She rented a hospital bed and other pieces of necessary equipment, and, as his condition deteriorated, she began to hire visiting nurses. At first I thought that she'd formed a romantic image of my father dying peacefully, in the living room, but then I saw how frantic she was. She believed that if she could just keep my father with her, he wouldn't die.

My father's cancer soon became unmanageable. His body was wracked, and he began howling in pain and convulsing. He was moved to a nearby hospital, which turned out to be a very good idea, because his pain was finally treated with a morphine pump, which is a device that allows a patient to monitor his own dosage, by pushing a button. Surprisingly, the doctor said that patients rarely overmedicate themselves. I instantly wanted one of these pumps for myself, just for dental work and certain cocktail parties.

Once my dad was more comfortable, my mom could relax as well. My older brother, Evan, also came to the hospital. Evan had a combative history with my parents, especially with my mother. As a teenager, and a child of the counterculture, he'd taken to telling my parents, in exhaustive detail, what was wrong with their conformist, capitalist values. Sometimes he would illustrate these lectures. Once, when my folks were out of town, he'd wheeled his motorcycle into the living room, and parked it on the wall-to-wall carpeting, and then he'd photographed this treason. He'd then wheeled the motorcycle back out, without leaving so much as a drop of motor oil behind, but a week later he left the Polaroids where my parents could find them. He was a passive-aggressive Che Guevara.

As the years went by, Evan continued to spar with my parents, over everything from his now waist-length hair, to his refusal to wear a tie to a cousin's wedding. At Evan's request, he and my parents finally went into therapy and vented, which helped, although Evan did accuse my mother of feeding her children unhealthy junk food like Drake's Cakes and Froot Loops, and I was then forced to remind him that this was an example of not merely good parenting but great parenting.

Once my father got sick, a truce was declared, although Evan still upset my mother by appearing at the hospital dressed as himself, in torn denim and a battered motorcycle jacket, with his hair tied back with a rubber band. My mother has always believed that Evan's wardrobe is a deliberate, rebellious insult, aimed at her, but she's wrong, because Evan is simply a good-natured Hells Angel born into a home without dust.

As the morphine kicked in, my father began to hallucinate. When a young, blond, Caucasian nurse came into his hospital room, my father asked her, in all seriousness, "Are you Nell Carter?" Nell Carter was the short, round, African-American star of a sitcom on which she played a wise, sassy housekeeper, and I was surprised, not just by my dad's question, but that he knew who Nell Carter was.

"No, I'm not Nell Carter," said the nurse, laughing.

"Please don't tell anyone he asked you that," my mother begged, but then even she, along with my father and the rest of us, started laughing and couldn't stop. My father's mind began to drift, to mostly welcome memories, of vacations and car trips. He and my mother held hands, as they always did. I usually hate couples who hold hands in public, as if they're advertising their storybook bliss, but when my parents held hands, the act seemed private and genuine.

Evan had read up on death and hospice care, perhaps a little too much, but Evan likes to do things his own way. When Evan was a child, an aunt once asked him what he wanted to be when he grew up, and he said, "Retired." He wasn't kidding, as he's fixed motorcycles and done construction work, but he's mostly lived on air. He's hardworking, in terms of chopping wood or planting an herb garden, but he thinks of actual employment as a government conspiracy. "Why should I get some ridiculous job?" he would say. "Just so I can pay for the president's fancy shoes?"

But Evan has a New Age soft spot, and he kept kneeling by my father's bedside, gently taking my father's hand, and murmuring, in a low, insistent tone, "You can let go now. We all love you. You can let go." He was completely well-intentioned, but after the first few attempts, it became clear that my father wasn't following the manual, and that my brother, without meaning to in any way, was starting to sound impatient, like the Grim Reaper with a golf date.

"Evan," said my mother, equally gently, "you're being incredibly sweet, but I think Daddy will go when he's ready."

4.

My father died a few days later, and Evan and I were sent to the casket showroom, to choose a coffin. The models ranged from basic pine boxes to an iridescent, candyflake, powder blue and chrome nightmare with a ruched, white-silk interior, which cost many thousands of dollars and looked like a country-western singer's tour bus. We were both taken with the pint-sized coffins for children, which the brochure delicately called "Shortees."

The funeral industry, as Evan pointed out, is designed to make the bereaved feel as guilty as possible and therefore willing to spend more money, as if the dead are hovering nearby, jeering, "Oh, so I'm not worth the down-filled pillow with the matching silk-covered buttons. I guess I'm supposed to spend eternity with my decaying skull resting on foam rubber. Well, thanks a casket-load, cheapskate." We settled on something mid-range, and at the funeral home, a few minutes before the service was set to begin, the funeral director asked the family if we'd like to see our father one last time, in private, before they closed the lid. Evan agreed to this, and went into the viewing room, but I held back. I was scared; and I didn't want my final memory of my father to be that of a cosmetically enhanced dead person. Also, my father had a low-down sense of humor and a reverence for burlesque comics. He was a big fan of Vanna White, the letter-turning hostess on *Wheel of Fortune*, and he liked to remind people that "vanna" means "bathtub" in Yiddish. And so I didn't want to see his body, and begin fantasizing about him abruptly sitting up, accompanied by the wooot! of a pennywhistle.

I hate funerals. While my father's service was brief and touching, it still did what funerals always do, which is to make death even more grim. Funerals are like birthday parties for dead people; everyone gets all dressed up, knowing they're going to have a bad time. Funerals can also make grief competitive, as everyone eyeballs the various friends and family members to rate who's the most stricken. My friend William told me that in the South, a mourner will often hurl him- or herself onto the coffin, weeping ostentatiously, and then teeter over the open grave, waving a tear-soaked hanky. "White trash love funerals," he said.

About a year after my dad died, I went with William to the 1993 March on Washington. This was a gay march, to promote visibility, and to protest the government's still atrocious record on AIDS funding, research, and care. People had been dying for years, and there was still only the most minimal treatment available, with no sign of the drug cocktails that would, years later, begin to keep those with HIV alive.

William and I took the train down and slept on a friend's couch in Georgetown. The spring day of the march was sunny and warm, and while there were organized delegations, and marching bands and the motorcycle-riding Dykes on Bikes, there were mostly just hundreds of thousands, if not millions, of people, walking toward the Capitol and the mall. There was true, infinite gay diversity, which meant that there were many people to admire, a more select group to ogle, and a copious supply of marchers dressed or undressed in ways that would embarrass the conservative gay politicos who yearned for timid respectability. My friend Candida's ex-girlfriend was there, riding with her own motorcycle gang, which had held a naming contest. The finalists had included the Wombs of Doom and the Menstrual Cycles, but the women had settled on the more prosaic Wildcats.

As we marched, or ambled, William and I ran into people we knew, from New York or elsewhere, and we all compared our rainbow trinkets, which are the Beanie Babies of gay pride. At a bandshell, a warbly lesbian folksinger tried to get the crowd to join in on the well-mannered anthem "We Are a Gentle, Angry People." William and I decided that this song was hopelessly wussy, and that the lyrics should include lines like "May I have the restroom key, please?" and "I'm so mad I could just . . . I'm sorry, you've caught me at a bad time."

I saw my favorite couple on a corner, waiting to cross the street. This was a surly, dominant lesbian in jeans, boots, a leather vest, and a leather cap tilted low on her forehead, and she was leading her submissive lover on a chain-link leash. This leash went from a rawhide loop in the top woman's fist, and then traveled about six feet into the open fly of her slave's jeans, where it was anchored to a labial piercing. While I admired this couple's confidence, all I kept thinking was, I hope no one jostles them.

Finally we reached the mall, which was filled with the AIDS quilt. For many years people had been sending along rectangles of fabric in honor of friends, lovers, and family members who'd died of AIDS. The panels were made from every possible material, from flannel and satin and bedsheets, and while

some were only marked with a name, others were more elaborately painted and embroidered and pinned with high school
yearbook pages and baby pictures and favorite T-shirts and
Mardi Gras beads. I'd read that this was the first and, possibly,
the last time that the quilt would be seen in its entirety. There
were aisles, and people were walking among the panels, which
seemed to stretch for miles, looking for someone they'd known,
and considering the lives, and debris, of strangers.

People were divided about the quilt. Some found it an appropriate memorial, while others thought it was quaint and fussy,
like a cemetery designed by the *Ladies' Home Journal*. But on that
day, the quilt was overwhelming. I don't cry easily, and I hadn't
cried at my father's funeral, or at any of the memorials I'd been
to for friends who'd died of AIDS. So many people were gone,
and so quickly, that tears had become a luxury, and endless
grief seemed useless.

Death had become deranged. A few months earlier Candida
had gathered with a group to surround the hospital bed of a
woman with a brain tumor. Everyone was instructed to join
hands, shut their eyes, and visualize the tumor, and then concentrate on shrinking it. Candida told me, "And I really tried to
focus and make the tumor evaporate, but we were all standing
there for a really long time and my feet hurt and I suddenly
realized that my mind had wandered and that I was trying to
remember which subway I needed to take to get home. And
then, later that week, the woman died. Do you think I killed
her?"

"Of course not," I said comfortingly, "you were there for her,
and I'm sure that her friends and family appreciated it." Then,

under my breath, but making sure that Candida could hear me, I whispered, "Murderer."

While I walked among the panels on the quilt, I saw that someone from New Jersey had died, and that their panel included a map of my home state. The panel was made from blue and gold felt, and it looked like a team banner, hanging from the rafters of a high school gym, maybe commemorating a basketball squad from a championship year. I didn't know the person who was being remembered, but I started to cry, and I couldn't stop. Looking around, all I saw were other people, in clusters or alone, sniffling and sobbing.

Later that night, there were parties all over the city, and I went to one being held in the cavernous lobby of a municipal building, a hall with soaring marble columns, mahogany-paneled walls, and burnished bronze railings. There was a top-flight DJ and a state-of-the-art sound and lighting system, and the place was thronged with all sorts of people, including plenty of staggeringly well-built, gyrating men, dancing with their shirts off and their jeans dipping low. It was like disco nite at the Lincoln Memorial.

I'd only just met John, back in New York, but we'd arranged to see each other at this party. We danced, and then, to prolong that early, hopelessly infatuated stage of our relationship, we went off to join our separate groups of friends.

Here's what I know about death and grieving: None of it makes any sense, although I will always cherish the words of a woman who spoke at a friend's memorial, and who began her affectionate remarks by saying, "God knows, Ed was cheap." Here's what I know about New Jersey: If you're a citizen, be proud of it. I knew a guy from Piscataway who would tell people that he was from the far more posh Princeton, which was forty-five minutes away. I always wanted to tell him, Darling, you're still from New Jersey. Who are you kidding?

And here's what I know about love: Don't let go.

I Shudder:

An Excerpt from the Most Deeply Intimate and Personal Diary of One Elyot Vionnet

Mr. Christmas

1.

Christmas is woefully misunderstood. Some believe that on Christmas we celebrate the birth of Our Lord Jesus Christ. This is ludicrous. Do you think that, year after year, Jesus wants to be reminded of how very old he is? Do you imagine that Jesus enjoys watching everyone else opening their own mammoth piles of presents on what's supposedly his big day? Do you feel, after the way humanity treated him, that a gala annual blowout might comfort Jesus, by saying, "We're all terribly sorry about that crucifixion business, but hey look, Jimmy got a catcher's mitt!"?

Others insist that Christmas is a time for giving, a day to reflect on our blessings, and an opportunity to share our love with our families and friends. Again, this is beyond repellent. Christmas, as it is practiced in the United States, is a season of excessive, credit-heavy spending, painfully awkward get-togethers with people we never liked to begin with, and the torture of children by never giving them enough gifts to satisfy their amoral, venal natures. The only appropriate holiday tokens would be to give every member of one's family a crossbow and a head start.

Christmas is, as any thoughtful person will concede, an occasion for absolute judgment, on each and every one of us. It is a day for the universe to decide, without prejudice, but also without pity, precisely who has been naughty, and deserving of, at best, nothing, and who has been nice, or who has at least pretended to be nice, by visiting the elderly or contributing to worthy causes, in the hope of using their faux-niceness as a bonus coupon, to be redeemed for Yuletide merchandise.

It has come to my attention that, in terms of strict and merciless judgment, Santa Claus has become, and there is only one word for it, sloppy. He's grown grossly overweight, and he careens through the sky, dropping garishly wrapped packages onto people who should more correctly be receiving envelopes of anthrax, crates of soap and deodorant, and subpoenas. When it comes to making well-considered and unassailable judgments, I am far more qualified than Santa. I am, in fact, the only person or being equipped to administer Christmas properly, since the entire grisly phenomenon began.

Of course, I don't have to do it. I could take the day off. I could let the planet wallow in its customary Christmas stench. But I won't do that, for one simple reason, for the reason which illustrates what should be the true spirit of what Jews prefer to call "the holidays."

I will fix Christmas, because I am, or I hope to become, a saint.

On the night before Christmas, I had to of course consider my ensemble. Santa's appearance is a cruel prank: red velvet on a fat man, with a wide, black patent leather belt to provide some laughable stab at a waistline? The beard and the boots? Over the centuries, Santa has begun to dress like an effeminate, drunken lumberjack, and without his watchful, presumably deeply embittered elves, he would most likely lurch out into a snowbank, fall asleep, and freeze to death, and his bloated, rigid bulk would be gnawed by his own reindeer, who would then develop crippling cholesterol problems.

As I stood before the full-length mirror attached to the open door of my single narrow closet, I asked myself: how can I show the proper respect for Christmas Eve, combined with an appropriately severe elegance? I instantly donned my tuxedo, a garment which still appears sleek and fresh, although it has been passed down through over eighty generations of Vionnet men, and, of course, Great Aunt Vestra Vionnet, who wore the family tux to bewitch half the women of Bucharest. No, Vestra was not Europe's first lesbian postmistress, but she was the first one to get it right.

Pleased with my tuxedo-clad reflection, I added a small sprig of berry-ripe holly to my lapel. For a moment I hesitated: was the sprig too much? Was I suddenly one of those matronly big-box store cashiers who overdo their snowflaked holiday cardigans by adding a plastic, battery-powered brooch of a reindeer head, where, when a small string is pulled, the tiny bulb at the end of Rudolph's nose lights up?

No. The sprig was perfect, as it gave the offhand impression, "Merry Christmas, but not that much."

I left my apartment and went down to the street, knowing that any animal-drawn sleigh was out of the question. Yes, it might be pretty and pictorial, but please—the aroma. The droppings. The incessant, nightmarish jingling. No, instead I decided to test my powers, as a saint-in-the-making. I wondered if, just maybe, I had developed, through my newfound allegiance to goodness, a miraculous gift: the ability to summon a taxi, just by thinking about it, the way Tarzan could silently mind-meld with lions and zebras. I stood on the curb, shut my eyes, and concentrated. I saw yellow, only yellow, of the most stirring, hopeful, soul-warming tint, as if a blazing comet of love were racing toward me. I briefly lost consciousness, but as I opened my eyes, there it was! My jolly Christmas cab!

The cab was being driven by a woman named, according to the barely legible license mounted on her cab's filthy Plexiglas partition, Ludmila Darp. Ludmila had thick, jet black hair which, for the season, had been braided with lush plastic poinsettia blossoms, sparkling with clear glitter. Like all cabdrivers, Ludmila refused to speak to her passengers, choosing instead to mutter, in seeming gibberish, into her headpiece for our entire journey. I would ordinarily find such behavior ill-mannered and offensive, except for this little-known fact: when cabdrivers mutter in this nonstop, stream-of-consciousness fashion, they are never, as is commonly believed, speaking to their spouses, their adulterous attachments who await them in motels near the entrances to various tunnels, their dispatcher, or their abandoned, greedy relatives halfway around the world. The cabdrivers are, in fact, maintaining a direct gravitational link with an alien space station orbiting Jupiter, and if the cabdrivers were to stop muttering for even a millisecond, Earth would spin wildly off its axis and hurtle into the sun. This is only one of the many reasons why I revere cabdrivers: they keep our planet safe. And, by the way, those small, shiny gold plastic crowns which are mounted above the dashboards of many cabs do not contain air freshener; they are real crowns, hammered from priceless gold nuggets, which the cabdrivers wear after work, as the rulers of their subterranean city.

Ludmila first brought me to an address in faraway Brooklyn, to a recently reclaimed factory building. I pressed a random buzzer, and, when a disembodied voice asked me who I was, I replied, "I'm from the *New York Times*, and we're thinking of including your apartment in our next Home section on Eco-Style." Before I even finished the sentence, the buzzer blasted eagerly and the door flew pantingly open, as if I were a returning war hero, or a spokesperson carrying an outsized lottery check.

Once I reached the fifth floor, a heavy steel door was opened by a thirty-five-ish fellow wearing the tight black stovepipe jeans of someone who either had his own band or sometimes claimed to; the scuffed, chunky motorcycle boots of someone who either rode a Harley or had named his daughter Harley; and the untucked, artfully creased and faded shirt of someone who either knows this dude who makes these really cool shirts or who at least knows the hole-in-the-wall boutique which sells these really cool shirts, a boutique which was especially designed to look like an abandoned sawmill. This fellow also sprouted professionally sheared sideburns, a thatch of only mildly thinning, product-rumpled hair, and the tiniest shadow of a fuzzy patch beneath his lower lip, as if the fellow knew that such facial hair was so eight years ago but he still couldn't let it go. It was a phantom soul patch, to match the empty, echoing three holes in his right earlobe.

"I'm Ned," the fellow said, holding out his hand, which was attached to a wrist draped with a vintage Rolex, a rawhide shoelace strung with a Zen brass disc, and a knotted strip of red twine, which signaled his interest in, if not the Kabbalah, then at least the celebrities who promoted the Kabbalah. "Come on in."

Ned ushered me into a long, many-windowed loft. Each element of the space's industrial heritage had been lovingly and expensively restored, so that every unvarnished, scarred oak beam and fist-sized iron rivet had attained the status of a Hemingway first edition. The furniture, by contrast, was ultramodern, a gallery of Italian and Dutch design, with the tubular chrome-and-cowhide chaise poised in precise conversation with the reclaimed bamboo armchair, and the transparent, undulating Lucite coffee table. There were a few overlapping, heirloom-quality oriental rugs, some enormous, jug-shaped lamps dripping with long-hardened green and brown glazes, and an open kitchen where the brushed-steel, restaurant-grade appliances guarded the poured-concrete countertops, which were kept bare, as poured concrete is more costly and delicate than the finest French porcelain.

"And this is Tash, for Natasha," said Ned, turning to his wife, whose real name I knew instantly was Amy, because a recent Nobel Prize winner has proved conclusively that no one has ever actually been named Natasha, let alone Tash.

"And you're from the *Times*, on Christmas Eve," said Tash, "that is so cool! It's like an early Christmas present! Ned, get him some wine. Our friends Breen and Casey have their own vineyard up in Maine, at their summer place."

As I contemplated both the thought of a Maine wine, and the possible genders of people named Breen and Casey, I saw that Tash was aggressively thin, as if she'd taped an Audubon watercolor of a starving wren to her refrigerator, for inspiration. Her hair drifted in deliberate wisps of a mousey-blond shade found only in girls who were ceramics majors, because Bennington had been forced, after much parental outcry, to eliminate its major in advanced bulimia, or as it's also known, dance. Tash's wardrobe was, I'm just going to say it, layered: I counted an ivory, spaghetti-strap camisole beneath a patterned rayon forties cocktail dress, beneath a beaded, black cashmere sweater with three-quarter-length sleeves, beneath many strands of pewter chains, amber beads that weighed more than Tash, and hemp knotted with bits of beach glass, all set off by openwork, crocheted fingerless gloves and black cotton-and-spandex leggings which exposed a shinful of gleamingly waxed flesh, ending in spike-heeled, mucus-colored, smushed-velvet half-boots. Just looking at Tash was exhausting; merely getting dressed in the morning was probably enough to keep her so arachnid slim.

"So how are you celebrating Christmas?" I asked Ned and Tash, who had now settled in side by side on their deep pumpkin, goatskin couch. Together, they looked like a Calder mobile which had fallen from the ceiling and landed on the furniture in an angular heap.

"I'll tell you what we'd like to do," said Ned, tilting his chin upward so that the light glinted off his thick black eyeglass frames, the frames which he'd ordered online from a site offering "Eyeglass Frames of the Great Midcentury Architectural Visionaries." "We'd like to somehow create a completely authentic Christmas," Ned continued, "an outsider Christmas."

"We want a Christmas," said Tash, "so that if someone came up here and saw us, they wouldn't go, 'Oh, right, Christmas,' they'd go, 'Christmas. Yeah. Cool.'"

"Especially for Jasper," said Ned, as a four-year-old wandered in from some tucked-away bedroom-pod. Jasper had blond, dreadlocked hair and he was wearing pull-up potty-training pants, printed with characters from the Shrek movies, and a sleeveless black T-shirt with the logo and schedule of a 1968 Rolling Stones tour, a brand-new T-shirt which had been sanded to a vintage limpness by a factory worker in Nepal.

"Jasper, honey," said Tash, "come over here, and tell this nice man about Christmas."

"Mr. Christmas!" said Jasper, excitedly catching sight of me. I wasn't surprised that Jasper recognized me, as I was obviously a friendly, mythical figure, like the Easter Bunny or the Tooth Fairy or Tash's first husband.

"We don't want to give Jas just some big, bogus, crap Christmas," said Ned, as his son nestled between his parents' bony hips.

"Jas, do you like our tree?" asked Tash, pointing Jasper's little hand toward a small blue spruce, still bundled with wire, and leaning against a nearby wall.

"It's really more of a piece," said Ned, regarding this tree. "That's why I leaned it. I don't want it to say, hey, we went out and spent a fortune on some pile of Christmas shit. I wanted us to have something that's sort of about Christmas, that makes a gesture toward Christmas but that's more of a comment on Christmas."

"It's like, that tree will be even cooler once it gets a little brown," said Tash, "and maybe on the floor we'll have one broken, clear glass ornament. Like the tree is weeping."

"Are you both artists?" I asked, and the couple became almost radioactive with gratitude.

"We're sort of life-artists," said Ned. "I mean, I'm in a band, sort of neo-soul-bluegrass, but during the day I'm a tech consultant, for people who want to create websites about wholly sustainable furniture, like end tables made from fossilized South African tree stumps, or dining room tables molded from thousands of compressed Evian bottles."

I found this mix of recycling and invention to be admirable, because I knew it meant that Ned also had family money.

"I'm working on a children's book," said Tash. "It's about a group of little girls who all have eating disorders, which allow them to fly."

"Because they're so thin?" I wondered. "So they just sort of waft upwards?"

"Yes," said Tash. "And of course they look great, but they fly to get the help they need. I'm calling it *The Airy Fairies*, and I'm still outlining and conceptualizing, but once I finish, I want the book to be printed on this amazing artisanal paper, crafted from oatmeal and gravel."

"Jasper," I asked, "what would you like for Christmas?"

"Jas?" said Ned, as the child looked from one parent to the next.

"Gun!" said Jasper merrily. "Big gun!" And then he pointed his finger around the room, making the sound of a sniper barrage. "Powpowpowpowpow!!!"

"Jesus Christ, Ned," said Tash, "why do you keep letting him watch your DVDs?"

"I was busy!" Ned protested. "I was working on a song, the one about my father's lawyers, and I had the headphones on, and those DVDs keep Jasper quiet."

"I *hate* guns," said Tash, "but Ned has this whole collection of Japanese gangster movies from the seventies. It's disgusting."

"They're incredible," said Ned, "and they've been unbelievably influential on an entire generation of American filmmakers!"

"Die! Die! Everybody die!" shouted Jasper happily, as he ran around the loft, hurling coffee-table books onto the floor.

"This Christmas," said Tash, trying to get things back on track, "we picked a theme, and we're all going to give each other gifts related to world music."

"And so I'm getting this amazing 1952 steel guitar, from France," said Ned, "and I got Tash this pair of diamond earrings that she wanted, from Cartier."

"Which I'm going to wear next week," said Tash, quickly, "when we go to see this Tongolese punk band, at this new club in this storefront where they used to sell corrective shoes. We heard about it from our nanny."

"And what are you getting Jasper?" I whispered.

"We're getting him gamelan lessons," Tash whispered back, "and a set of Balinese shadow puppets, so he can create his own ritualized dance/theater evenings."

"MERRY CHRISTMAS!" Jasper was now yelling. "KILL BASTARD! DIE DIE DIE!"

2.

As I returned to my cab, I thought to myself, being a parent is never easy, especially at the holidays. And I wondered what would happen tomorrow morning, when Ned and Tash and Jasper ripped off the hand-blocked rice-paper wrapping from their gifts, which had been lovingly tied with strips of cypress-infused raffia, to discover that all of their boxes, large and small, were now empty, and that their contents had somehow made their way into the trunk of my cab. At first I considered distributing these gifts to the less fortunate, but then I decided that if I gave the less fortunate Balinese shadow puppets, they'd only get irritated and groan, "Balinese shadow puppets? *More* Balinese shadow puppets?"

I was feeling smudged with Brooklyn hipster sophistication, so I asked Ludmila to bring me to a home where a more traditional Christmas was being celebrated. But how, you may ask, did Ludmila then pilot her cab from New York to the snow-battered plains of Twineheart, Kansas, in what felt like an instant? Did the car actually leave the ground, silhouetted against the Christmas moon? Did partygoers from over twenty states look up and wave their arms, in a vain attempt to hail Ludmila, forcing me to lean out the window and point ostentatiously to the cab's darkened rooftop light, while howling, "Occupied!" Can a taxi take flight, like a sleigh or a Learjet or an anorexic fairy?

I will only say this: never underestimate the driving abilities of a Manhattan cabdriver, or the fact that Ludmila was from the backcountry outside Kiev, so she had no concept of red lights.

From the darkness, I saw a set of squarish, invitingly yellow beacons, which, as they grew steadily larger and more distinct, I found were the windows of a generously scaled Kansas farmhouse. Ludmila pulled up beside a snowbanked picket fence and uttered her first understandable words of the evening: "Go insidt. Haf de fun. Meter ees steel runnink."

The contours of the farmhouse were framed in those richly hued Christmas lights, which I much prefer to the bland, year-round, noncommittal twinkle of those all-white strands. The snow was many feet deep, exposing only the top hat of a molded plastic snowman, the curving tips of several six-foot-tall striped Styrofoam candy canes, and the heads of at least three plastic Santas—the front yard of this farmhouse was like the grim aftermath of some Yuletide ocean-liner disaster, as survivors paddled around, miles out at sea. I stamped my way toward the front door, which had been covered with tinfoil and wide, red plastic ribbon, to resemble a wrapped package, and which was also outlined with evergreen garland and hung with a mighty hollyberry wreath, embedded with golden spheres and lit-from-within plastic angels with ruddy, airbrushed cheeks. I wondered if this wreath could be tossed out into the yard, as a life preserver to be grasped by the buried snowman and the surely frostbitten Santas. But still, this was clearly a house where Christmas was lived, and lived well.

I pushed the doorbell, which rang with a recorded chorus of chipmunk voices chirping "God Rest Ye Merry Gentlemen," and then the door popped open to reveal a cheerfully stout middle-aged woman who had, I felt, been hosed down with Christmas. Her head of joyously abundant corkscrew curls had been severely parted down the center, with one side colored iodine red and the other AstroTurf green, as if Christmas were a brutal, take-no-prisoners arena sporting event. Her face was wonderfully puglike and flushed, as if she were not only happy to see me, but equally ecstatic to just be opening her front door.

"Well, howdy-ho!" the woman said. "I don't know who you are or why you're here or why the hecky-hay you're not wearing a winter coat, but come right on in!"

As she led me inside, I smelled her home's many holiday fragrances, from the musky pine of her twelve-foot tree, to the cloves that had been studded into the oranges which were stacked in pyramids on footed cake plates, to the baking gingerbread from the kitchen, to the thick candles which filled the mantel and gave off an additional, trademarked Baking Gingerbread scent. The woman had even perfumed herself with drops of peppermint oil, as the perfect top note to her oversize holiday sweatshirt, which had been extravagantly sequinned and hand-painted with a mural of not just Santa's workshop, but also the North Pole train station, Mrs. Claus's sewing nook, the elves' cafeteria, and, running down onto her coordinated sweatpants, a reindeer red-light district, complete with a pimpish looking Blitzen in a wide-brimmed fedora.

"Look, everybody—we got company!" said the woman, as she presented me to her expansive parlor, which was packed with hundreds of pieces of skirted colonial reproduction furniture, and even more high-spirited relatives. The room looked like a global summit of the happiest, friendliest, and most stain-resistant coven.

"I'm Linda Lou Smacker," said the woman, "and these are my mom and my pop and my husband and my kids and the grandkids and my sisters and my brothers and their kids and what can I say? It's Kansas and we ran out of condoms!"

"I'm Uncle Stan," said someone else, thrusting a mug of steaming cider into my hand, complete with a dollop of whipped cream jabbed with a cinnamon stick.

"Second-Cousin-Once-Removed-But-Not-Far-Enough-Carolynn-With-Two-N's!" said someone else, offering me a plate where a decal of Jesus' pale, thoughtful face peeked out from beneath a mountain of sugar cookies shaped like chiming bells, with gumdrop clappers.

"And I'm Big Paw Paw, Linda Lou's way-better half!" guffawed a Paul Bunyan–like figure in a bulging plaid flannel shirt, suspenders, duck boots, and a trucker's cap, with the peaked brim safety-pinned with mistletoe. Thankfully, or perhaps sadly, I wasn't expected to kiss Big Paw Paw, although he did shove something shaped like a snowball and encrusted with meringue into my mouth. "And I'm only askin' so we can put your name on some presents," said Big Paw Paw, "but who in the name of the sweet baby Jesus and my wife's big ol' butt are you?"

"Big Paw Paw!" protested Linda Lou, as he grabbed that big ol' butt with gusto; Linda Lou's blushing grin assured me that the couple's sex life, even after thirty years of marriage, was more than mutually satisfying, and may even have included a drunken videotape which featured not only the couple's robust lovemaking but a partial view of Linda Lou's collection of Victorian dolls.

"I'm Mr. Christmas," I announced to the room, and everyone nodded, as if I was sent each year by the Junior Chamber of Commerce. "And I'm here to determine just who's been naughty and just who's been nice."

There was a pause, as everyone mulled this over and glanced at other family members. Then, as one, all of the men shot their hands vigorously into the air.

"NAUGHTY!" the men all shouted.

"THEY WISH!" the women all shouted right back, with their hands instantly reaching even higher.

"My Lord," I said, "you seem like the most genuinely happy and sweet-souled people I've ever met, and without your being a huge, sanctimonious pain. You make me believe that there just might be something called a real Christmas spirit."

"Aw, heck," said Big Paw Paw, "I don't know if any of that's true, but it sure is nice to hear you say it."

"We just like to drink eggnog and eat anything that isn't nailed down and see who can put on the most pounds by New

Year's," said Linda Lou, but, looking around, I saw that, while no one in the room could be called sylphlike, they were all more strong and sturdy than overfed.

"But what's your holiday secret?" I asked, mystified. I felt like a pith-helmeted explorer who'd stumbled upon a blessedly untouched, utopian tribe in some well-hidden rain forest. These people might be simple but never simpleminded; their clothing was comfy and entertaining, rather than painfully chic, and they seemed to have an untroubled, straightforward grasp of life's pleasures.

"Should we tell him?" asked an outlying brother-in-law.

"Tell me what?" I said.

"Why the heck not, he's practically family," said Big Paw Paw, chugging back what looked like a tureen of hot chocolate; Big Paw Paw prided himself on his ability to eat and drink without needing to chew or swallow.

"Well," said Linda Lou, as everyone smiled and closed in a bit, as if they were gathering around a campfire, with weenies and s'mores, "you see, for us, for the whole extended Smacker-Cannastock-Kellerhitt family Christmas isn't just your average let's-get-together-and-watch-Big-Paw-Paw-pass-out-in-his-recliner-in-front-of-the-game holiday."

"You got that right!" agreed Big Paw Paw, giving Linda Lou's cheek a little preliminary smooch.

"Paw Paw!" said Linda Lou, pinching him, and then, "Here at our house, we have a very special tradition, which has been passed down to us over all the generations, from the folks who settled Twineheart in covered wagons and log cabins. And I suppose they invented this tradition because they didn't have cable TV or Foosball or snowmobiles or any of our other ridiculous so-called advantages. But to honor those wonderful hard-working, hard-living people, each Christmas, at midnight, we pass around the family Christmas stocking."

A trim-looking grandmother, wearing a pair of bobbing, spring-mounted plastic antlers on a headband, held up the treasured, threadbare, moss green velvet stocking, with patchy fur trim and some unraveling crewelwork spelling out half the word "XMAS." She shook the stocking and it jingled gently.

"And then everyone puts their name on a little slip of paper," said Linda Lou, "and then we dump all of the slips into the stocking and we shake it up real good, so there's no cheating and no tears. And then at the stroke of midnight, the youngest child reaches into the stocking and pulls out a name. Oh, I know it's just an old family hoo-ha, but it's really very exciting!"

"It gets me every time!" piped up a pretty teenager, who was wearing a Santa cap over her meticulously shampooed and conditioned blond hair, which cascaded to the hem of her frayed denim miniskirt, which had been embroidered with sassy female elves with huge, come-hither eyes and candy-cane striped bras and panties.

"But what happens to the person who gets picked?" I asked.

"Well . . ." said Big Paw Paw, with a grin, as if he were cuing a rousing musical number.

"We eat 'em!" said Linda Lou.

"We chase 'em around," said Big Paw Paw, "then they get pretty tired, and so we grab 'em and carve 'em right up, with cranberry sauce and those little-bitty jet-puffed marshmallows!"

"I hope it's not one of the toddlers again," groused a sour-puss

261

uncle, who was passing out sheets of Xeroxed lyrics to Christmas carols. "Whenever that happens, there's never enough to go 'round. This year, I hope it's one of you nice big-boned ladies!"

"Uncle Jerry! Stop!" scolded Linda Lou, as all of the women shrieked with affectionate laughter.

"You eat the person?" I asked, trying not to sound like some fussy, epicene restaurant critic, turning up his nose at cobbler or meatloaf.

"Oh, it's silly," said Linda Lou, "but come on, it's Christmas!"

"So how's about it?" Big Paw Paw asked me. "At least stick around for the stocking. But I gotta warn you, if you don't put your name in, you're gonna only get gristle!"

"Oh, I'd love to stay," I said, with bewitching sincerity, as I'm a master at always leaving a party on the early side, before anyone starts to sing, or get devoured. "But I've got a cab waiting."

"Awwww," said the entire room, with heartfelt disappointment, as all of the women began to fill plastic containers with cookies and puddings and fruitcake slices, so I'd have something for the road.

As I backed out of the house, spewing gratitude but building speed, I leapt into the cab and said, "Ludmila, step on it! Too much Christmas!" I tried to settle on some definitive opinion of the cozy homestead I'd just visited, and here's what I came up with: as I'd long suspected, when it comes to festive depravity, New Yorkers are rank amateurs compared to anyone from the Midwest, or any region without all-night newsstands and leash laws.

As our evening continued, Ludmila and I made many more stops. We visited a nomadic tribe, midway on their trek across the Kalahari. These people and their camels had no concept of Christmas, and their possessions were limited to a few tents and an iron cooking pot. To express my admiration for their anti-consumerist, uncorrupted lifestyle, I gave them a blender, with the special attachments for shredding ice and making carrot curls, a set of hot rollers, and a device I'd ordered from television which allows sweaters and out-of-season down comforters to be compacted and stored in see-through, vacuum-sealed polyethylene bags.

I was less pleased with a mob chieftain in Moscow who was gifting his money-laundering and heroin-dealing associates with prostitutes and strippers. Ludmila and I rescued all of these young ladies and enrolled them in junior colleges in New Jersey, where they could continue to dress like prostitutes and strippers while studying to earn a decent living as dental technicians. An Amish family in Pennsylvania refused to accept any Christmas gifts at all, insisting that their love of God was all they needed for a satisfying holiday. This struck me as both rude and high-handed, so without telling them, I listed each member of the family on one of those find-your-perfect-mate websites, and I had each person's profile say that they were into "prayer, working with my hands, long buggy rides, and anal."

By the time Ludmila pulled up in front of my apartment building it was almost dawn. "Git oudt," she said, as I calculated her tip. Since it was Christmas Eve, I went all the way up to thirty percent, which, given the duration of our travels, allowed Ludmila to bring her entire family over from Kiev and buy them their wildest dream, which was a home in the Bronx with a television in at least one of the bathrooms. "Tank ju very mooch," said Ludmila, pocketing the roll of bills, "andt merry Chreesmuss, andt pliss check de beck seat for jour belonkinks."

3.

As I walked down the hallway toward my apartment, I heard the strains of pop Christmas standards leaking from behind another door; there were a few final bars of "Frosty the Snowman," followed by my favorite song, "I Saw Mommy Kissing Santa Claus." I love this song because it sounds like the opening of a child's testimony at a murder trial. I knocked gently at the door, and found it was open.

"Hi there," said a woman who was sitting cross-legged on the floor in front of a coffee table, without looking at me.

"Yo," said her husband, seated across from her, as they continued playing a marathon game of Monopoly. Their apartment was far larger than mine, with many rooms, and it was furnished in what I can only call a warm, contemporary yet classic style of timeless elegance, or at least that was what the catalogue from which the couple had purchased virtually all of their belongings must have called it. The look was an amalgam of rich, dark-wood furniture set against Aegean blue walls with a chair rail in white enamel, with many sets of matching vases in groups of three, each holding a single, dramatic, whitewashed branch, and there were lots of nubby, muted-plaid chenille throws, tossed uselessly but decoratively across round, saddle-stitched leather ottomans that opened to provide storage for more chenille throws. There was a decent-sized Christmas tree displaying only Aegean blue and glossy white ornaments, for a mood that most textbooks refer to as "matchy-matchy," or "pure small-town decorator's powder room, and yes, he calls it the powder room."

"There's a carton of eggnog in the fridge," said the wife, still not looking up from her game, "and there's a big thing of Danish cookies on the kitchen island." As she rolled the dice, she told her husband, "I'm going to make you cry like a little baby girl right out of Harvard Business School."

"It's on, bitch," said the husband, who then, also without looking up, told me, "We also have beer and some hard stuff, help yourself, it's Christmas or whatever, if you're a Muslim or something, I don't know, in the cabinet next to the sink there's some cracked-wheat crackers."

I realized that I knew this couple, or had at least chatted with them by the elevator. She was Sara, who ran a hedge fund, and who was renowned for returning to work while giving birth. "Oh, come on," she'd told the obstetrician, "the head's out, give me my BlackBerry." Drake, the husband, was a top-tier litigator for a white-shoe law firm, where he'd represented a corporation that had imported Chinese-made toys coated with lead-based paint. In his tide-turning summation, Drake had held up something called Tommy the Towtruck, and he'd then momentously revealed the label on the underside, which read, in Chinese, "Do Not Lick."

As far as I could tell, Sara and Drake Morelle were the two most competitive people on earth. Even at the elevator, they'd either bet on how soon the car would reach our floor, or Drake, who participated in Ironman triathlons on five continents, would race down the stairs, to beat Sara to the lobby. Sara, for her part, was always either using her many wireless devices to do business, or to grill other mothers at her children's schools and top them in fund-raising and cupcake production, and to demand that various teachers be fired "for slowing our kids down with that nap-time bull." When I would say, "How are you?" to Sara, she'd jerk her head toward her husband and say, "Better than him," and when I'd say "Good morning" to Drake, he'd say, "Great day!" Once they'd even asked me to shut my eyes and choose which one of them radiated, as Sara put it, "a more powerful vibe," and when I picked their dog, Drake almost punched me, shouting, "That dog's a loser!"

As the Morelles continued to play cutthroat Christmas Eve Monopoly, I noticed that they'd replaced the game's small, multicolored play money with actual cash. Drake had also tossed his great-grandfather's gold pocket watch onto the board, and Sara had offered her wedding ring. As I sampled a Danish cookie, which I'd grabbed from one of those circular navy blue tins which can be found in the gourmet-treats aisle of any mid-range supermarket, and which are given as the most generic gifts at holiday open houses, I tiptoed through the apartment. Brant, the couple's twelve-year-old son, was in his bedroom, and at first I assumed that he'd been in some catastrophic accident involving his skateboard and a sanitation truck, because the boy seemed to be on life support. He was lying flat out on his bed, with a molded plastic headpiece covering his face, and he was tethered to a writhing mass of jumper cables, keyboards, and beeping video monitors. Then, from his profane grunting, I realized that he was actually playing one, if not more, of the most advanced virtual-reality video games. His arms and legs jerked spasmodically as he began to build a virtual city on a barren, unclaimed asteroid, where he would then construct a tractor beam which would draw lingerie models to his home base and detonate their boyfriends.

Returning to the apartment's living room, I opened a towering armoire made of burnished, coffee-colored wenge wood and inlaid with bands of ivory which had been compassionately harvested from elephants whose families had signed a release, by stomping on it. The armoire was packed, on every shelf, with board games, including the most vicious, irredeemable, inhuman evil ever devised: Scrabble.

I should explain. My parents, while loving, were not unlike the Morelles, in that their lives were ruled, and ultimately destroyed, by a relentless lust for competition. My earliest memory is from the second day of my life, when, as I lay cooing in my mother's arms, I heard my father say, "He looks like me," to which my mother instantly retorted, "Only younger." They were constantly at war, over the ideal amount of vermouth in a martini, over who was the most unqualified secretary of defense in American history, and over which parent would die first, and in more harrowing anguish. And that was just breakfast.

As I grew up, my parents' one-upsmanship only blossomed: for whatever nonsensical reasons, they were desperate to determine who was better at croquet, at badminton, and at ranking all of the state capitals, by population density. They needed to see who was better at dressing up for Halloween as a superhero's girlfriend—Dad won, for coordinating his two-tone Lois Lane purse with his two-tone spectator pumps—who was better at trimming our boxwood hedges into the profiles of their own parents—Mom won, for duplicating Nana's lazy eye—and who could hold their breath longer, and who could hold their breath longer underwater, and who could hold their breath longer underwater while the other one poked them with a harpoon.

While my parents' impossible and ever-rising standards may very well be reflected in my own astringent nature, I have always despised games. My parents played them all, upon waking, over the phone with each other while at work, long into the night, and during every vacation moment. They played children's games where the playing pieces were small plastic lollipops, they played chess until their fine marble chess pieces were worn to indistinguishable nubs, they played checkers and Parcheesi and Risk and Life and games based on unpopular, long-canceled TV shows that neither parent had ever watched. But Scrabble was their favorite, their clawing addiction, their ultimate madness, and they owned sets of every vintage and size, including not just the small, plastic, snap-shut version which could be played on airplanes, but an even tinier variation which fit into both my mother's compact and my father's wallet, and which could be played surreptitiously, under the table, at dinner parties. My mother had earrings made from the familiar, wooden, lettered tiles, and my father owned similar cuff links, and, when playing, they would both use these accessories to try and cheat.

It all came to a head when I was thirteen years old, on my parents' twentieth wedding anniversary. Of course they had competed to see who could outdo the other in presenting lavish, carefully chosen, impossible-to-find gifts, and of course they both wrote poems in which they tried to outdo the other in the depth, beauty, and pain of their love for the other. Finally, after the numbingly competitive toasts and cakes and kisses— don't ask—a commemorative, cut-crystal and sterling-silver Scrabble board appeared, with tiles hewn from thousands of those miniature Japanese bonsai trees, with the letters and tiny numerals hand-painted in gothic script by imprisoned Soviet dissidents. This board was my mother's gift to my father, so she pulled ahead. The first game went on for over two days, and my parents didn't eat, sleep, or drink, and their eyes grew red-socketed and feverish, but they didn't care. I begged them to stop, to call it an anniversary draw, but they didn't respond, and I doubt that they even heard my screams, as I insisted that using the word "emu" more than once was just too easy.

At five a.m. on the third morning, my mother smiled knowingly at my father and used her last remaining tiles to spell "loser," and thereby ended seven points ahead. My father then smiled even more diabolically and used his last tiles, with the help of the "e" in "loser," to spell "emerald," thereby winning the game by a single point. My mother stared at the board for the next two hours. She looked up. She said, "Congratulations. And by the way, what's a three-letter word, consisting of only vowels, which means 'corpse'?"

"A three-letter word, all vowels, which means 'corpse'?" my father repeated, and then he spent the next two hours in paralyzed silence, wracking his brain, and forcing his hand to resist lunging for any of the dictionaries, thesauruses, or encyclopedias that sat on a bookshelf just a few tantalizing feet away. At last he inhaled sharply, looked my mother right in the eye, and said, "You're bluffing. So go ahead, tell me—what could possibly be a three-letter word, with all vowels, meaning 'corpse'?"

My mother replied, in a tone I still want to believe was at least lightly brushed with regret, " 'You.' "

She then took the revolver which she'd hidden in the box for the board game of Barbie's Dream Date—Special Oscar Nite Edition, and shot my father right through the heart.

Later that afternoon, I helped my mother to bury my father out by our gazebo, and I explained to my younger sister that his death had been yet another tragic, Scrabble-related accident, just like all the ones we'd read about in our local newspaper. Late that night, I heard my mother scream, from her bedroom. I rushed to her side, and found her holding a small, velvet-covered box which she had just discovered under her pillow, with a note from my father reading, "Happy Anniversary—I love you more." She opened the box, which contained a priceless emerald ring which had once been owned by Queen Isabella of Spain, by Elizabeth Taylor, and, without Ms. Taylor's knowledge, by her envious maid. My mother slid the ring onto her finger and held out her hand at shoulder height, admiring the stone's facets and color. Then she looked to heaven, shaking her head ruefully. Still to heaven, and to my father, she whispered, "You win."

"I now own over half the board," Sara sneered to her husband. "Merry Christmas, pussy boy."

"You're not even gonna see me coming, pencil dick," Drake crowed, kissing the dice.

Reeling with trauma, I was about to leave this den of Yuletide horror, when I caught sight of something, which turned out to be someone, huddled against the wall midway between the Christmas tree and the roaring fire in the fireplace. I'd forgotten—the Morelles also had an eight-year-old daughter, Stella Morelle. Now, as at all other times, Stella was wearing a gray wool almost military-style jacket and matching skirt, along with black wool knee socks and sturdy cordovan walking shoes. This outfit looked like a uniform, only Stella had insisted on attending public school. She also had a helmet of prematurely silver hair, cut in a brisk Dutch bob, and the loveliest green eyes, the green of an Irish meadow in a retouched brochure. While Stella's face was both grave and adorable, everything else about her suggested the Slavic villainess of an early James Bond film; she looked like a honed steel blade might snap out of her shoe at any moment, and kick someone in the crotch. Right now, however, Stella was seated on a child-sized folding chair, and she was trying very hard, against difficult Christmas Eve odds, to finish reading her book, which was an especially long and depressing novel, even for Turgenev.

"Stella?" I asked. "Are you all right?"

"I'm fine," Stella said, in a voice which implied, "If you ask me what grade I'm in it will be the last time you ever use your larynx."

"Are you having a nice Christmas Eve?"

Stella looked off to one side and sighed, as her parents' Scrabble-related wrangling escalated, and the hum and clatter from her brother's video game became migraine-inducing.

"My parents kept asking me what I wanted for Christmas," Stella said, "and I kept telling them that they're very sweet to ask but I get all of my books from the library, so I really don't need anything. Although . . ."

271

"Yes?"

"There really is something I want more than anything else in the whole world. I should've written to Santa about it but I was embarrassed."

"So what do you want?"

"It's awful, I'll sound so ungrateful."

"But you don't want toys or dolls or electronics or anything else. You're the least spoiled child I've ever met."

"No. I still can't tell you."

"Stella, do you know who I am?"

"You're Mr. Vionnet, from down the hall."

"But who am I tonight?"

Stella put down her book and studied me. And while she tried to hide it, her green eyes began to sparkle.

"You're Mr. Christmas," she said.

"So, Stella, you can tell me. Because I won't tell anyone else, or leak it to the media or ever hold it against you."

"Really? Do you really want to know? You don't have to get it for me, you shouldn't, but it's just something I keep thinking about."

"Of course. So, Stella, what do you want more than anything else in the whole world?"

She bit her lip and then said shyly, without a shred of ego, "I want . . . I just want . . . I would like—some privacy."

I was struck by this request, because it was exactly what I'd asked for, in a detailed diary entry, when I was just Stella's age, some fifty-five years earlier. "I'll see what I can do," I told her.

"No!" she protested. "Please, I'm fine, I'm being a baby, please, just—have another cookie."

I almost patted Stella on the head, but I knew that this would be condescending. Instead, we solemnly shook hands and wished each other well.

4.

Back in my own quarters, as I slipped into my scarlet satin pajamas, which I wear only on Christmas Eve, I kept thinking about Stella. While she was self-reliant and held strong opinions, she was still a child, and children, more than anyone, need Mr. Christmas. Mr. Christmas is the best sort of therapist because, rather than doling out humdrum advice or barely effective prescriptions, he can provide efficient magic.

A few hours later, there was a brisk knock at my door. It was Stella, now in a gray homespun nightshirt and gray leather moccasins. Stella, it must be said, had the fashion sense of a warden.

"I'm sorry to ask, and I don't want to be a bother," she said, "but could you help me with something?"

When we got to the Morelle apartment, it was obvious what had happened. Sara, Drake, and Brant had all finally fallen asleep, slumped over their games. That was when the flames from the fireplace had licked out and caught the lowest branches of the Christmas tree on fire. As the tree was gradually consumed, the thick black smoke had crept through the apartment, filling the slumbering lungs of Stella's parents and brother, quickly annihilating them. They now lay quietly, and I dearly hoped that the family headstone would read, in granite: "Game Over."

Once the tree had been reduced to smoldering ashes, the fire had been sated. Because Stella had retired to her own small room, once a maid's quarters, and because she'd been reading by flashlight, with the sheet over her head, she'd been left unchoked and unharmed. The cotton balls in her ears, intended to eliminate her parents' ceaseless war cries, had also prevented Stella from hearing the fire's crackle, or her family's final moans, which must have been, in any event, indistinguishable from their usual sounds of game-playing triumph and dismay.

Stella and I placed her family's bodies on bedsheets and dragged them into the recycling room at the end of our shared hallway. After the holidays, our building's superintendent would bundle the bodies along with the accumulated newspapers, magazines, collapsed cardboard gift boxes, and discarded wrapping paper, and leave everything stacked neatly by the curb. This was New York City, where three dead bodies would only draw attention, and rebuke, if they were not properly disposed of in a manner which would make everyone in our building swell with civic pride and climate-change responsibility. Bodies are like Christmas trees; if you follow the rules and put them out on the correct day of the week, they'll be mulched and used to fertilize those wonderfully well-thought-out little parks along the Hudson.

"Stella," I said, once our task was complete and we sat on her late parents' boxy, mocha-toned sofa, with the Aegean blue and white houndstooth-check accent pillows. "What an interesting Christmas."

"It's very strange," said Stella, slowly munching the last of the Danish cookies.

"How are you feeling?"

"Well, I'm in mourning. That's one of the reasons why I always dress this way, because you never know what's going to happen. All of the other kids at school, they wear all those bright colors and they have all of those souvenir key chains and little stuffed animals hanging off their backpacks. And I always think, but what if something terrible happens? Their outfits will look so inappropriate."

"I'm sorry about your parents, and your brother."

"Thank you. I did love them so much. In an abstract way."

"Of course."

"And I'll miss them terribly—whenever I see any sort of game." We both shuddered, involuntarily.

"And now," said Stella, "I suppose . . . I'm an orphan." She said this with both an unreachable sadness and a dawning sense of wonder.

"Stella," I said, now sipping the tea which she'd brewed, "perhaps this isn't the time or place, but I've been thinking about something. You know, the heroes and heroines of almost all of the best novels are usually orphans."

"That's true," said Stella thoughtfully, "and I suppose, if I decide to become a writer or a poet, or even just an afternoon talk-show guest, this Christmas will give me an awful lot of credibility."

"Exactly."

"Are you an orphan?"

"Not completely," I said, and while I love my mother, I was a touch jealous of the dark glamour of Stella's new situation.

"I'm probably in shock," Stella said, as she squinted at the couch and, I suspect, began thinking about slipcovers.

"And, Stella," I said, as gently as possible, "I know that you have so much to think about and deal with right now, and I'd never presume to know what you're feeling. But let me just say this: life is never easy, and it's filled with change, for good and for otherwise. But if we're going to, at some point in the far, far distant future, if we were to even think about listing the more positive aspects of your . . . current Christmas, we could consider the following—you still have the best dog in the world."

At this point Stella's beloved collie, Ivan, leapt up and began nuzzling Stella's knees. Stella had adopted Ivan from a local shelter and had named him, all on her own. Her parents, once they'd decided that Ivan wasn't dog-show caliber, had barely noticed him.

"Ivan is the best," said Stella, as the dog licked her face, "and I think he didn't suffocate because of all his fur. It was like a gas mask." Ivan was indeed long-haired and, like all collies, he had the shiniest, most trusting eyes and the most guileless, devoted expression. Collies aren't the brightest dogs, but they're the most heartbreakingly eager and upbeat, as if they've undergone the cheeriest sort of lobotomies. A collie is here to help.

"So you have Ivan," I continued, "and, well, despite all of this unfathomable tragedy—you do now have your own three-bedroom apartment. In a doorman building."

As Stella stroked Ivan's long head, she looked around her home and began thinking about changes, of course, and about the wholesale elimination of the various games, perhaps with a hatchet. But she was also thinking, tentatively, that, aside from the human factor, there really wasn't any significant smoke damage.

"If you need anything," I said, politely taking my leave, "just knock."

A few hours after I'd returned to my apartment, there was a tap at my door. It was Stella, now in her uniform, holding a gray shoe box; Stella ordered her footwear from a Scottish company which supplied mostly Bavarian tour guides and bird watchers.

"This is for you," said Stella, and as I opened the box, I didn't find shoes, but a length of yellowed human bone, mounted on a tarnished gold-filigree stand. It was a handsome item.

"It's a holy relic," Stella explained. "It's the thighbone, the femur, of Saint Nicholas. I found it on eBay, and I wasn't sure what to do with it. But I want you to have it, because it reminds me of you."

I marveled at the femur, and at Stella's uncanny knack for gift giving.

Good manners and a memorably perverse imagination are such a rare combination, particularly in someone so young. Stella and I smiled at each other, but with a certain reserve, because we were both New Yorkers, and neighbors, and that meant we'd rather die than impose on one another, but that we'd always be available to gossip viciously about anyone else who lived in the building, especially the people we knew nothing about. As Stella returned to her own apartment, I dissected my Christmas labors. I'd tried, but I wasn't sure if I'd reorganized the holiday, on any meaningful worldwide level. But still, thanks to the moon and the Kansas snow and the poor ventilation in the Morelles' apartment, a true Christmas miracle had occurred: I was no longer alone.

At the Chelsea Hotel

1.

I was in college, and, on an errand, I passed by the fabric storage room on the second floor of the graduate drama school. From inside this room I heard someone say, "On the French brocade!" and then fart loudly. A few seconds later I heard someone else announce, "On that hideous blue corduroy!" followed by another seismic fart. Then I heard a distinctly southern voice declare, "I don't care what anyone says, on that repulsive lime green polyester!" punctuated by an even more sustained and trumpeting fart. These voices and these farts, it seemed, were critiquing the various bolts of fabric. I was intrigued.

The last voice belonged to an aspiring costume designer named William Ivey Long, and I'm not sure when we were formally introduced, but later that year he hired me to be his assistant at the Summer Cabaret, where I was also the janitor and snack-bar waiter. The Cabaret troupe performed a different full-length play every week, and William, using more imagination than cash, had to come up with hundreds of costumes. This is why I was no help at all:

1. Early in July, William handed me the delicate silk belt of a priceless vintage evening gown, and asked me to shorten it by one inch. I destroyed the whole dress.

2. William asked me to cut twenty yards of imported chintz into twelve-inch-wide strips. I sliced everything in the wrong direction, and the fabric could then only be used to stuff pillows for my apartment.

3. William worked very hard to reupholster a valuable Victorian sofa, for his own apartment. He then asked me to help him carry the finished sofa for three blocks, from the costume shop to his home. To this day no one's absolutely sure what really happened, but someone dropped his end in the middle of High Street, and the sofa split in two, with one chunk rolling into the gutter while the other half was hit by a car. William stared at me as if I'd slaughtered his child, although, as he told me later, "No, I'm sorry, but what you did was much worse. The world has plenty of babies, but that sofa was an *antique*." William stopped speaking to me for three days, until I pretended to be his elderly housekeeper, following him everywhere with a broom and asking him when I might polish the silver and if I should use bleach to

remove the skid marks from his undershorts—"And Mister Long," I clucked, "with the way you been fartin', it ain't gonna be easy." Finally he laughed, and our friendship truly began.

About William's name: I usually hate people who use three names, as in Gary Marc Bluner or Winston Marley Coates. But William was from North Carolina, he was William Ivey Long III, and as he put it, "William Long sounds like an insurance salesman, and I'm just not a Bill Long, can you imagine?" We agreed that Bill Long was not a bad name for a porn star, and William later thought about opening a costume shop with another designer named Zack Brown, so that their business could be called Long and Brown. People who knew William as a child can, and do, comfortably call him Billy, but William Ivey Long seemed just right, because it didn't sound like anyone else.

William also looked like no one else: he had a mop of curly blond hair, flushed cheeks, and bee-stung lips, and his eyes shone from behind round, wire-rimmed glasses. He was always on a diet, and once, when I tried to sketch him on a cocktail napkin, he advised, "Just use a lot of circles." He most resembled a happily demented cherub, although, years later, we discovered that he also looked exactly like an oil portrait of the seventy-ish, distinguished female detective novelist Dorothy Leigh Sayers. Because he was a costume designer, strangers expected William to dress flamboyantly, but he refused, limiting his wardrobe to jeans, khakis, heavily starched white dress shirts, rep ties, and navy blazers. "It's my uniform," he explained.

"My personality is already far too colorful, and I don't need to compete with my work."

William could burst breathlessly into a room, hurling sketches and swatches and God knows what else from the twin L.L. Bean canvas tote bags that never left his sides, or he could sit cross-legged on the carpet, solemnly absorbed in Proust or a coffee-table book on the Great Homes of Ireland. He'd found a plaster bust of a woman with a strong face and a forties hairdo, on a department-store loading dock, and he'd brought her home and put her on his mantel. "Her name is Sally Windsor," he told me, "and she's a simple Englishwoman who takes in sewing while her husband, Lance, is away at the war." He paused for a moment, then decided, "I *am* Sally Windsor."

After graduating a year ahead of me, William moved to New York and into the Chelsea Hotel. As soon as I could, I took the train down for a visit. The Chelsea is a grand, battered, red-brick Victorian pile on Twenty-third Street, with a faltering neon sign and rows of ornate balconies worked with nodding, cast-iron sunflowers. Built in 1883, it's a lurid bohemian landmark, and while the Chelsea takes overnight guests, many people stay for years, and it's been home to everyone from Walt Whitman to Arthur Miller to the Rolling Stones.

The lobby was filled with pop and abstract paintings, along with tilting mobiles and tortured statuary, because some of the hotel's resident artists would exchange their work for rent. The night I got there, the lobby was also packed with a shouting, shoving mob of reporters and photographers, and I could barely push my way through. Then the elevator doors opened, and a gurney carrying the shrouded body of Nancy Spungen, the heroin-addicted girlfriend of punk idol Sid Vicious, was wheeled out, because Nancy had just been stabbed to death on an upper floor. Standing on tiptoe, I glimpsed ragged, bleached-blond hair and a pale knobby hand hanging out from beneath a sheet. This was all very tragic and, of course, thrilling.

William would be late, so he'd left a key for me at the front desk. His fourth-floor, one-bedroom apartment was high-ceilinged, with a marble fireplace, pitted parquet floors, and the largest, most aggressive cockroaches I'd ever seen; they were like skittering Matchbox cars. The apartment faced Twenty-third Street and shared a balcony with whoever lived in the apartment next door. As I took a seat, the balcony's French doors opened and a naked nineteen-year-old boy with self-inflicted, rust-colored hair appeared. He stared at me for almost a minute, with a look of intense dislocation, as if he'd crash-landed on the wrong planet, and then he left the same way he'd come in, without saying a word. As I settled into one of the plump armchairs that William had rescued from the street and slipcovered in a gardenia print, the French doors reopened, and the boy came back in, now wearing only a pair of completely see-through parachute nylon hot pants, with a large zipper that ran back to front.

"Um, like, I am really sorry," the boy said. "But, like, I din't wantcha to think that I was, like, the kinda person who walked around naked." This was such a heartfelt introduction that I tried to stop looking at the boy's penis, although, thanks to his transparent shorts, he now seemed even more naked.

"I'm like, Michael, and William said I could come over and borrow a beer. I'm waitin' for this dude, he's one of my regulars, he's, like, on the Board of Directors of Time-Life."

Michael, William later explained, was a hustler who identified all of his clients as being on the Board of Directors of Time-Life. He wasn't deliberately lying, because Michael's drug use made reality a flexible concept. Over time, William and I would wait out on the balcony and watch as Michael's many sugar daddies left their cabs and limos. They were almost always silver-haired and well-dressed, so it seemed possible that Michael was servicing the *entire* Board of Directors of Time-Life. Michael was also constantly changing his last name and no one could keep up, so for convenience William started calling him Michael Neighbor.

William had chosen the Chelsea because his idol, Charles James, had been living in a suite on a higher floor for decades. Mr. James, as William reverently referred to him, was a mad genius. He'd been a visionary couturier since the 1930s, and if you ever want to know what that means, just check out a double-page spread in the December 1948 issue of *Vogue*. In this photo, twelve models all wear gaspingly beautiful, draped and cantilevered gowns. The dresses are lunatic and timeless, and the women look like some goddessy tribunal on Mount Olympus. Such impossible perfection could never be mass-produced, and few women could afford the cost, or the multiple fittings, required. Every time Mr. James tried for a commercial career, he'd be acclaimed, and then he'd get frustrated by his backers' need for a saleable product, and then he'd quit in a rage and be institutionalized. He now lived on private commissions, and Anjelica Huston or Bianca Jagger were always stopping by for the eighteenth adjustment to the pilgrim collar of a majestically simple ivory silk blouse.

Mr. James himself was under five feet tall, and his remaining hair was dyed with a black shoe polish that dripped onto his forehead. I first met Mr. James a few weeks later, in the elevator at the Chelsea, where he was walking Sputnik, his small, arthritic, incontinent dog. Mr. James eyeballed me and then, in a shaky but irrefutable tone, decreed, "Your nose is *enormous*. You must cut your hair and be proud of your nose! You must tell the world, *look* at my nose! *Behold!*" At that time I had shoulder-length hair that made me look like an unkempt Jewish pony, so I wisely listened to Mr. James and the very next day, I got myself a nice short haircut.

Heroin, hustlers, and hairstyling tips from an inspired dwarf; plus, as William gleefully added, "There's a deli on the corner!"

2.

A few months later, William was depressed. I had graduated and was now living in the West Village, and he called me up: "I can't pay my rent, no one wants to hire me, and I'm getting as fat as a pig. If I jump off the roof of the Chelsea, will I die?"

"No, it's only eight stories, so you'll probably just be crippled for life. And if you keep whining, no one will want to push your wheelchair."

"Well, what if I spray Raid right into my mouth and then jump off the roof, then will I die?"

"No, then you'll be crippled for life and you'll have no esophagus, and because you brought it on yourself, no one will want to liquefy a hamburger in the blender and squeeze it into your feeding tube."

"Fine, well, what if I cut my throat with a razor, jump off the roof, and when I hit the street a truck runs over me, then will I die?"

"Worth a shot."

William's suicidal tendencies were matched by his highly original hypochondria, and late one night I got a tearful call: "Rudnick, I don't know what to do! I was walking down Twenty-third Street and my colon fell out!"

"Your colon fell out? Onto the street? Like a carburetor?"

"Yes! I was walking down the street and I could feel some-thing moving in my pants! Something dropping! And when I got home, I looked in my boxer shorts, and there were all these strange pieces of skin! It was my colon! What should I do?"

"Do you have pinking shears?"

"Yes . . ."

"Do you have a needle and thread?"

"Of course!"

"Do you have any light-colored fabric, maybe just a muslin?"

"I think so . . ."

"Do you have a pattern for a new colon?"

William slammed down the phone, but he called me back twenty seconds later. "All right, I get it. All I'm doing is whin-ing and complaining. I have no money, I have no career, I have no life, boo hoo hoo, poor little William. Well, there's only one thing I can do."

"Yeah?"

"I need to have a party."

William decided to cheer himself up by cheering everyone

up. He scheduled his party for Valentine's Day, and the hand-written pink-and-gold invitations promised "A Night of Liberty and Love," because the evening was in honor of two of William's favorite historical figures, Abraham Lincoln and Cupid. "Lincoln freed the slaves," William told me, "and then Cupid made them fall in love." "Cool," said Michael Neighbor, "can I come?" "Of course," William replied, "and I need your help."

For the week before the party, William rented an extra room down the hall, to store all of his furniture. He then called in every possible favor, and recruited an army of florists, scenic artists, carpenters, and unskilled labor, like me. First we repainted his entire apartment a pale, flattering pink—"Because this is New York in February," William explained, "so people need all the help they can get." Then several hundred strands of white Christmas twinkle lights were dipped in pink glaze, and William teetered atop a high ladder, stapling the lights in snaking patterns across the ceiling. "Oh no!" he wailed, trying to reach a far corner, "My arm's too short to box with God!" This last phrase was the title of a popular, touring gospel musical, and I had once seen a poster for a similar show, which listed "Executive Producer—Jesus Christ."

After the lights were up, we inflated hundreds of pink helium balloons, which flew to the ceiling and filtered the glow. Every balloon trailed yards of golden ribbon, with each ribbon knotted at the opposite end with a pink carnation dangling in midair. The floor was drenched with glossy white enamel, and a professional portraitist created a mural over the fireplace, with the profiles of Lincoln and Cupid, gazing longingly into each other's eyes. The room looked like an enchanted rain forest, or the inside of a priceless Fabergé egg, as dreamt by a feverish twelve-year-old girl.

On the night of the party, William clustered hundreds more balloons on his balcony, and dumped pounds of glitter marking a path from the street, up four flights of stairs, and down the hall to his apartment. He'd invited over 300 people, including most of the hotel's residents, especially Neon Leon, who lived across the hall. "I'm not quite sure what Neon Leon does, or why he's called Neon Leon," William said, "but he's very nice, even if he likes to set his apartment on fire almost every day. So if we invite him, maybe he'll just let the fire wait until the next day." William wasn't kidding, as the hall would frequently fill with smoke, and William would just stuff wet towels under his own door, wait for the fire trucks, and comment, "Neon Leon. I think he just smokes things and falls asleep."

Because the party was a celebration of romance, William asked Michael Neighbor to recommend a male prostitute whose favors could be raffled off at midnight. A good-looking, sandy-haired guy arrived, and William gave him a tight red T-shirt that said "Mr. Valentine" across the chest. Mr. Valentine then circulated affably as the apartment filled to bursting, because everyone William invited had shown up, and they'd brought friends. There was pink champagne, heart-shaped sugar cookies, and hors d'oeuvres laid out in the shape of Lincoln's stovepipe hat. There was a shoe box on the mantel that had been découpaged with doilies and construction-paper hearts, and beside it was a ribbed glass tray stacked with children's dime-store valentines. If guests wanted to bid for Mr. Valentine, they had to write their names on one of the cards, and then tuck it into a slot in the shoe box. William had made sure that Mr. Valentine was equally able to pleasure men and women, and while all sorts of people submitted their cards, one actress in particular bid at least fifty times.

Like any near-virginal, sheltered boy from the suburbs, I was fascinated by prostitutes. It was less about sex than sheer confidence, because imagine being so hot that people would pay you. This seemed like a far greater accomplishment than, say, a merit badge in forestry or decent SAT scores. I was far too intimidated, and way too broke, to ever hire a prostitute; I'd be more likely to ask for their autograph. Over my years in New York, I've met many prostitutes, and I've stopped generalizing, because as with anyone in a service profession, hookers vary. There was a tough call girl who was being kept by three rich men, and she seemed damaged and defiant. There was a sunny guy from Arkansas, who only complained about having to load up on beer before visiting a casting director who liked to be peed on. And there was Michael Neighbor, for whom hustling was a natural fit, because he was too easily distracted to keep a day job; he loved attention, and he spent most of his earnings on high-tech video games and gadgets.

Many of the guests at William's party had gone to the Yale School of Drama, and as Mr. Valentine socialized, he noticed a recently graduated playwright and asked, "Ed?" Peering through the throng, Ed replied, "Dan?"

"Is that Dan?" asked a woman who'd graduated two years back, with her degree in theater administration. "Becky! You look fabulous!" declared Mr. Valentine. It soon became evident that almost half the party knew Mr. Valentine, since he'd graduated three years earlier, from the directing program.

"I haven't seen you in forever!" exclaimed a woman who was currently an assistant dramaturg at a regional theater. "What have you been doing?"

"I'm Mr. Valentine!" said Dan, without a trace of embarrassment. "Do you know how hard it is to break into directing? You can't get a job until someone can come and see a show you did, and you can't get a show without a previous credit. It sucks!"

Most of the guests were pretty much unemployed, so everyone hugged Dan and congratulated him, for at least being able to take home a tax-free paycheck. The music blasted, everyone danced, all of the designers paid homage to Mr. James, and Mr. Valentine eventually went home with another aspiring director. I suspect that while they probably had sex, they really got off on bitching about how tough it was to land even an assistant directing gig.

"So, do you feel better?" I asked William, as we collapsed at six a.m., onto his furniture in the room down the hall.

"So much better," he said. "But do you think people had a good time?"

"Fuck, yeah!" said Michael Neighbor. "Your party was hot! Shit, I'm goin' to drama school!"

3.

William at last began to get design work Off-Broadway—specifically, on a show called *Earthworms*, which was a lacerating attack on the playwright's Catholic boyhood. It was about to star a very young Richard Gere, who left during rehearsals when he was cast in a movie. William was impressed by Gere's sullen good looks, but more by the fact that, even as a union-minimum performer, Gere had his jeans custom made. "So right there I knew he was going to be a big star," William predicted.

A scene called for two vicious nuns to carry a twelve-year-old boy across the stage, slung from a rail by his bound wrists and ankles, so William needed to find two nuns' habits. To save money, he phoned a Brooklyn convent and told them that Playwrights Horizons was doing a revival of *The Sound of Music*. The nuns were naturally delighted, and soon two complimentary habits were lying across William's bed at the Chelsea.

We looked at the habits. We did what we had to do. We put them on. I defy anyone, male or female, Jew or Gentile, gay or straight, if left alone with a nun's habit, not to try it on. And model it.

The body-skimming, summer-weight, slimmingly black wool habit was shockingly sensual. The slits at the hips weren't pockets, but went right through to the skin. The wimple was more confining, first the snug white under-bonnet and then the heavy black veil, but soon William and I were swirling around his two rooms.

Somehow we became convinced that we had sailed far beyond drag. We were *nuns*. To test this conviction, we left the apartment. We took small, swift steps, like devout geishas. We kept our chins down, humbly. As we moved through the lobby, there was a wild burst of cheering and applause.

"Did everyone clap because they'd never seen nuns at the

Chelsea Hotel?" William wondered, once we were out on the street.

"They were probably clapping because they'd never seen nuns with five-o'clock shadow and Adam's apples," I said.

"Well, I'm a *nun*," William insisted, as he shook the coffee can he'd brought along at passersby. We'd already dropped some coins into the can, to make some noise and encourage donations. "Won't you help?" William asked a young mom who was pushing her infant in a stroller and clutching her four-year-old's hand. "We're building a new convent," William told her, "in—Ohio."

"We need hymnals," I added.

"All of our old hymnals are falling to pieces."

"It's because we can't stop praying. It's like a drug."

"Don't talk to them," the woman warned her toddlers, yanking them away.

"Selfish," William muttered. "I hope that God makes her children into serial killers. With thick ankles. With piano legs."

"You need to be more spiritual," I told him as we approached a businessman getting out of a cab.

"It's for the children," William begged the man, shaking his coffee can. "The children who can't walk."

"The lazy children," I added.

"What *are* you?" the man asked, aghast.

"Michael Neighbor is on the fourth floor," William said.

"Thank you," the businessman replied, scurrying into the Chelsea.

"He's going to hell," I decided.

"Unless he buys Michael Neighbor a new Walkman."

We weren't making any money, so we walked into a nearby

apartment building lobby, where we sang "Climb Ev'ry Mountain."

"Welcome, brothers and sisters," William began, to the doorman and the guy behind the desk and the tenants waiting for the elevator. "We are the Little Sisters ... the Little Sisters ..."

"We are the Little Sisters of The Swollen Colon," I declared, "and when was the last time any of you went to church? Or said a novena? Or enjoyed a truly cleansing bowel movement?"

"Amen, Sister!" cried William.

"This city is filled with evil, and false emotion, and bad performance art!"

"Sing it, Sister!"

"In fact, this city has become so clogged with sin, so jammed with heathen heartache, so blocked with wrongdoing, on every street corner, and in every downtown apartment building lobby with sad flocked wallpaper, this city has become so backlogged with bile, that poor Sister Chloe Hypatia, the nun standing right beside me now, Sister Chloe Hypatia has not experienced a successful bowel movement in over two long years!"

"It's true," Sister Chloe Hypatia confessed, "but it's God's will!"

"Can you imagine what that feels like? Chloe Hypatia spends her days kneeling and scrubbing and teaching oral hygiene at St. Bartholomew's, and yet at any second she knows that she just might explode, and that parts of her body, and not the pretty parts, those body parts might maim or injure or even murder hundreds of innocent people within a five-block radius!"

"I'm a powder keg!"

"So if you won't give, if you won't dig deep, if you don't cry out, 'Yes Jesus, I want Sister Chloe Hypatia to find release, in an empty, tiled chamber!' well then, we cannot be responsible! It's up to you!"

"I feel it! It's coming! I can't stop it!"

"Run, everyone! Run for your lives! Run and pray!"

With that, we hiked up our skirts and ran for home, bursting through the front doors of the Chelsea, where we smacked right into Mr. James, who was taking Sputnik out for a stroll. Mr. James glanced at our habits and then finally asked, in a slightly bored tone, "Chanel?"

Crossing ourselves, we climbed four flights and didn't stop until we were back in William's apartment, behind a locked door, panting and mortified.

"Oh, Rudnick," William gasped, "are we going to hell?"

"Excuse me, do you think this is the only reason?"

I did wonder if we'd actually blasphemed, by running around in borrowed habits. My religious convictions were shaky, but I was always superstitious.

"But what if we get to the Pearly Gates," William asked, "and what if Saint Peter is there, waving a Polaroid and asking, 'Were you those horrible, ugly, constipated nuns?' What will we say?"

We stared at each other. William's gold, wire-rimmed glasses and his cherubic features lent him at least a slightly pious, kindly aura. I looked in the mirror over the mantel and all I saw was nose. I also saw that Michael Neighbor had appeared at the French doors.

"Yes, my son?" William asked him. "Shall we pray for you?"

"Nah," said Michael, barely noticing our outfits, "I got a headache. Do you got, like, a Motrin or something?"

"Come here, my child," William told Michael. "Don't be afraid."

"What are you gonna do?" Michael asked, backing away.

Standing, William laid his palm on Michael's forehead. Shoving hard, he shouted, "Demon, be gone!"

"Whoa," said Michael, rubbing his head and feeling better. "*Whoa.*"

4.

I learned the history of William's family mostly from his mother's letters. Once a month a fat, typewritten parcel would arrive at the Chelsea. Sometimes William would get the original of these jumbo newsletters, and sometimes a Xerox copy. Getting the original was somehow more special; William's mother was a Freudian tease.

As an introduction to these letters, William pulled out a back issue of *National Geographic* from the early 1960s, with a travelogue cover story called something like "Carolina Wonderland" or "Welcome to the Sunshine." He flipped to a full-color photo of his family, with his youthful parents serving lemonade to their towheaded kids, all gathered, sitcom style, around a redwood picnic table. "Look at us," William said. "Don't we look normal? I swear, you'd never know."

William's parents were schoolteachers, but they devoted much of their year to *The Lost Colony*, an outdoor North Carolina pageant-drama. These pageant-dramas were popular through-out the region, offering either historical recreations or Bible stories; the *National Geographic* spread had included photos of actors in a Last Supper scene, with their faces painted with psychedelic colors and thick black lines, to mimic stained glass. *The Lost Colony* ran from May through October at a roughhewn amphitheater, and it told the stories of Columbus, the first Thanksgiving, the founding of the earliest Virginia Colony, and the birth of Virginia Dare, "the first white child born in the New World." "Actually, they've changed that 'white child' business," William assured me. "People are so sensitive." The pageant included a massed choir, in which William's sister sang, a comic, man-hungry Native American squaw named Agona, and tribal dances performed by local college boys, who played Native Americans by wearing loincloths and the thick, brown body makeup called Texas Dirt. The performance ended with an epilogue set in the Present Day, where a happy American family, the dad in a suit and the mom in a shirtwaist, stride into the bright Carolina future.

William had been raised at the pageant, where his father was the long-time technical director and his mother acted; William handed me an elaborate souvenir program with a photo-portrait of his mom in her curled, plasma red wig, whiteface, stiff lace ruff, and garage-size, bejeweled gown, as Queen Elizabeth I. "That's Mary Wood," he said, using her maiden name.

"So your mom walked around dressed as Queen Elizabeth?" I asked.

"Of course, and she sent Sir Walter Raleigh to oversee the settlements."

"Wasn't that weird for you, as a child?"

"You don't understand. My mother *is* Queen Elizabeth."

While in grade school, William had painted scenery and mended costumes, "And I loved it, it was just where I wanted to be. Until one day, I must've been eight years old, I found this old farthingale, it was a sort of Jacobean hoopskirt, in the costume shop. And I put it on, and I wore it everywhere. But then my mother saw me, in my farthingale, and she burned it."

"That's the meaning of life," I concluded. "You fall in love, and then they burn your farthingale."

As an adult, maybe because of the farthingale incident, William had been determined to leave the theater behind. "Oh, yes," he explained, "I even got engaged."

"To whom? To what?"

"To a very sweet young lady who thought that I was very nice and who just wanted to be married to someone."

"Did you have sex?"

"Of course, and it was just fine, because I just fantasized about these four brothers whom I would watch playing touch football on the beach, and I'm sure that she was probably thinking about the exact same thing."

"And what happened?"

"Well, I had it all planned, and I was in graduate school at Chapel Hill, studying Renaissance art history and architecture, and I was going to get married and have children and be this nice small-town college professor, and be all decent and dignified. And I was just three credits short of my doctorate, but that summer I went to Europe, and I saw all of the most beautiful paintings and tapestries and crown jewels, and I thought, I don't

297

want to just look at beautiful things. I want to somehow—create them. I want to help tell stories and meet amazing people and put on shows and just—see what happens. And finally I just stood on a mountaintop and I said to myself, 'William, you are not a college professor, and if you marry that woman you are going to make both of your lives miserable.' And so I applied to the Drama School and I broke off my engagement and I said, I am just a big ol' silly queer fool, and so be it!"

William was the most original, talented, and generous person I'd ever met, so I was stunned to hear that he'd ever doubted himself. "But, William," I asked, "you have such a major personality. Didn't you always know that? Didn't that farthingale tell you anything?"

"Wait," he cautioned, picking up one of his mother's lengthy, single-spaced letters. "Listen."

"Dear Ones," the letter began. "It's April and everything is starting to bud and flower, and our hydrangeas are especially lovely this year. Who among us doesn't appreciate a happy hydrangea?"

"I love 'em," I said.

"Hi, drangea," William agreed, and then he continued reading aloud. "Last Thursday after work your sister and I went to visit Miss Iolanthe, Phyllis Mandermint, and poor, brain-damaged Lucretia Stillman. Ever since the accident, Lucretia doesn't seem to recognize anyone, or to eat anything except rice. She complimented my silver necklace, and asked if I might introduce her to Fidel Castro. She looks well and her health is good, but all I could think was, you know, perhaps sometimes a coma is a blessing."

William skipped ahead, to a section about his dad. "Your father is doing just fine, and the doctor says that his ankle has completely healed, and I said, well, that's good news, but he had no business trying to play basketball with a team of college boys. But to show the boys that there were no hard feelings, your father invited the whole team over for lunch again last Saturday, and he took Bobby Bantry into Raleigh to buy him some new sneakers and a warm-up jacket. Well, as to your father, I will only say this: let him dream his dreams."

"Oh my God, William, is your father gay?"

"Of course."

"But haven't your parents been married for, like, forty years?"

"Yes, but many Southern men, they get married, and then they entertain other gentlemen. It's a tradition."

"But that's nuts."

"Only if you try and play basketball with Bobby Bantry."

"But what does your mother think?"

"You heard, she lets him dream his dreams. She's Southern. So she ignores everything that she doesn't care for, and then moves on. And I don't think she likes sex all that much, and I do at least partially agree with her. I think that's it more important to help people and to create a lovely home."

"Okay, which one is more insane—your mother, your father, or you?"

"You Yankees don't understand anything. Now, you're Jewish, and I respect that, I wish I was Jewish, because then I'd be much smarter, but I'd never have a Queen Anne sideboard or a chifferobe."

"What's a chifferobe?"

"Oh, so you don't know everything. Are you sure you're Jewish?"

William's parents became like fictional creations, like superheroes whose adventures were delivered in monthly installments. William's father produced and directed his local community theater production of *Equus*, a play in which a naked outcast blinds six horses, snorting beasts who were mimed by shirtless actors, or, as William's dad called them, "strapping young fellows." Mary Wood began appearing on her own local cable TV show, a weekly half-hour called *Mary Long's Yesteryears*, in which she toured plantations, formal gardens, and lovingly tended cemeteries filled with the Civil War dead. William got a videotape of a season's worth of shows, and my favorite had Mary Wood, in a peach shantung suit, holding a microphone as she stood in front of a particularly well-kept, colonnaded estate, planted with weeping willows and wisteria. "And just back here are the old slave cabins, which have been completely restored," Mary Wood told her audience, with a warm, inviting smile. "Aren't they lovely?"

Finally, worlds collided when William's parents decided to fly up to Manhattan to find out just what William was doing with his life. William was determined to show them that he was doing just fine, so he planned a tea party, and invited Mr. James, because he was older and accomplished; me, because I'd promised to behave; and Claire Mallory North. William and I had both met Claire at Yale, and she was William's ideal. Claire was radiantly blond, her tousled pageboy always held in check by either a tortoiseshell headband or tortoiseshell combs. She had a sophisticated prettiness, with cornflower blue eyes, the poreless complexion of a Fragonard milkmaid, and a slightly husky, amused speaking voice. Claire's father was an Ivy League attorney who'd divorced her mother and become a cocktail pianist, and Claire was never quite sure if she approved. Claire was both elegant and accepting; at school, she'd refused to wear jeans, but she was happy to hang out at the Chelsea.

"I can't wait to meet your parents," Claire told William, as she perched on the eight-foot-long psychiatrist's couch William had found at the Goodwill and placed in front of his French doors.

"But, everyone, just remember," William cautioned us, "they haven't been to New York in years, and we want them to think that everything's just fine."

"And where are they from?" Mr. James tried to remember. "Georgia? One of the Dakotas? Will they wear shoes?"

"Oh my God . . ." said William as the doorbell rang.

"We're going to love them and we're all going to make an effort and everything will be splendid," said Claire.

"Why are you looking at me?" I asked her. Claire and I got along just fine, if a little warily. I thought she was wry and dauntingly well-bred, and she had once told William that I might be the devil. I wasn't sure if this was because I was gay or Jewish or from New Jersey, but I was flattered. Claire was genuinely spiritual, about both her single strand of graduated pearls and her soul. She'd once told William and me that she intended to become "the first saint on the Best Dressed list," and she was well on her way.

"Well, hello, everyone!" said Mary Wood, as William led her into the room. "Billy, I hope you haven't made a fuss!"

"I still don't get it," said William's father, who was also named William but who was called Bill or Mr. Long. "This is supposed to be a hotel, but people live here, like squatters. Is it some kind of flophouse?"

Mary Wood looked like a human-size, delicately groomed, infinitely gracious mouse. Her thin, pale brown hair was fluffed into a becoming cloud, and she squinted appreciatively through pinkish eyeglass frames. Mr. Long was tall, stooped, and ornery, a suspicious Ichabod in math-major perma-press short sleeves.

"How was your flight?" asked Claire, after the introductory hugs and handshakes had been exchanged.

"Oh, it was just perfect," said Mary Wood.

"If you like sitting jammed up against God knows what sort of people," added Mr. Long, "and, Billy, who the hell are those characters in the lobby, with the purple hair and the black T-shirts and the combat boots? Are they moon men?"

"They're my neighbors," said William, evenly. "This is Manhattan."

"The Chelsea is completely—simpatico," said Mr. James, "for the artistic temperament. Although I do not care for all of this drug-taking. Except perhaps opium."

"Isn't that grand?" said Mary Wood. "Now, Mr. James, Billy has told us so much about you, and he's sent us photos and newspaper clippings. You're the most wonderful designer."

"Tell that to Mr. Halston," Mr. James harrumphed.

"Halston, the designer?" asked Mary Wood.

"Halston the *thief*," spat Mr. James, "Halston the *criminal*." Halston was at that time a hugely successful American designer, and Mr. James felt, and not without cause, that many of Halston's designs had been based on his own, from decades earlier. "He's making millions!" Mr. James insisted. "And he's stolen my work!"

"That's just what I'm saying," agreed Mr. Long, "I think this building is in a high-crime area. We read about it all the time, we see it on the news. People in New York getting mugged, people getting shot, probably right on this block. Is there prostitution?"

"On this block?" I asked. "Or this floor?"

"Where are you staying?" asked Claire, for a change of subject.

"We're at the Marriott," said Mary Wood. "It's, well . . . it's a Marriott. So I'm sure they know what they're doing."

"And they're charging an arm and a leg," said Mr. Long. "Billy, this city costs a goddamn fortune, and it's a hellhole. How are you going to stay here? Are you making a living?"

"William is making the most wonderful life for himself," insisted Claire. "You must be so proud of him."

"And he's getting more and more work," I chimed in. "He just did a play with all of these nuns."

"Rudnick," said William, sweetly but sharply.

"Nuns," said Mary Wood. "Billy, do you remember Sharon Bastkerry? Her cousin Florene became a nun. Some people said it was because of her having that one normal arm and that one tiny arm, but I'm sure she's just a very good person."

"It's all about tailoring," said Mr. James. "Look at the Duchess of Windsor."

"So, Mr. James," said Mr. Long, "tell me the truth. Your frank opinion. Is Billy throwing his life right down the goddamn toilet?"

"Bill," said Mary Wood, as the tendons in her neck pulled taut.

"Someone has to ask the question," said Mr. Long. "Billy was on track, he was aiming right for that doctorate, like gangbusters. We were just bursting. And then one day, out of the blue, bingo, he's off to New Haven, he wants to design costumes, and he wants to move up to New York City! We thought he was out of his mind!"

"We were thinking about his future," soothed Mary Wood. "Do you remember Cal Craybart? Mildred's boy? He wanted to be a racecar driver. And do you know where he is today?"

"Is he a nun?" I asked.

"He came to his senses," said Mary Wood, "and he got married and he went right back to school. I believe he's going to be a nutritionist."

"You see?" said Mr. Long. "Billy, I'm not saying you have to be some goddamn nutritionist . . ."

"Not at all," said Mary Wood, "although these cookies are delicious . . ."

"Daddy," said William, "I'm doing what I want to do. I've told you a million times, I have to try this, this is who I am, or who I think I am, and I'm sorry if that upsets you, or embarrasses you . . ."

"Look at yourself!" said Mr. Long. "You're not getting anywhere! You've been up here for two years, you're living in this . . . this . . . whatever it is, with con men and heroin shooters and bloodthirsty murderers . . ."

"Bill, there aren't any murderers here," said Mary Wood.

"Only that fellow on the second floor," said Mr. James. "He shot his wife. Because she kept staring at him."

"*Billy!*" shouted Mr. Long, now completely exasperated. "This isn't going to work! You're just fooling yourself! You can still go back to Chapel Hill and get your degree, you can still do what's right! You can fix this! Are you listening to a god-damn word I've said?"

The room grew very quiet, as Claire and I glanced at each other.

"Daddy . . ." William began, standing up, about to leave or explode or throw something.

"Bill . . ." said Mary Wood, raising her hands and looking around frantically, for a throw pillow or a floral arrangement to fuss over.

"Yo," said Michael Neighbor, at the French doors, between clients. He was wearing white spandex bicycle shorts, flip-flops, and a ribbed tank top printed with the phrase "I ♥" and the silhouette of a rooster.

"Well, hello, young man," said Mr. Long.

I was never sure if Michael had overheard the Long family warfare, and had dropped by to help out, or if he was just looking for a snack. But soon Mary Wood and Claire were competing to see who could compliment the other, the day, and William's job prospects more profusely; Mr. James was examining my haircut and predicting the return of the Nehru jacket; and Mr. Long was absorbed in a richly satisfying conversation with Michael, about subway lines, the safety of Times Square, bus exhaust, and whether or not tennis was a good workout for the biceps.

After tea and pastries, most of the guests left, but I stayed and watched a PBS documentary with Mary Wood, a historical program that involved slavery and the antebellum era. "Slavery," said Mary Wood, thoughtfully. "It was all really so very long ago, and no one really knows what happened. So at my school, with my sixth graders, I just don't teach it."

I didn't think that Mary Wood was being racist; she simply believed that any historical discussion should emphasize the more positive aspects of, for example, floggings and executions. As we talked, I realized that Mary Wood was no fool. This was a woman who, throughout her life and certainly her marriage, had known great challenges, and in each case she'd weighed her options and made a judgment call. Her family, I felt sure, was her main priority, followed by God, community service, and maintaining a pleasant tone of voice at all times. She'd made the best of things, she'd raised spectacular children, and during the summer months she got to wear a crown, tax the colonies, and maybe consider having certain people beheaded.

Once William's parents had gone, I told him, "Your father is really something."

"My father . . . ," said William, and he took a deep breath. "My father is a very difficult man. But I can't hate him. And I won't let anyone else hate him."

"Why not?"

"You have to understand, my father's family had a farm. And he left that farm and he worked in the theater. That was like— running away to join the circus."

"So what happened?"

"Well, he wanted to be a playwright. And I know that in high

306

school and at college, he wrote all sorts of plays, and the schools would put them on. He loved it."

"So why did he stop?"

"I don't know, he doesn't talk about it. But there was the war, and he was in the army, and then he got married. He had a family. But he always told me and my brother that someday, he'd drive us all up north, and he'd let us see New York. But only the skyline. It was clear that we could see it, but we wouldn't go into the city."

"But why not?"

"I'm not sure. Maybe he was scared, or maybe it just didn't suit him. But that was a very different time."

I was suddenly ashamed. I'd been angry at William's father, because he'd seemed like a bully, and because I didn't think he understood his son. But just like me, Mr. Long had wanted to be a playwright. And maybe he'd moved on, to something more satisfying, or maybe he still wondered what might have been, if he'd checked into his own version of the Chelsea Hotel. Maybe he was jealous of William, or maybe he was rightfully concerned about his son's life—what if, for William, New York went terribly wrong?

"We had such a marvelous time with you all in NYC," wrote Mary Wood, in her next letter, "and Billy, I'm certain that, in time, you are going to do so very well. Please give my best to all of your friends, and to that person who lives next door. Isn't he something! Selah." I wasn't familiar with the word "selah," with which Mary Wood closed all her letters, but it turned out to be derived from a difficult-to-translate Hebrew term, meaning something along the lines of "Amen."

5.

One day, not long after his parents' visit, William sent out invitations to a really joyous occasion: his twenty-one-year-old sister, Laura, was coming up for a visit, and William was throwing a birthday party for her, at the Chelsea. I hadn't met Laura, but William had told me this: she was retarded.

This was in the 1980s, before the word "retarded" was replaced with "developmentally disabled." When William said that his sister was retarded, there was nothing belittling or derogatory in the term. William adored his sister, and he was very matter-of-fact about her life; as always, I was the one with the problem.

At my elementary school in New Jersey there had been special classes for the retarded students, divided between the less highly functioning kids, called the Trainables, and the more adept kids, called the Educables. While some of these people had physical features that marked them as retarded, most of them looked just like the rest of us, meaning the kids who couldn't be helped at all: public school students from New Jersey.

I'd seen misguided TV movies about the retarded, and there was usually a male and a female, who would fall in love and yearn to be married, "like people." The actors playing these roles would use ridiculous, mushmouthed vocal patterns, and the guys would wear baseball caps and baggy pants yanked to mid-chest, to expose their pasty, hairy shins and white tube socks, while the actresses went for shapeless housedresses and multiple barrettes. I was always thrown by the scientific designation "profoundly retarded," because it sounded so bottomless and final, and I could hear a neurologist telling my parents, "Oh, Paul isn't just run-of-the-mill. Oh no, Paul is profoundly retarded." The only phrase that was anywhere near as upsetting was "morbidly obese," which sounds like a Sherlock Holmes solution: "Evelyn was killed by her own enormous thighs. She was morbidly obese."

When I was in seventh grade, I got a job working as a counselor at a Headstart program, and the bus that picked me up also drove many retarded kids to a nearby day camp. These kids were all perfectly well-behaved, but they often sat next to me, and this was my fear: I became convinced that the bus driver would assume that I was retarded and force me to get off the bus at the day camp. I would protest, and offer to take an IQ test, but of course no one would believe me. "That's what they all say," the driver would chortle. My parents would either lose track of me in the system, or they'd refuse to identify me: "Maybe now you won't be such a smart-ass. No, Officer, we've never seen him before in our lives. I mean, just look at him—he's retarded."

I survived that summer, and I assumed that, once I was out of schools and colleges forever, I'd never mix with retarded people ever again; our social circles just wouldn't overlap. And while I knew that William's sister was retarded, I never thought there'd be actual contact. William, sensing my discomfort, said, "You don't understand. This is my sister. I expect you to marry her."

William's parents, he eventually explained, had been determined to offer Laura the most equal and loving upbringing. She was included in all family activities, and was encouraged to develop every possible talent. Her favorite book was *Gone with the Wind*, and she was not only a trained singer but had won a medal at the Special Olympics in horseback riding. She'd met with the governor of North Carolina, to discuss his programs for the handicapped, and she was a fan of the opera star Beverly Sills, who had a retarded son. The more I learned about Laura's accomplishments, the more intimidated I became; now I wasn't just scared, I was jealous.

William wanted Laura's visit to be perfect, so he became unbearably bossy. I should mention here that bossiness is one of William's most finely honed traits, and that he had been expelled from kindergarten for threatening the other children, until they agreed to wear his homemade robes and burnooses and pose in biblical tableaux. I was told to buy Laura a birthday gift, only "Don't get anything too complicated, or something that could break, or anything disgusting."

"What about a nice scarf?" I asked.

"Fine, but not a square, it should be a rectangle, so she can tie it."

"What about a nice cream-colored rectangle?"

"No, that could show stains, buy it in navy, and make sure it's a hundred percent silk, so it can drape."

I did as I was told, and as I was wrapping the scarf, and writing a message on the gift card, William kept hounding me. "What are you writing?" he demanded. "Don't write anything repulsive. I know you, and Laura is a proper young lady, so just write something sweet and decent. I can't see what you're doing, what are you writing?"

" 'Get well soon.' "

By the time Laura arrived, William and I were both nervous wrecks. She was being kept so occupied that I wouldn't meet her until the birthday party itself. I dressed respectably and gathered with twenty of William's friends in his parlor, which had been made even more genteel for the occasion, with lace heirloom tablecloths, monogrammed linen napkins, tiered, pressed-glass serving pieces arranged with finger sandwiches, and a china tea service hand-painted with roses. Whatever William hadn't inherited, he'd bought from thrift stores, so many of the monograms belonged to, as William put it, "very nice dead strangers." Among the guests were Christopher, a sly and dashing set designer, and Candida, who was then in film school and supporting herself by working as an assistant to a hard-core pornographer. "I'm his right hand," she liked to tell people.

Laura was still out at a matinee, so we all sat balancing our tiny dessert plates on our knees, and sipping Earl Grey from doll-sized cups.

"So, Billy's sister, she's, like, retarded, right?" asked Michael Neighbor.

"Uh-huh," I said, trying to sound blasé, as if I attended birthday parties for retarded girls every day.

"Is she, like, totally retarded, like, is she gonna roll around?"

"No, I think she's . . . I don't know, I think she's . . . fine. She won a medal at the Special Olympics."

"I once had a cousin who was retarded," Michael remembered, "but he was totally cool, he'd, like, pinch me, but then he'd hug me. He was so nice, he was always hugging everybody."

"*Everybody*," said Candida, leering at me.

"Shut up!" I told her.

"Hello, hello, we're late, we have no manners, we're terrible, but we're here!" William called out, from the front door. "Laura, look, it's your party!"

Laura entered, regally. She made one thing instantly clear: while her brother might be bossy, there was only one Guest of Honor. Her face had a certain roundness, and when she spoke she often rolled her eyes upward, but the real word for Laura Ann Long was ladylike. She had short, henna-tinted hair brushed into neat bangs, and she was wearing white button earrings, white cotton gloves, glossy black patent-leather pumps, and a sharply tailored aqua doubleknit shirtwaist dress with gold buttons; William later mentioned that "Only the elderly and the retarded are allowed to wear doubleknit, in case something spills." Laura carried an oval, black patent-leather purse and immediately greeted her guests: "Hello, everybody, I'm Laura Ann Long, and I'd like to thank you all for coming to my party! Aren't you sweet!"

William escorted Laura to a central armchair, where she managed the true first lady technique of speaking to several people at once, and making everyone feel cared for. "Why, Ronnie," she told a Broadway dancer whom she'd known when he was a teenager in Rock Hill, "I haven't seen you in ages. You are looking very nice and skinny, I must say. I have put on a few pounds, and so has William."

"Laura!" William sputtered.

"But we are trying to diet. And, everyone, this is Claire Mallory North, who took me to the Metropolitan Museum and showed me the most beautiful French paintings, you must all see them, although Claire told me that people who live in New York are lazy and never go to museums. Is that true? No, William, I do not need another cookie, and neither do you. And, Christopher, you were so kind to take me to the nicest dinner, and your red sweater is very becoming, but I don't know if I approve of your mustache. But it does make you look very handsome."

Laura was not only by far the best-mannered person in the room, she was flirtatious. She spoke with a slight singsongy lilt, and I kept thinking about the opening, outdoor party in the movie of *Gone with the Wind*, where Scarlett O'Hara bewitches the Tarleton twins. All of the new faces were introduced to Laura one at a time, and finally I was presented. Because Laura was seated, and because she so thoroughly outclassed me, I knelt. "Laura, this is Paul Rudnick," said William, as if he were peering at my calling card through a lorgnette.

"Well, of course it is," said Laura, "and I have heard just so much about you. My brother William says that you are very nice, for a Yankee."

"And a Jew," Christopher whispered in my ear.

"Laura, you look beautiful," I said, because suddenly all I wanted was her approval, as if she could bestow knighthoods.

"Why thank you, you are very kind. I bought this dress with my mother at the Galleria in Raleigh, and I have saved it for my very first visit to New York. Because it is a special occasion, and I do not like to wear slacks."

"Me neither," Christopher whispered.

"Now, Laura," William prompted, "Paul has a birthday gift for you. Rudnick, give her your present."

"Why, thank you, I am just getting too many presents,

although can a girl ever really have too many? Oh, isn't this nice. It's a scarf. William, should I wear it right now?"

As William helped Laura to knot and arrange the scarf, it occurred to me that Laura had her own in-house designer and stylist. I later saw a snapshot of Laura wearing a costume William had recut for her; she was posed in her front yard in a cotillion-on-the-levee hoopskirt with a fringed shawl and a swooping picture hat. William believed in the curative power of clothing. As an undergraduate he'd earned money by looking after an ailing, local lady novelist. He'd kept her fed and clean as her Alzheimer's had progressed. She liked parties, so William would dress her in a long velvet tunic and a wizard's pointed hat, and push her wheelchair up to the punch bowl. "I loved her very much," he'd told me. "But I had to watch her, because she'd take off her shoes and chew on them."

After the birthday cake was served, we all moved our chairs into a circle, for the concert portion of the party. Laura stood at the center of the group, and nodded to her brother Robert, who was three years younger than William, and who'd graduated from the Drama School himself, where he'd studied the actual design of theaters, the architecture and acoustics; "Man stuff," William had sniffed, "plus he's married, so my parents approve." Robert was tall, trim, and owlish, with gleaming eyes and a neat, natty mustache, and he was remarkably good-natured about being the spawn of an unusual family.

Years later, Robert became engaged to the woman who would become his second wife, but she was Danish, so the